The Wolf Children of the Eastern Front

In Memoriam
Jürgen Albohn
(1965–2017)

Also by Sonya Winterberg

Gebrauchsanweisung für Kanada (Piper, 2021)
Kollwitz: Die Biografie (Bertelsmann, 2015)
Kleine Hände im Großen Krieg: Kinderschicksale im Ersten Weltkrieg
(Aufbau Verlag, 2014)
Kriegskinder: Erinnerungen einer Generation (Piper, 2010)

Also by Kerstin Lieff

*Letters from Berlin: A Story of War, Survival, and the Redeeming
Power of Love and Friendship* (Lyons Press, 2021)

Visit the authors online at
www.thingwithfeathers.ca
and on

The Wolf Children of the Eastern Front

Alone and Forgotten

Sonya Winterberg
with
Kerstin Lieff

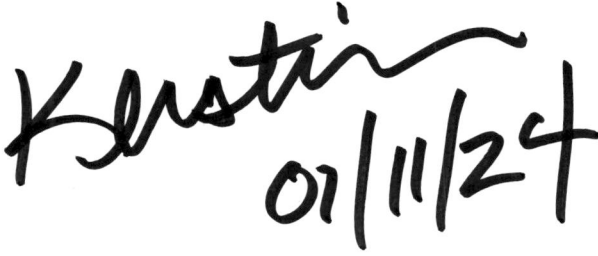

Pen & Sword
MILITARY

First published in Great Britain in 2022 by
Pen & Sword Military
An imprint of
Pen & Sword Books Ltd
Yorkshire – Philadelphia

Copyright © Sonya Winterberg & Kerstin Lieff 2022

ISBN 978 1 39901 460 1

The rights of Sonya Winterberg & Kerstin Lieff to be identified as Authors of this work has been asserted by them in accordance with the Copyright, Designs and Patents Act 1988.

A CIP catalogue record for this book is
available from the British Library.

All rights reserved. No part of this book may be reproduced or transmitted in any form or by any means, electronic or mechanical including photocopying, recording or by any information storage and retrieval system, without permission from the Publisher in writing.

Typeset by Mac Style
Printed in the UK by CPI Group (UK) Ltd, Croydon, CR0 4YY.

Pen & Sword Books Limited incorporates the imprints of Atlas, Archaeology, Aviation, Discovery, Family History, Fiction, History, Maritime, Military, Military Classics, Politics, Select, Transport, True Crime, Air World, Frontline Publishing, Leo Cooper, Remember When, Seaforth Publishing, The Praetorian Press, Wharncliffe Local History, Wharncliffe Transport, Wharncliffe True Crime and White Owl.

For a complete list of Pen & Sword titles please contact

PEN & SWORD BOOKS LIMITED
47 Church Street, Barnsley, South Yorkshire, S70 2AS, England
E-mail: enquiries@pen-and-sword.co.uk
Website: www.pen-and-sword.co.uk

Or

PEN AND SWORD BOOKS
1950 Lawrence Rd, Havertown, PA 19083, USA
E-mail: Uspen-and-sword@casematepublishers.com
Website: www.penandswordbooks.com

Königsberg, July 1945

On one of those glorious days, I walked along the deserted Hagenstrasse. A small cart rolled past me. Two children had their hands on the drawbar and were trotting along the road to Juditten. On the cart, however, lay a wooden box just large enough to hold the body of a small child, a bouquet of field flowers on top of it. Next to it there was still room for the shovel. Two children were preparing to bury a third. Far and wide no adult!

Paul Ronge

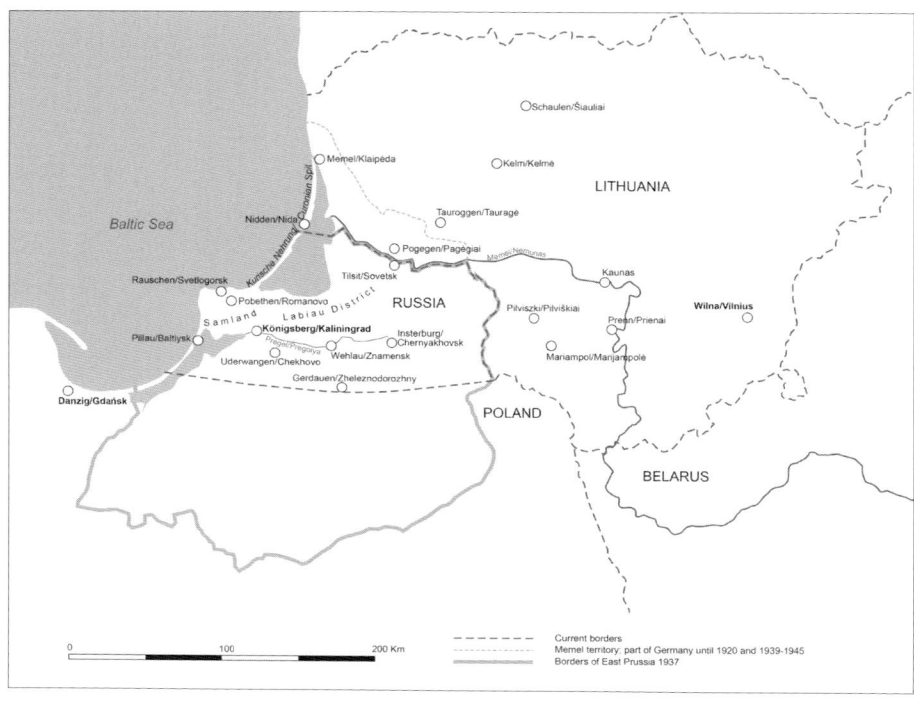

Map showing today's countries and the area of the former East Prussia, *c.*1939.

Contents

Preface by John Kay — ix
Prologue — xii

Chapter 1   A Day of Reckoning   1
Chapter 2   Memories of Königsberg   9
Chapter 3   Peace and War   14
Chapter 4   The *Stunde Null*   33
Chapter 5   Abandoned   46
Chapter 6   The Land of Bread and Cake   58
Chapter 7   Wolf Children and Forest Brothers   70
Chapter 8   Shelter and Kindness   78
Chapter 9   The Decision   89
Chapter 10   Captured and Deported   103
Chapter 11   The Allure of the New Germany   111
Chapter 12   In the West   126
Chapter 13   Strangers in a Strange Land   136
Chapter 14   Then and Now   153
Chapter 15   Policies and Politics   187
Chapter 16   Longing for Königsberg   202

Epilogue by Kerstin Lieff — 221
Editorial Note by Sonya Winterberg — 224
Bibliography — 226
Illustration Credits — 228
Index — 229

The Red Army entering Tilsit in early 1945.

Preface
by John Kay

I've always considered myself to be fortunate but, after reading this gripping book of horrific and terrifying tales about the lost children and orphans left behind in East Prussia in 1945, I now know how *truly* lucky I am. Had it not been for the death of the father I never knew, my mother and I would have remained in Tilsit and been forced to flee East Prussia to escape the advancing Russian army, like thousands of refugees who died of hunger and cold or worse during their desperate trek in pursuit of safety. It's doubtful that I, as an infant, would have survived such a deadly ordeal.

I was born during the Second World War in April 1944 in Tilsit, East Prussia, which was then still part of Germany. My father, who was in the German army, was killed on the Russian front a month before my birth. Because she was now a 'war widow', the Nazi authorities permitted my mother to take me and travel by train to 'visit' my paternal grandmother. At my grandmother's, the two women commiserated about my father's death and my 'Oma' saw her new grandchild for the first time.

When word reached my mother that Tilsit was being heavily bombarded by the Russians, she decided not to return but instead boarded a westbound train which stopped in Arnstadt, a small town in Thuringia. At war's end, Arnstadt was under Russian control and became part of communist East Germany. After almost five years of living under this regime, my mother summoned the courage to try to escape to American-controlled West Germany, a risky and dangerous undertaking, but we were lucky and made it across the heavily patrolled border into freedom. We then lived in Hanover until my mother, my stepfather (my mother had married a good man who had survived years in a Russian POW camp) and I emigrated to Toronto, Canada, in 1958.

There, after high school, I decided to try my luck in the world of music. After joining forces in 1965 with Jutta, my lifelong love and muse, I formed Steppenwolf in Los Angeles in 1967. A year later, my teenage fantasy was no longer a daydream, for Steppenwolf became an enormously successful band and life has been an adventure ever since. It is difficult to put into words this bizarre, unnatural feeling that my father's premature death is why my mother and I survived and were spared the horrors of the death march out of East Prussia in 1945.

During the final months of the war, thousands fled East Prussia to escape the advancing Red Army. Some in horse-drawn wagons piled with people and scant possessions, others on foot with just a suitcase and their children in tow, struggling to keep up. Through freezing temperatures and blowing snow they trudged endlessly in a frantic attempt to reach safety. The escape route soon became a highway of horrors: women throwing babies onto vehicles; dead horses lying frozen in the road; human corpses in the roadside trenches. All this with pounding artillery filling the air.

In the ensuing chaos, it is estimated 20,000 children lost their families, children who watched helplessly as their siblings starved to death or their mothers died from illness or simply from exhaustion. These children, suddenly finding themselves alone, formed bands that wandered the countryside of East Prussia and Lithuania for months and even years. They lived in forests and fields, hid in bullet-riddled farmhouses, and begged for, or stole, what food they could find, some no older than 4, often carrying a younger sibling on their hips. Those who managed to survive were mostly saved by Lithuanian farmers. Today they are known as the *Wolfskinder* or Wolf Children. This is their story, a story which has touched me like no other I've read in years. If it doesn't move you, I suggest you check your pulse.

John Kay (born Joachim Fritz Krauledat, 12 April 1944) is a German-born Canadian rock singer, songwriter and guitarist known as the frontman of Steppenwolf, whose signature hit is 'Born to be Wild'.

Memories of a bygone era.

Prologue

It is 21 March 1992, in a small apartment on the third floor of an old brick building in the northern German town of Flensburg. Anna Unkat's hands are trembling as she holds a typewritten letter she has just received from the International Red Cross. Tears run down the old woman's furrowed face. She hasn't cried like this in a long time. Nearly fifty years have passed since the day she lost her youngest son, Günther, while fleeing the Red Army in East Prussia. They have been endless years in which she worried, day upon day, running the scene over and over through her mind of those last moments before the train took off and she realised that her little Günther had been left behind at the station. But she never gave up believing he was still alive. Over the years, she has tried everything possible to find him, but always came to a dead end—until now. It took fifty years for this moment to arrive.

The elderly woman wipes her face and asks her caregiver—someone without whom she has not been able to manage for many years now—for a pencil. With much effort, she tries to put down on paper the emotions and thoughts that are going through her head that very moment.

> My dearest son!
> Today I received the letter from the International Tracing Service, saying that you, my dear little Güntherchen, are still alive! I broke down in tears of joy.
> You write that you have taken a new name. Is that the name of your foster parents? Do you live alone or do you have a family?
> Please bring everything that you have. I have plenty of room. My dear Güntherchen! God finally heard my prayers! Come as quickly as you can. I won't write much, but I want to see you right away. I am so excited that I simply can't write more.
> Many heartfelt greetings from the distant Flensburg.
> Your loving mother

Hans Neumann is at the railway station in Braunschweig in the late evening hours of 2 September 1991. He is overcome with emotion. Standing in front of him is his brother, Gerhard, whom he hasn't seen since a warm spring day in 1945. Hans was 7 years old when he was separated from both his mother and his brother while on the flight out of East Prussia. Left on his own, he wandered the borderlands of Königsberg and Lithuania, living in the forests along the Memel River for two years, always hoping to reach Germany one day and find his family once again—to no avail. He has been living with a Lithuanian farming family since 1947. The German Hans became Jonas, a Lithuanian boy. However, he never forgot his German roots, and he never forgot his parents and his three siblings.

It was not until early 1991 that, through the tracing services of the Church and the Red Cross, his German family were able to find him. It took several months to clear some bureaucratic red tape, but now the two brothers hold each other in their arms. Hans struggles to find words: 'The heavens have opened their floodgates …'

Even his father is still alive and has come all the way from Dortmund to see him. Hermann Neumann is 89 years old and lives in a retirement home. Unable to believe his own eyes, he takes his lost son's hand. The whole family, but for his mother, have come. Hans will never see her again. Shortly after the war she was imprisoned in a Gulag in Siberia, where she died in 1948.

The miracle of a reunited family after such a long time does not always happen. Another Wolf Child, Inge Fischer, does not know to this day what happened to her mother. 'I was probably 5 years old. The farmer's wife kept me in the pigsty with the pigs. When my mother unexpectedly arrived to take me with her to Germany, the woman was ashamed, and she lied. She told her I was dead.' The girl stayed with the Lithuanian family near the city of Kaunas and was renamed Janina. On her deathbed, the Catholic farmwoman who had taken her in confessed her deceit. It was an unabsolved sin that had haunted her conscience for her entire life, and she begged her foster daughter for forgiveness. After the farmwoman died, Janina reverted to her German name Inge and tried to find her mother. But it was all in vain. There is not a trace to be found, anywhere in Germany.

These are but three stories of the roughly 20,000 German children who lost their parents during the last days of the Second World War. It was a time when hundreds of thousands of families fled the Red Army from the north-eastern German province of East Prussia, with countless instances of children being left behind during the flight. Some of these children watched as their families were shot to death. Others stood by helplessly while their younger siblings starved. Often no older than 4 or 5 years old, they found themselves alone, and, for months and even years afterwards, managed to survive by banding together, living under the open skies of East Prussia, Königsberg and the Baltic States. They call themselves 'The Wolf Children'.

Those Wolf Children who did not survive either died of starvation or were shot by the Red Army, caught while desperately searching for food. Sometimes they were shot for the mere reason that they were German. Of those who did survive, up until 1951, thousands were loaded onto cattle cars and transported to East Germany—the GDR—where they were taken to orphanages, forbidden to talk about their pasts. Some were lucky enough to be reunited with relatives in West Germany. An equally large number were left behind in the Soviet Union. Many of them, though, arrived in Lithuania, where they were often put to work as little better than slave labour. Because it was illegal to be German, or to care for German children, in order to protect themselves and their Lithuanian families, these children often took on Lithuanian names. In the best scenarios, they were cared for as foster children and later, some were even adopted. Yet most of them never went to school and never learned to read or write.

Some were led to believe that Germany went under after the war and did not exist anymore. They believed it still when they were contacted through the International Tracing Service (ITS) in the early 1990s. For decades they had to deny their real names and weren't allowed to speak their mother tongue. Some were young enough to have forgotten their past. Others were devastated by it. And for many of them, a surprisingly strong and defiant child's soul had survived. Even though they had known their birth parents for only a few short years, they maintained a lifelong yearning to find their families of origin—even into their old age.

I had heard about the Wolf Children sometime in the early 1990s and their stories interested me tremendously. Then, one day, I read some remarks that the former German MP Wolfgang von Stetten had made in 2007:

> Even now, in their old age, they continue to live in abject poverty. It is a disgrace that, even with all the hardships they have had to endure, the German government has not been able to offer these people even a small pension to alleviate their miserable circumstances. After sixty-two years of waiting, these not even one hundred survivors are still losing the war. They feel betrayed, abandoned and, in the final analysis, forgotten by their fatherland.

I knew then that I wanted to write about them.

In 2011, I accompany a group of Wolf Children from Lithuania on a visit to Germany. One of them is Waltraut Minnt. 'She's a roamer,' someone who has known her for years whispers to me. What he means is she is a 'drifter', someone who never found her footing. Waltraut tends to hold herself back and, even in group photos, she usually stands to the side, a few steps apart from the others, as if she doesn't really belong.

I notice Waltraut appears to be quite restless during our travels. Over and over, she holds up the group; she doesn't return to the bus on time. Finally, when we're in Berlin, we discover what is bothering her. She tells us about a brother, Fritz, who lives in the area. She smiles and cries all at the same time and is so happy to have an address, to know that he still exists. But she doesn't trust herself to look him up. For three days and three nights, she can't stop thinking about if and how she could meet up with him. 'But how are we to understand one another?' is her greatest concern.

Like so many of the Wolf Children who stayed behind in Lithuania, she has forgotten most of her German. She finally finds out that her brother doesn't even want to see her, and she is devastated. It seems she's an embarrassment to him. After all, she was 'just' a half-sister, and anyway, 'One really doesn't know what kind of expectations these people from the East have of us.' The only thing Waltraut has left is her happy memories. At least that is something no one can take away from her.

Waltraut loves to wear blue with small geometric designs. Her clothes are mostly polyester, from a bygone age. Her black hair, not fully greyed, is pinned back in a bun. She no longer sees well, so she is wearing a distinct pair of curved glasses in the shape of a butterfly that, admittedly, have seen better days. She can't remember the last time her eyesight was checked. Often, she'll lean her head slightly to the side, look skeptically with her small brown eyes at who she's talking to, and then slowly shake her head. In these moments, I think she has missed her calling. She should have been a schoolteacher. There is one more accessory that is inseparably connected to Waltraut. It is a yellowed handbag that looks to be from the 1950s.

While in Germany, one day we have lunch together in a cafeteria. Everything is a new experience for her—the bright colours, the light-filled rooms, and now the many selections of both warm and cold dishes at the buffet, soups and salads. She is visibly overwhelmed. I watch as she balances her tray with uncertainty, trying to choose from this abundance of German food. In the end, she takes a small bowl of soup and three bread rolls. When she sits at the table, in a seemingly guarded moment, she lets two of the rolls fall into her bag. 'You just never know,' she explains to me later. She has never seen this much food in her entire life. 'And so beautifully arranged … Like in a fairytale!'

But it isn't just food that makes its way into Waltraut's bag. It is everything she could possibly ever need. In fact, her entire life fits into this bag—because you never know.

When she tells me this, I want to know everything—about her life and her handbag. I realise how little I really know about the Wolf Children. And I understand that I won't find the answers to my questions in Germany. For that, I will need to travel to Lithuania.

Unarmed civilians defending the Lithuanian Press House against Soviet troops, Vilnius, January 1991.

Chapter 1

A Day of Reckoning

Vilnius, on a Thursday in January 2011. I've been in the city for only a few days. I'm here with Valdas Petrauskas. He was a young man at the end of the Second World War and can still remember the *vokietukai*, the 'little Germans', as the Lithuanians affectionately called the children from East Prussia who wandered, hungry, through the countryside. He is telling me about the 'Bloody Sunday' of January 1991, and his eyes grow wide when he recalls this Lithuanian day of reckoning. As I listen to his story, I realise how much this was a momentous day of reckoning for the Wolf Children as well.

Two days before that Bloody Sunday, Soviet tanks arrived to occupy the capital city of Lithuania. The new 'Republic of Lithuania' had not yet been recognised, and Mikhail Gorbachev wanted it back in his fold of the USSR. He had given them an ultimatum: Rejoin the Soviet Union or the USSR will continue the invasion.

To push his agenda, a few months earlier he had called for a commercial blockade of Lithuania, causing severe economic hardship. As so often happened in the history of the Cold War, tanks were deployed once again to secure the cohesion of an already crumbling Eastern Bloc. Although the situation in this young republic had become precarious, the Lithuanians were not about to acquiesce to Moscow's demands.

Amongst the many courageous people of this historic hour was the newly elected president of the parliament, Vytautas Landsbergis. He and a few of his deputies hid inside the parliament office in the Gediminas Avenue, the main avenue of Vilnius, and, in a dramatic television appearance, he appealed to his people and begged them to come to protect the building. By the thousands, Lithuanians arrived and pushed the KGB-organised demonstrators back. Day and night, the Lithuanians guarded their parliament building, willing to die for their newly won freedom. As in pre-Soviet days, priests were among the throngs, taking confessions of believers and offering them their last rites.

'Many Lithuanians were banished to Siberia under Stalin,' Valdas explains. 'Nearly everyone had someone in their own family who had been taken. Many of them never returned.'

Those who had dodged that fate were now at a crossroads when Russia invaded Vilnius, and they figured they had more to win than to lose. The fall of the Berlin Wall had created a rift in the Iron Curtain, and Lithuanians were not about to let this once-in-a-lifetime opportunity slip away.

By late afternoon that Sunday, people had gathered not only at the parliament building but also at the broadcasting offices of the national television station. They stood in tight rows and sang. But it did not take long for the situation to escalate. Soviet tanks pointed their gun barrels at the people. Soldiers rushed in and brutally beat the demonstrators with guns and iron rods. Eventually, they opened fire and shot randomly into the crowd without mercy. To this day, Lithuanians cannot forget those television images. One could hear the fear in the newsreader's voice as she reported from inside the locked studio. 'They're here! They're hammering against the door!' Then, suddenly, the transmission was interrupted, and a Soviet station took over the broadcast.

Landsbergis managed to find a way to speak to his people anyway, and never once did they lose faith. About 150,000 Lithuanian men and women formed an impenetrable human wall around his building, using whatever they could find to stop the onslaught. Gorbachev, wanting to mitigate any further bloodshed, eventually pulled his Soviet troops back. In the end, there were fifteen dead and hundreds of wounded. They were to be the sacrificial lambs that sealed the final independence for Lithuania.

On this winter evening in 2011, the anniversary of this day of reckoning is being celebrated for its twentieth year. It has become a national holiday. All night long, small fires burn in the streets. Men, women and children stand and warm themselves as they did then at the square in front of the parliament building and at the television station. One can hear the magical sounds of countless choirs and people joining in, singing the songs of freedom. They are traditional folksongs from long ago sung with a new meaning, restoring a sense of Lithuanian identity. As of the 1980s, folklore and dance groups were the one way the people could get around Soviet suppression, and this 'Singing Revolution' is what led to their independence.

Valdas takes me under the arches of the city wall and leads me to the old city of Vilnius. It is evening and the shadows have grown long. They look sinister and a chill runs through me. We arrive at the parliament building and here Valdas shows me the concrete barricades that still remain as a reminder of that Bloody Sunday. Today they sit on the other side of a glass enclosure behind which are walls painted with graffiti and murals to commemorate what took place on that day.

It has become dark, and we turn to leave. As we part, Valdas takes my hand and holds it a long time. His eyes are filled with emotion.

What happened in Vilnius on Bloody Sunday is mentioned as a mere footnote to history by the rest of the global community. The Gulf War had just begun and it had taken centre stage in the media. Yet for a small group of Germans known as the Wolf Children who have been living in Lithuania since 1945, a tiny opening of hope had blossomed, an opening to a world that, for them, had been as distant as it was unknown—the land of their mothers and fathers.

With the Cold War coming to an end, and the events that led to the Lithuanian revolution, an opportunity arose for these Wolf Children for the first time. It was a small opportunity, but hopes were high of re-establishing a bond with the land of their birth, Germany. Just the name, 'West Germany', kindled a longing in them and sounded much like paradise. Surely, so many of them thought, their people would now receive them with open arms. They, the abandoned children from the war, would finally return to that place in the world where they belonged. Because they were, without question, German.

Yet the supposed fatherland did not have its children at the forefront of its mind. There were still 340,000 Soviet soldiers stationed in East Germany, and the Two Plus Four Agreement—the treaty that was negotiated in 1990 between the two countries, East and West Germany, and the four occupying powers, France, Great Britain, the USSR and the United States—had not yet been ratified by the Supreme Council of the Soviet Union. The final signature that would seal the agreement did not materialise until three months later, in March 1991. Even as late as July of the same year, Chancellor Helmut Kohl still spoke of the 'unilateral support of the independence of individual Soviet republics' as 'dangerously stupid'. He simply did not want to jeopardise the relationship that had developed between himself and Gorbachev.

'Reunification' for the Wolf Children needed to wait until diplomatic relations between Lithuania and Germany were established. Nevertheless, the first window of hope had been flung open, and the International Tracing Service recorded increasing inquiries from both countries.

A handful of the Wolf Children did connect with family, but this was not the rule. Many family members had already died, and for the others, because so many of them had changed their names, relatives were difficult, if not impossible, to find. Then there was the reaction to the Wolf Children. Because of their unimaginably sad stories, their poverty and poor appearance, and their uneducated manners, many of the Wolf Children who found their relations in Germany were not well received. They were perceived as an embarrassment and many Germans denied they even knew them. The prevailing fear the relatives in Germany had was that they must now also care for, and pay for, these 'new poor relations from the East'.

Quite to the contrary, though, for most of the Wolf Children, financial support was the least of their concerns. For them, first and foremost, they wanted clarity about their roots. They longed for photos of parents and siblings from when they were children. They simply wanted affirmation. That so many of them were so poorly received was something the Wolf Children were not prepared for. Such blatant and unexpected rejection traumatised many of them even further.

For those who had been left behind in Lithuania, the question that haunted them for their entire lives was: How would life have turned out had I succeeded in escaping to Germany? Or, as Christel Scheffler, who was born in Königsberg in 1939, puts it, 'How would life have turned out if I had not been thrown into the shadow side of life?'

But how did things go for the former Wolf Children who did manage to get to Germany? Gerhard Gudovius lives in the foothills of the Swabian Alps. He has not spoken about his past for many decades. Not until he reads a book review in the newspaper, the *Reutlinger General-Anzeiger*, in 2011, does he begin to remember any of it. The review covers a young adult novel about a Wolf Child. As he reads, he realises the story is not even correct. It is merely fiction and he is sorely disappointed. 'This is just kitsch!' he says. 'And the author never even experienced it herself. What does she know?' For weeks he is upset over this and decides to write a letter to the editor and ultimately tries to find other 'real' Wolf Children who he thinks might be living in the area.

When I first meet him, it becomes clear to me quite quickly that there is a question that has plagued him his entire life. The 16-year-old war-orphaned Gerhard, after half a year of wandering and begging in Lithuania, was taken in by a farmer's family who treated him as their own son. The family had other children his age, and this half-starved boy adjusted to his new life easily. Gerhard proved to be clever and a hard worker, gladly helping with whatever needed to be done on the farm. Eventually, they even trusted him with a very important task. Every day he was to take the milk to the nearby town of Kalvarija.

'I lived with this family for five years. They called me Gerhardas, and other than the colour of my hair—I was fair-haired—there was nothing that differentiated me from the rest of them.' Yet in the early summer of 1951, two Soviet soldiers surprise him at the door and give him the orders to leave immediately. Everything goes very fast from here on out. Gerhard does not even know what is happening. They tell him they will be coming to pick him up the following day.

When he tells his Lithuanian family about the visit from officials, they burst into tears. Gerhard is so touched by this moment he will remember it for the rest of his life. He has never forgotten how emotional the parting from the only real family he'd ever had was—on this, his day of reckoning.

'What would have become of me had I stayed in Lithuania back then?' But who could answer his question? I suggest that we meet up with the Wolf Children travelling from Lithuania while they are on their tour of Germany. Perhaps they have an answer. He responds without hesitation, yes.

Gerhard Gudovius has lived in Reutlingen in southern Germany since the mid-1950s. This is where he met his wife, Gerlinde, it is where his children were born, and it is where he has a plot of land on a hill overlooking the city. He and his wife like to garden here. Although the Swabian mannerisms are foreign to his East Prussian heritage, he finds that there is a sense of order that is shared by both the Swabians and the East Prussians. And, in the end, he feels lucky to have come to this place he now calls home. 'When I was on the transport from Lithuania and heard that I was on my way to East Germany, it became clear to me that nothing good was to come of it and that I needed to escape as soon as I could. And I would have to do so quickly.'

His wife has worked for many years in the sacristy of the parish. She's originally from the Saxon Vogtland. Like her husband, she came to Reutlingen in the 1950s. Together they have made this foreign land their home. 'We've had good times, and we've had hard times as well,' says Gerlinde Gudovius. 'But, for the most part, we've had what you could call a normal life.' Except that sometimes her husband became uncommunicative, and refused to speak about the past. 'Sometimes he was not the best of fathers. And there were times when he would get extremely drunk.'

Yet today they seem to lead a contented life. They live in a small terraced house in a quiet neighbourhood that they rent for a good price from the parish. They enjoy taking bus tours so that at least in their old age they can see a bit of the world. They are modest people who do not seem to lack for kindness nor hospitality. 'But there is an uneasy feeling that nags at me,' Gerhard finally tells me. 'It is this: Would life, would everything, possibly have been just a little easier, if I had stayed in Lithuania back then?'

As we set out on a sunny May afternoon to meet up with the Wolf Children from Lithuania, Gerhard is in high spirits. He had a sleepless night in which he constantly tried to reconstruct where exactly the Lithuanian family who took him in had lived. 'Unfortunately, I don't remember their name and I also don't know the village where we lived. I know it was near Kalvarija, because that's where I always brought the milk to the dairy. I remember there was a sort of pond nearby where we swam to cool ourselves off in the summer.' Then he is silent.

'Do you think there might be someone here who's from Kalvarija?' he finally asks me. I don't know but I assume that with thirty-five participants, the chances are quite good.

When we finally meet up with the Wolf Children, he can no longer contain himself. 'Is there someone here from Kalvarija?' he shouts out excitedly. But the communication is not that easy. Most of the Wolf Children from Lithuania speak very little German, if any at all.

'And where have they left their husbands?' Gerhard asks me. I look around and, like him, notice it is predominantly women and hardly any men who are here.

One of the interpreters approaches him and says, 'There is, in fact, a woman here from the area around Kalvarija,' and she introduces Erna Schneider. Unfortunately, Erna barely understands her mother tongue any longer. But she is elated to know there is someone in Germany who remembers the area in Lithuania where she is from. At the end of the war, when she lost her family, she was only 9 years old. Even with the fragmented memories that Gerhard shares with her, she cannot, unfortunately, help him.

But Gerhard is not to be discouraged. He finds there are a number of Wolf Children with whom he is able to share stories—although the communication is not easy. He passes most of the afternoon with Rudi Lindenau who lives in Šiauliai, in northern Lithuania. Both were born in Königsberg and both in 1932. Since the Reunification in 1991, Rudi has been able to make a number of connections in Germany and has relearned German. Both men talk about the old Königsberg, and then about the famine, and the endless begging that followed. They talk about how they came to Lithuania, and joke about the tricks they were able to pull off that ensured the survival of these clever young boys. They discover many similarities, but the difference is in the parting, the time when Gerhard leaves Lithuania in 1951. Rudi is one of those who stayed behind in Lithuania, but he isn't bitter about his life. 'I've always had it good, even in the hard times,' he muses. But his cheerful manner and soft friendly face cannot hide the fact that it wasn't really an easy life that he led as a Wolf Child.

Gerhard is especially shocked at the financial situation of this man, a senior citizen. The poverty line in Lithuania lies at 700 litas per month, which translates to 200 euros at the time. There is hardly a Wolf Child that receives more than 400 litas in state pension.

Now the question about the lack of men becomes clear to Gerhard. Most of these women are widows. The life expectancy of a Lithuanian man is 65 years of age, about ten years less than that of a German. Alongside the larger economic problems in this country, there is widespread alcoholism. And Lithuania is among the highest in suicide rates in the world, our interpreter explains. In this moment a light goes on in Gerhard's head. He suddenly realises that his memories of a blissful life in the countryside in Lithuania are nowhere near reality. 'I would probably not be alive today,' he reflects as I drive him home. He's grateful for the new friendships he's made, but more importantly, he has been able to answer possibly the most pressing question of his life: What would have become of him?

Rudi Lindenau's only childhood photo.

View of the Hundegatt branch of the Pregolya River, Königsberg, 1920.

Chapter 2
Memories of Königsberg

What connects the Wolf Children of Germany to those still living in Lithuania are the memories they hold so dear—of East Prussia, of their childhoods, of pre-war times when the war had not yet reached their homes.

Let us go back in time to the Königsberg some of its former residents hold in their memories. But there's a problem: the places they remember, the places they have longed for, are no longer there. Today they only exist on old photographs and maps from before the war. All has disappeared with the tragic history of the twentieth century and is irretrievably lost forever.

Yet this longing for the home that no longer exists has an aspect of forgiveness to it. Marion Countess von Dönhoff wrote in her memoir: 'Perhaps the highest form of love is loving without possessing.'

When the Wolf Children talk about the past, about East Prussia and its picturesque capital city Königsberg, the stories they tell have one thing in common: they are always beautiful memories. They remember an open landscape, its stillness, its soothing solitude—aspects that defined East Prussian virtues such as sincerity, modesty and discipline.

Famous as well as ordinary citizens of Königsberg recall similar images of their early years in this city of Germany's easternmost lands. For generations back, people have remembered their childhood in Königsberg as 'idyllic', reminiscent of the Romantic and Biedermeier eras.

Königsberg, today's Russian exclave Kaliningrad, lies between Poland and Lithuania on the Baltic Sea. The Pregolya River, once known as the Pregel, runs through the city, making a fork in the centre, creating a city island, the so-called Kneiphof. To the west, the two forks meet again and flow as one into the Frisches Haff, or 'Fresh Lagoon', emptying into the Baltic Sea. Of the five bridges that once spanned the river, only one remains—the Cathedral Bridge (the *Dom Brücke*), also known as the Honey Bridge.

The German artist Käthe Kollwitz was born in the borough of Sackheim on the old Pregel River in Königsberg in 1867. In her diaries, she describes her home.

> We lived on the Weidendamm number 9, in Königsberg. I can only vaguely remember the parlour where I was inking a drawing. But I can clearly remember the courtyard and the gardens. A small front garden opened to a larger courtyard that stretched all the way down to the Pregel. There, flat-

bedded barges packed with bricks were offloaded and then stacked in our yard. The stacks the men created had cavities in them in which we could play as children.

Sixty years after Käthe Kollwitz, the violinist Michael Wieck was born in Königsberg in 1928. For him, the city was:

> a fairytale land, with its imposing castle that sat right in the centre. A statue of the crowned Kaiser Wilhelm I, holding his sabre high to the sky, stood prominently out in front. In the castle's courtyard there was a tavern, frighteningly named the Blutgericht, the 'Blood Court'. Not far from it was a lovely castle pond with swans and ducks, and boats to rent. Picturesque bridges to the Kneiphof spanned the Pregel all up and down the river; on each was a drawbridge that often made us late for school.

The Blutgericht tavern he speaks of—its assigned punishments can only be imagined—just like Auerbachs Keller in Leipzig, was widely known across all

The Blutgericht tavern, Königsberg, 1937.

of Germany and beyond. The legendary *Königsberger Klopse* (meatballs) come from Königsberg, as does *Ochsenblut*, which, because of its gruesome name, 'ox blood', frightened generations of children. And yet, it is only a cocktail made with champagne and a splash of burgundy.

In her memoirs, Erika Morgenstern, who was born in 1939, remembers the castle 'where Prussian kings once were crowned, as a place of fairytales. My eyes would scan the tall windows. I always hoped, just once, to see a princess there, wearing a long white gown and a crown on her head. And I was sure she most certainly was allowed to eat an entire bar of chocolate whenever she wanted.'

Gerhard Gudovius was born in Königsberg in 1932. About his childhood, he recalls:

> It was a city in which there was always something going on. Even for children there was constantly something new to discover. An outing to the Pregel was the ultimate. At the piers, we watched as the steamships unloaded their cargo. Young men carrying large burlap sacks on their backs ran in and back out of the half-timber warehouses, while streetcar bells clanged and steam engines whistled in the background. In the middle of the city stood the castle with its stately church tower. Chestnut and linden trees lined the castle's walkways where people strolled on Sundays. And here, we could always find shelter from the hot summer sun.

The landmarks of this old Hansestadt, or 'Hanseatic city', were the half-timbered warehouses on the Lastadie, even though they no longer had any economic significance. During the 1920s, a new loading dock was built at the lower end of the Pregel River, making this warehouse district officially obsolete. The area, however, continued to be magical to children who played in and around it. Trains were an added attraction as they could be observed while goods, such as the legendary Tilsiter cheese, were offloaded.

Often on Sundays, whenever his grandparents sneaked him some pocket money, Gerhard would take the streetcar number 8 to the Münzplatz, where he could visit the cinema. 'That's when I really felt like a grown up!'

The square had an obelisk with a clock in it, called the Normaluhr, the 'normal clock'. Young lovers used to meet here, remembers Erika Sauerbaum, a Wolf Child who was born in Königsberg in 1928. From there, one could take a lovely stroll down into the city centre. 'The promenade on the castle pond's left bank was by far our favorite. In the summertime, it was virtually impossible to find a place to sit there on the terrace of the Café Schwärmer, and yet it was the hope of every young girl to be invited to do just that by a young gentleman.'

Even the dance floor in the garden of the Parkhotel's Promenadenweg was a summertime attraction. At the northern end of the promenade, a small cascade trickled gently from the Oberteich, the 'upper pond', into the castle pond below. And the upper pond! It was where generations of Königsberger children learned to swim, 'because not everyone could afford to spend their summers at the fancy Baltic beaches of Cranz and Rauschen', Erika explains.

Even the East Prussian author Burkhard Sumowski, born in 1936, wrote about the upper pond in his memoirs:

> It was the most magnificent of all of Königsberg's waterways, as large as a lake and surrounded by some of the most beautiful parks and promenades. There was a small building, an electrical substation, which looked much like a gingerbread house. It was tucked behind a thicket of bushes near my grandparents' home and was quite close to the pond. To tease my grandmother, my grandfather used to say the Boshebaubau, an evil god, lived there, and he loved to snatch away naughty children.

At the southern end of the city, between Haberg and Nasser Garten, the 'Wet Garden', was the central railway station. This was where trains from the nearby village of Ponarth arrived—a favorite excursion for Königsbergers. From Ponarth you could view the cityscape while enjoying some locally brewed beer. Many of the Wolf Children came from this south-western corner of the city.

East Prussia with its former capital city, Königsberg, does not exist anymore. This area, once it was ceded to Russia, became Oblast Kaliningrad. The region was once the breadbasket of Germany, and, along with the Hanseatic Königsberg and all the surrounding villages, was destroyed during the war. In fact, the entire land was laid to waste. Where German was once widely spoken, where East Prussia with all her history had reigned for centuries, the last traces of the diaspora have vanished.

As we leave the memories of Königsberg behind, let us take one last look from the Honey Bridge over the Kneiphof. There we see the pastel-coloured traditional *Fachwerkhäuser*, the half-timbered houses of the Fischdorf, the 'Fishing Village', and watch the tourists strolling carefree in the summertime. On the other bank of the river, a modern glass palace was recently erected. The gorgeous views of the cathedral with its backdrop of the beautifully restored historic buildings are most likely only accessible to the Russian aristocracy, who have apartments here.

But on this day, Kaliningrad seems to embrace us. The sun is peeking from behind the clouds. A few golden rays are reflecting off the Pregel. A fisherman is lazily throwing his lure while a young father plays with his daughter. She is lost in the wonder of the shimmering bubbles her father is blowing for her. For just one moment, the world appears, once more, to be at peace.

The Lastadie docks of Königsberg, 1935.

Chapter 3

Peace and War

The end of the First World War brought significant changes to both West and East Prussia. Large parts of West Prussia, Gdańsk, the East Prussian city of Soldau and the Memel Territory were separated from the German Reich under the Versailles Treaty without a referendum. These regions were given to Poland, except for Gdańsk, which became a free city, and the Memel Territory, which was to become a free state but in 1923 was annexed to Lithuania.

Other parts of West Prussia as well as southern East Prussia were to vote whether they wanted to belong to Poland or to East Prussia. This vote was cast on 11 June 1920. No one was surprised at the outcome, not even the Poles. In every sector, over 90 per cent of the voters decided in favour of staying with Germany. The Polish Chief of State, Józef Piłsudski, told the German Secretary of State, Gustav Stresemann, 'East Prussia is undeniably German. That has been my opinion since I was a child. And it did not need to be validated by a plebiscite vote. This is my opinion. You are welcome to publicise it in an open forum to reassure your East Prussians in Königsberg.'

It was united and yet separated from the heartland. This new division, separated from the rest of Germany, also meant East Prussia became isolated from the country's economy, and for East Prussia to survive, it was going to need huge financial support from the federal government. Several steps were immediately taken to help create a robust East Prussian identity. For example, the *Deutsche Ostmesse Königsberg*, the German National Trade Fair, East, was founded in Königsberg in 1920 to promote trade. The economically weakened region also received a new sea connection. *Seedienst Ostpreussen*, a combined passenger and freight ferry, served the sea ports of Swinemünde (Świnoujście), Pillau (Baltiysk), and later, the Bay of Danzig, Travemünde, Kiel and Helsinki. The use of freight trains was considerably increased when the airport in Königsberg was built. This first German civilian airport was inaugurated in 1922. Its maiden flight was the route Königsberg–Rīga–Moscow. Soon flights also serviced Berlin and Stockholm.

Despite these tremendous steps towards commercial expansion and the determination of the German government to strengthen the economy of its eastern regions, the ideals of National Socialism quickly gained ground with the East Prussians, who saw the Versailles Treaty as nothing but a humiliation, even though the ideals of the Nazis were not at all in sync with the Prussian virtues of humility, a sense of justice, and a fear of God. That such a political minority party could so unabashedly proclaim a totalitarian leadership was a surprise. No one believed this could happen, but, with the consequences of Versailles, a worldwide economic depression, and communism gaining popularity, the loud voices of the Nazis seemed to promise a solution to the people in this isolated province.

In the years leading up to 1933, these hopes of a better future were fuelled by the many early successes of the new regime under Hitler. Commerce in the East suddenly blossomed. The *Deutsche Ostmesse Königsberg* became the second-largest trade fair in all of Germany, topped only by that in Leipzig. Even in foreign policy, East Prussia became the stabilising factor. In fact, a non-aggression pact, the so-called 'Friendship Agreement' between Germany and Poland, was signed in 1934. But, as history revealed, a 'friendship' between Germany and her European neighbours would soon be broken by Hitler and his Third Reich.

This animosity is what Czechoslovakia felt in the autumn of 1938, when it ceded the Sudetenland to Germany, hoping to mitigate any further conflict. However, in March 1939, the German Wehrmacht marched into Prague anyway, and announced that this land was now Germany's 'Bohemian and Moravian protectorate'. Within days, Czechoslovakia ceased to exist.

In a desperate attempt to avert a similar fate, only a week later, Lithuania offered to return all of the Memel Territory to Germany. With this, it appeared Hitler had achieved all his foreign policy goals, and to the East Prussians, the possibility of a war was as good as nil. If at all, it was something that could only happen in the distant future. To the children of this area, the idea was unfathomable.

Ursula Haak was born in 1935, the only daughter to a land labouring family on the Birgen estate, about 5 kilometers from Tilsit. She was the seventh child. Her younger brother, Horst, was born a year later and remains the baby of the family. The estate on which her parents, Anna and Albert, work is over 100 hectares in size, with twenty horses and seventy head of cattle. The famous Tilsiter cheese is produced in the estate's creamery. Like other families that work here, Ursula's family live in a community of servants' quarters. Next to their home, they have a small garden in which they grow vegetables and have a few animals for their personal use.

Her father is a tall man with blue eyes. At first glance he resembles the writer Thomas Mann. Her mother, dressed in her Sunday outfit, looks much like a teacher, and the description is fitting. To Ursula's parents, it is important that the family go to church each Sunday dressed in their best clothing. Although they are poor, they wear proper clothing, and it is important that even the children look good. Sundays and holidays are holy days on this estate, and Ursula's mother, Anna, bakes a cake every Saturday that is served on Sunday afternoon with coffee. Just before Christmas and Easter, a pig is slaughtered.

Preparing Tilsiter cheese, East Prussia, c.1930.

Dorothea Bjelfvenstam lives in Stockholm today but was born in Königsberg. When she thinks of her childhood in that city, images of a Russian *matryoshka* doll come to her. 'When I open them, I find another figure inside that always gets smaller. The first, the smallest one deep inside, is the child who I was in Königsberg.' The memories of her first years in the upper-class borough of Amalienau are fragmented images: sandboxes, arbours and apple trees in her grandfather's small garden. There is a Bechstein grand piano on which her grandfather plays while Dorothea sits underneath and 'disappears into the music'. Then there is 'Christmas with Oma, Mutti and Auntie. But not my father. Kindergarten and school, parks and friends, one of whom was the daughter of the Nazi-mayor.' The neighbours next door have a small dog, as small as Dorothea herself.

Eva Briskorn is the same age as Dorothea and is also from Königsberg. Eva was born in 1933, just before Hitler came to power. She is her parents', Otto and Gisela's, first child. In short order, six more children are born. As she is the oldest, from an early age, Eva learns to help with household chores as well as care for the younger children. On the one hand, she considers it a burden, but on the other, she has a sunny disposition and enjoys the praise she receives from her parents for the good work she does. The family lives in an unassuming home in the eastern borough of Liep.

What was once a fishing village established during the time of the Teutonic Order, Liep became the hub and end point for log-running down the Deyma River, and here a pulp factory was built in 1906. As industry increased in the region, housing developments for the workers grew up around Liep, and in 1905, the village was incorporated into Königsberg. Not long after, a rail connection was established.

Eva's family lives in a two-bedroom apartment in the workers' housing on Troppauer Weg, which includes a bath and a kitchen. With each new addition, the living conditions grow evermore crowded. Her father, Otto, is a master carpenter and works in a carpentry shop. Eva is a daddy's girl and loves to sit on

Eva on her first day of school.

Eva Briskorn, left, with her parents and siblings.

his lap and listen while he tells her stories. To him, she is not Eva, but rather 'the little Evchen' or 'my little darling'.

Otto Briskorn is a devoted father through and through. He loves to spend time with his family and when the war begins, he joins a unit that is stationed near Königsberg, so he can come home as often as possible.

Eva starts school just as the war begins in 1939. A photo of her first day shows a cheerful little girl with head full of curls tied back into a thick braid. School is a happy time for her, and she finds it easy to learn to read and write. She learns the *Sütterlin* script and achieves good grades for her penmanship. She dreams of becoming a doctor.

Eva goes to the Horst Wessel School, as do all the children in the area. When she's not in school, she socialises at the Sackheim Gate. There is a public beach at the Kupferteich, or the 'Copper Pond'. Here, the lifeguard teaches the children to swim by wrapping them in a harness attached to a fishing rod. There is also a diving tower from which they love to plunge into the water.

Not far from there is a small fair, and behind that is the community garden at Lieper Weg. It is a dreamland, especially in the summer months. It is where Eva plays hide-and-seek with her friends and where she jumps rope for hours on end. On Tapiauer Strasse is the athletic field of the Horst Wessel School; next to it is a military cemetery. Eva's father works nearby. When Eva comes home from school, her first question is always, 'Is Papa not home yet?' —and the scene becomes a ritual. Eva throws her school bag demonstratively in the corner, causing her mother to sigh, but 'Evchen' is already out of the door to go to pick up her father from work. For her, the short walk home with her father is the highlight of her day. This is when she can have her father all to herself without having to share him with her younger siblings. This is also when she can bare her soul and ask him for advice.

After the warm rain showers cool the summer heat, Eva loves to run barefoot up the hill behind her house. In her hand she carries little paper boats that she races against her playmates down the gutter that runs alongside the road. During bad weather, the children endlessly play the favorite German board game *'Mensch ärgere Dich nicht'* (Man, Don't Get Angry), much like the English game Ludo. Eva finds that this is a particularly good way to learn to lose: years later, she will remember this. In the winter, the children love to throw buckets of water into the street so that when it freezes, they can slide down the small incline on their bottoms.

In the garden behind the apartment building, the family has a small shed in which they store wood and coal for the winter. This is also where Otto Briskorn pursues his great passion, breeding pigeons. For hours, Eva watches as her father cleans the hutch, feeds the birds, and coos to them.

Her mother sews all the clothes for her many children herself. She is a talented seamstress, and also does knitting and embroidery. Often, Eva and her sisters,

Sabine and Gisela, come to their mother to beg for her to sew them a new dress. As soon as their mother agrees, the youngest, Sabine, pipes up the loudest: 'I'm the youngest. You need to sew the first little dress for me!' When Eva looks back, what she remembers is the very last dress her mother sewed for the girls. It was a sailor dress with blue fabric and a white collar with embroidery along the edges.

Gerhard Gudovius is an illegitimate child, born in Königsberg in 1932. His unmarried mother, Herta, leaves her newborn with her parents, who raise him as their own. He never learns who his father is. When he is 5 years old, his mother surprises them by returning home. She is deathly ill with gangrene from an infected appendectomy and the doctors have given up on her. For a short while his grandparents take care of their daughter, but then Gerhard watches his 26-year-old mother die from her infection.

The highlight of his week is when Gerhard gets to go with his grandparents to visit his mother's grave. It is a beautiful grave, Gerhard thinks, always bedecked with pretty flowers and its white marble stone framed in black. In the cemetery, with its peaceful surroundings, death does not scare him.

Gerhard often plays with Michael, a boy from his neighbourhood. Michael's parents have a busy bicycle shop that is next door to Gerhard's house. Michael has a marvelous train set, a Märklin. The two boys live in their own world when they play together, building and rebuilding the tracks where they let the trains run.

It is a Thursday morning in November 1938. At breakfast, Gerhard's grandparents talk about what an unquiet night it has been. Over and over, they heard loud screaming in the streets and window panes being smashed in. Before Gerhard can even ask what happened, the doorbell rings. It is his uncle, who immediately asks whether everything is all right with them. Gerhard has never seen him so animated. He talks nonstop and cannot settle down.

'Did you not hear what was going on last night? What do you think happened?' Gerhard has no idea what to make of the adults' behavior. His uncle urges them to come see for themselves. When they step into the street, the first thing they see is glass shards everywhere. The walls of the bicycle shop are painted with slogans, and the showroom window has been smashed in. Quietly they walk down to Synagogue Street, not saying a word. Everywhere in the quarter they see chaos. When they get to the old synagogue, a crowd has already gathered. This house of God has been ransacked, and there is evidence of a fire. Even here, Gerhard sees shattered glass everywhere.

His grandmother turns around; she has seen enough. Holding Gerhard by the hand, she runs back home. He still doesn't understand what has happened. Yet in view of the destruction everywhere, he decides not to ask.

In September 1939, Gerhard starts school with a candy-filled cone nearly as tall as he is, called a *Zuckertüte*, the 'sugar bag', which all German children take with them on their first day of school. When he reminisces about this moment, he calls it his 'miracle bag'. His grandparents had filled it with all the best sweets they could think of for their darling. His school is the Hoffmann School for Boys, which is not far from his grandparents' home. The teacher's name is Nachtigall. Gerhard loves this name because it means 'nightingale', but the teacher in no way resembles what the name promises. He is unreasonably strict. Gerhard, in fact, thinks him rather malicious. He beats his students much harder than is common, even for these times.

Gerhard goes to school and plays with his friend, Michael, for quite some time, before one day his grandfather takes him to the side and advises him that it is no longer safe to visit this friend. He is not allowed to be seen with those who are now required to wear the Star of David. It could bring the whole family into trouble. Gerhard cannot understand why he can't be with his best friend. What has changed? Michael is still the same.

Now, when he wants to play with Michael, he must wait until the streets are empty, and no one can see him enter his neighbour's house. A few weeks later, the Jewish family disappears. When he asks for an explanation, his grandfather shrugs his shoulders. He does not know if they were picked up, or if they went underground. Gerhard hears the explanation without digging any deeper. It seems that every day there are mysterious events that happen in this young child's world.

Life goes on as usual. Lessons don't always go according to plan, and school has lost its charm for Gerhard. Life in the streets and playing with his friends give him more freedom with every year and are much more exciting than the long hours spent in the classroom. Pranks are on daily order and the city is a huge adventure playground. A favorite pastime of theirs is rubbing two bricks together, making a red powder. They then pee on the dust, and, with the mud, they write things on the walls of the houses. Sometimes it is slogans, but sometimes, too, they draw indecent pictures. There is always something new they come up with.

The neighbour's bicycle shop has been abandoned and plundered, and it is a forbidden place to go. When he sees what has happened, Gerhard wonders, over and over again, where Michael might be. He and his friends wander into the workshop, even though it's not allowed, and find pots of glue that they dump into a pile in the back yard and set on fire. Then they run away.

But Gerhard doesn't have only mischievous pranks in mind; he wants to make money too. So, for a few coins he helps the customers of the local general store, the *Kolonialwarenladen*, by carrying their shopping bags to their homes around the corner, earning a little extra pocket money.

In the waning months of 1938, Hitler began to show his true face. Terror reigned, not just with his enemies, but within Germany as well. Jewish citizens, who were discriminated against as of his inauguration, were now openly persecuted. Most children in East Prussia—and Gerhard's story is a prime example—could not grasp the events that were happening, nor did they understand any of it. Unless, of course, they were Jewish.

In September 1939, the German Wehrmacht invaded Poland and unleashed a war of unprecedented magnitude. The speed of the German (troops') victories there surprised friends as well as foes. To the East Prussians, however, the occupation of Poland was a gift, because now, once again, they were reunited with the German mainland. But, for the children, nothing changed—for now.

Liesbeth Dejok was born in December 1931 in Erlenrode in the Elchniederung, a name that means the 'Moose Valley'. It's true that in the winter, moose often wander into the surrounding fields, eating discarded vegetable rinds or Brussels sprouts that have been left on the stalk to ripen. The valley is crisscrossed by creeks and irrigation ditches and runs alongside the Memel River, which borders Lithuania. The valley also has an intricate canal system, there to divert flooding and to keep the wetlands arable, which took farmers centuries to build.

Liesbeth's parents have a small farm where they grow their own food. Her father also works in construction. Liesbeth is the youngest, with four brothers and one sister. In the autumn of 1937, she starts the first grade. Liesbeth loves going to this small one-room schoolhouse. In the front is a large yard where she passionately plays ball during her playtimes. In the school's garden, the children plant their own vegetables and flowers. Otherwise, lessons are about practical things, like baking bread and making handicrafts.

For this little girl, soldiers have long been a part of daily life, even before the war began. Young men in uniform have been quartered in the village for as long

A quaint fishing village in the Neman River Delta, Elchniederung, *c.*1930.

as she can remember. On the farms and in the village, they are a welcome sight. 'The soldiers had a good life with us at our house,' Liesbeth remembers. They catch fish in the waterways and fry them over open fires. Often, they sing while they do this, which enchants the children, just as the soldiers enchant the young girls of the village.

By the time the third grade begins, military men have begun living in the schoolhouse. Liesbeth and the other schoolchildren are moved out; their desks are put in the barn. In good weather, lessons are given out in the field. A cook who cooks for the school also caters for the soldiers, but there is always something that falls by the wayside for the children—a slice of cake here, a piece of candy or a sugar cube there.

Soon her brothers are 'drafted'. Liesbeth does not understand this word and wonders why her mother cries all the time now. So, her brothers are also soldiers—what's so wrong with that? Her father has already served in the First World War, and, because of his age, he is not called up to enlist. All he is required to do is dig trenches in the surrounding fields. When her teacher, Naujoks, is drafted, his wife takes over, giving lessons to the primary school students without further thought.

One morning everything is different. Liesbeth's father is already at work when she wakes up, and she notices how silent the village is. Only slowly does she grasp what has happened. During the night all the soldiers have disappeared. But Liesbeth still needs to give the cows water before school. She runs to fill her bucket and pour it into the long wooden trough. As she is tipping the first bucket, she hears an ominous rumbling in the distance. As fast as she can, she fills the trough with more buckets of water and runs to her mother in fear. 'Mama, a thunderstorm, a thunderstorm!' she screams. But her mother takes her face into both hands and says solemnly, 'No, my child, this is the war …'

Her sisters send packages to the front in preparation for the upcoming winter. To keep their brothers warm during the war, a sheep is purchased and the oldest daughter spins wool so that she can knit socks and gloves. Liesbeth is a cleaver girl and soon learns how to spin and knit herself.

In June 1941, Eva Briskorn's childhood ends abruptly. The war has arrived in Königsberg and her parents are visibly upset. Eva does not understand what's going on. Her school has been intermittently closed over the last several months; she does not see anything wrong with that. But then a day comes when her mother insists that Eva should stay at home. She needs her help in the household, she says. The atmosphere in the home changes dramatically. Her father, who is usually quite cheerful, is now nearly always serious, if he is even ever home. Her mother cries all the time and is worried about how to feed her children. Food, because of the war, has been rationed—a rumbling stomach can ruin any good mood. This is something even Eva understands by now.

Gerhard Windt lives with his parents in Königsberg-Ponarth. He was already a young man when the family unexpectedly received a new baby to foster in April 1939. At the age of 24, Gerhard no longer expected his mother Gertrud's undying wish to have a daughter would still come true. But Christel Scheffler was born out of wedlock to a mother who saw no possible means of being able to raise her. The family is delighted and hopes to eventually adopt her.

When Christel learns to talk, the pronunciation of her name is difficult and she begins to call herself Kitty. Everyone else follows suit. Kitty is the sunshine of the family's life and truly a beloved child. Her blonde curly hair is tied into two lively pigtails that bob up and down as she learns to walk. Her eyes, according to her father, are of the 'palest cornflower blue'. Her mother loves to sew for Kitty. She makes all her clothes by hand and sews them with loving care. Although Gerhard is much older than she, Kitty grows up admiring her big brother. He's a soldier and is in the navy, and when he comes home on leave, he wears a smart sailor's uniform. Even this 24-year-old man adores this little girl. And he loves the fact that his mother, Gertrud, is so happy in her renewed role as a mother.

On weekends, Kitty and Gertrud go to visit both the grandmothers. One is a fisherwoman and sells the fresh catch every day at the Königsberger fish market. The *Oma* on her mother's side can usually be found working in her community near the Sackheim Gate. On the way there, they pass the meatpacking house. It stinks so badly that Kitty needs to hold her nose long after she's arrived at her grandmother's house.

At the beginning of 1941, her father is drafted into the army. He is sent to Yugoslavia. Now Kitty and her mother live alone. Only occasionally do they receive mail from the front. The first airstrike on Königsberg takes place in the summer of 1941. For the time being, this seems to be the exception. Nonetheless, Kitty is terrified and becomes an anxious little girl. In 1943, her father returns from the Balkans with battle injuries to his shoulder and back. He spends the first few weeks in the military hospital where his wife and little Kitty visit him often. 'My little angel,' as the head of this family always calls his foster child, helps him to recover quickly.

But soon, the tranquil life of the Windts is definitively over. The houses at the Fichteplatz lie in a horseshoe shape inside of which is a grassy field where the children like to play, but now the field is being torn up. Kitty watches from the kitchen window. She feels outraged and helpless at the same time. Slit trenches appear, and an underground bunker is built. Like all the other children, this 4-year-old does not want her playground to be taken away, and so they continue to play there anyway. One day she cuts her face badly while playing inside one of the unfinished trenches, leaving her with a permanent scar.

Lothar Wegner and his siblings live not far from Kitty's house. His older brother, Horst, and younger sister, Ingrid, who is two years his junior, mean the world to him. What he remembers most of his first years of life is a happy childhood. On Sundays, the family goes to church, after which they visit the zoo or go to one of the many museums in the city. Education for the children is important to the parents; otherwise the children enjoy a carefree life.

When Lothar starts school in September 1941, he feels quite proud. Finally, he's allowed to do what his older brother does. Now he, too, is a big boy. But the year 1941 brings serious changes to the family. His mother, who has always worked as a dedicated housewife managing the home, must go out to find a job. She is hired as a seamstress by a large sewing firm that manufactures uniforms for German soldiers. Lothar's father is a manager at the Nazi-run Organization Todt, a construction group established by the Nazis to build 'all things required'. All that Lothar understands is that the work his father does is called 'mobilisation'.

Prior to this, his father worked in the private sector, but now he is to supervise the construction of roads, bridges and defence systems that will be needed for incoming soldiers who, apparently, will soon be arriving in large numbers. Lothar has not yet seen a soldier face to face. For him the war is altogether an abstraction, but over and over again he hears his older brother and his parents discuss war and its fronts.

In the summer of 1944, Lothar's happy childhood life in Königsberg is shattered forever. Nights full of fear and dread suddenly rule his life. Every night, before putting her children to bed, his mother sets rucksacks packed with all the essentials next to their beds. Every night, the shrill wailing of sirens startles the family awake, and they need to run into the bomb shelter. Lothar barely finds a spot to lie down before the walls begin to rattle from the English bombers that fly over Königsberg in waves, dropping their explosive loads. The deafening noise and ensuing tremors paralyse this 9-year-old boy, who cannot understand any of it. In his terror, he sees his surroundings as if through a magnifying glass. While some people weep and whimper, others roam about and scream, and yet others pray to God that it may all end quickly. Lothar hides his head in his mother's lap. After the attacks, after they leave the bomb shelter again, he sees that all the buildings are in flames. In only a few nights, the historic inner city of Königsberg will lie in ash and rubble from the fire and phosphorus bombings.

'So, have I forsaken my childhood years in Königsberg?' Dorothea Bjelfvenstam asks in her memoir, *They Called us the Hitler Girls*. 'They were burned.'

Dorothea writes in the third person, the only way the memories of August 1944 and the two airstrikes of the British bombers are bearable enough to speak about:

> Königsberg, the burning city. The streetcar still ran all the way to the zoo. But how did the mother and child get into the inner city on foot? They had to get papers that needed to be certified, because the next day the Kindertransport, the transport to take the children to safety, was to leave.

All day long they ran through the burning city, looking for the Swastika flag and the eagle emblem that denoted a government office.

One building that sat between two burning houses was still standing. It was cordoned off all around. People ran, screaming, in and out. All around it was burning. The child saw only fire, buildings on fire, people on fire, flames up to the sky, children at a front door, waiting for their mother. Children who were to jump from the second floor through the flames, children who were waiting, children who were to run away, because the whole building was in flames. Charred trees. A child with a pillow in her arms. Screams. A woman sitting on a suitcase with her hands in front of her face, continuously saying, 'My eyes, my eyes.'

They needed to get over a bridge, over to the other side of the Pregel. The bridge was suddenly blocked off so that the fires could not reach the other side. They had to wait, locked in on the Kneiphof Island. They needed to cross before the Krämer Bridge collapsed! They needed to get to 'the horseshoe', they needed to get home so that the child could be sent away the next day. It was burning everywhere. Burnt people. Flames as tall as buildings, fire to the heavens.

More and more often, Gerhard Gudovius's grandparents spend the summer nights of 1944 in their garden plot at the northern edge of Königsberg, and during the two nights of the British air raids, on 27 and 30 August, the family also stays here in their garden cottage. There are still shelters from the First World War nearby, and when the sirens drag them from their sleep, that's where they run to, to wait it out. Not far from the shelter is an anti-aircraft gun. The soldiers stationed there only seldom risk launching a rocket, wanting to protect the people who have come here seeking refuge. They want to avoid, at all risk, returning fire from the enemy. Gerhard is very lucky. Neither artillery nor bombs land on the little shelter where he and his grandparents have been hiding.

Yet to get home, they once again need to traverse the city. The destruction that they see is horrific. The handcart carrying all their belongings can hardly pass through the streets. Everywhere there are hoses from the firefighters. It all seems so hopeless. The fires overwhelm even the firefighters and destroy their equipment. All the warehouses are aflame. Glowing steel beams turn soft like rubber in the heat and fall under the weight of the buildings.

Phosphorus bombs and flamethrowers have turned the city into a never-before-seen firestorm. Corpses float in the Pregel; people, in their despair, must have jumped into the water, where they burned to death or drowned. There is a biting smoke all around. Gerhard cannot breathe. The smell of burnt flesh and an unbearable heat permeates the air. When they arrive at their house, like a miracle, it is still standing. His grandparents weep. From then on, they move into the cellar. They have no other choice. The fear of being surprised once again by bombs and then not be able to get to safety on time is too overwhelming.

It is estimated that the wave of bombings upon Königsberg by the Royal Air Force cost the lives of 5,000 civilians; 200,000 lost their homes. But the grandparents' will to live is extraordinary. Above all, they would do anything for their grandson Gerhard. For him, in the face of the destruction, what he has witnessed over the past few days takes his innocence away forever. And an angry defiance takes its place.

While the children in Königsberg have no options after the city is destroyed, things in the outlying provinces look quite different. Right up until January 1945, 6-year-old Dieter Gröning from Mednicken, west of Königsberg, has no idea what war means. He does not even know that war exists. When his father was drafted, he was only 2 years old. That his father is rarely home is something he does not wonder about. He does not know anything different. His memories of life on the land are those of a simple and content childhood. In the summer they bathe in the lakes around his home, and little Dieter learns to swim rather quickly. In the winter he plays in the snow with the other boys from the neighbourhood. He toboggans and admires the snorting and steaming horses as they pull their sleighs through the pristine winter landscape. He learns to ride horses on the estate where his parents are hired as farm labourers. He is close to his siblings and he often needs to look after the younger ones, while his mother works or takes care of the household. In 1945, his older brother is 9, his sister is 3½, and the twins are 1½ years old.

The Grönings are not paid in cash. Instead, they are rewarded for their work with food. They also own a cow and several pigs, chickens, ducks and geese. Regularly, they butcher their livestock, and there is always plenty to eat. The whole family participates in the butchering; even Dieter considers these days to be something special. Regularly, too, his mother bakes bread, and on holidays, a cake. Dieter loves to be with his mother in the kitchen. This is where he feels loved and cared for; this is where the world is safe.

The children who live in parts of the Elchniederung experience the start of the war in much the same way. It is not until the beginning of 1944 that Liesbeth Dejok receives news of disasters that appear in short order. All four brothers have fallen. Then there is the time when no member of the Nazi Party dares visit them anymore as her parents never registered as Nazis. Then Liesbeth's oldest sister Helene's husband is killed. Nazi officials come to the door for the fifth time bearing the bad news, and Liesbeth watches as Helene completely falls to pieces. In the end, the adults always force themselves to bravely pull through and move on with their daily lives. Liesbeth is resigned. The only thing in her life that matters now is that the remaining family members stay together.

In contrast, Tilsit had already been bombed as early as June 1941 during the first Russian air raids, and the Russians attack them again the following year. Ursula

Haak, who lives in Tilsit, believes the world is coming to an end. She buries her head in her mother's apron while the thundering bombs outside frighten them both. Ursula prays that death won't hurt so badly.

Her childhood comes to an abrupt end when her father is drafted into the army. 'Well, it is the war …' her mother says, resignedly. This answer does not explain things to the little girl. Not long thereafter, her older brothers, Franz, Erich, Paul and Heinz, are drafted. Eventually there are very few men left at all on the estate, and the women must take over even the hardest labour in order to keep the business running. Only one of her brothers returns home one last time on leave from the front. When he shows up, Ursula is beside herself with joy. Perhaps this means the war is almost over. But Paul can stay only a few short days because he must return to his unit. War must go on.

A year later—it is now 1943—her mother's worst fears come true. Two of her sons were killed in the Battle of Stalingrad. She bravely continues her daily routine, and by 1944 she gets no more news from the front. Not from her husband, not from her two remaining sons. She will never hear word from any of them again. In July 1944, Tilsit becomes the target of heavy bombardments. A month later, all mothers with children are the first to be evacuated. Anna Haak and her three youngest children, Ursula, Horst and Willy, are amongst them.

The day after a fire storm destroyed 90 per cent of the city of Königsberg in August 1944, Dorothea Bjelfvenstam, without knowing it, is given the opportunity of her life. She is evacuated to Saxony along with her classmates. Even then, the situation is perilous, and incomprehensible, to her. In her memoir, she writes:

> The pictures of the departure the next morning are black. At the central railway station, the train has darkened windows. There are sixty children in the first and second grades from the Hindenburg Lyceum. The group director, fully outfitted with Nazi Party regalia, points out the seats in the train compartments where the children are to sit. They are to be separated from their parents. The child is an 11-year-old Hitler-girl; she does not cry. She carries her 'Iron Rations' in a shoulder bag along with some raisins and a packet of sugar, in case of an emergency. Along with that, she has an identification card that entitles her to be on the transport. It is stamped 'Heil Hitler!' Then the train leaves the inferno behind and brings the children to safety.

For many other children her age, the suffering has just begun. But for Dorothea, she is at least spared from the fate of the Wolf Children.

Late in September 1944, 5-year-old Helmut Falk is to go on a big journey, just like Dorothea. He will be going to Saxony. His mother wants to leave the Memel

Territory with her four children and go to live with her relatives. While his mother is worried about the family and the advancing Red Army, Helmut is excited about the upcoming adventure. He's never travelled this far! At the railway station there's a lot of commotion going on. And, in the midst of all the chaos, the family must sit and wait. How long, no one can say. His mother packed their most necessary belongings into two suitcases and each child was allowed one small rucksack. A few clothes, a pillow and a ragdoll are what Helmut packed for himself. And three blue marbles. These he hides in his trouser pocket.

One day and one night they sit at the station and wait for the train that should have departed a day ago. More and more people arrive and squeeze onto the narrow platform. The train attendant has lost control over the situation long ago. Helmut thinks nothing of what he sees around him and finds a corner where he can play with his marbles. How lovely they glint in the sunlight, he thinks. Lost in his thoughts, he plays *Lochklickern*, a game in which his marbles must hit a small hole. A crack at the edge of the station wall works perfectly.

Helmut hears a train coming but doesn't wonder when he hears it departing the station again. After all, all kinds of freight trains came through during the night. Yet, with this train, the entire crowd disappears. Only a few soldiers remain on the platform, smoking cigarettes. Now Helmut panics. Where is his mother? Where are his siblings? He starts to walk around the station building, wandering without aim, but he finds only the train conductor, who shakes his head at him. As far as he knows, that was the last train leaving for the West.

Until today, Helmut has no idea how this could have happened. It's possible that his mother, in all the mêlée, did not notice that her son was left behind. But, for Helmut, a new life begins on this day—without a family.

New Year's Eve 1944/45 is the last time Kitty Windt remembers her family all together in a seemingly carefree atmosphere. By now, Königsberg has been surrounded by the Red Army and is only a few kilometers from the city limits. And yet life inside the city continues on. There is a constant stream of refugees from the East. The Nazi officials, who still run the government posts, are fully unprepared but try to keep the businesses running, using all means and resources.

Kitty's brother, Gerhard, comes home on leave for the New Year and has brought his fiancée. Friends of his parents, a couple, also come to visit. The husband works at the shipyards in Elbing, where they are still manufacturing torpedoes for that 'final victory'. The wife had already been evacuated to Saxony and was now returning to the besieged city once again to spend the holidays.

Kitty doesn't understand any of the worries the adults talk about. Even in the night of New Year's Eve, she stays in bed a long time and sleeps a deep sleep. Suddenly, at midnight, she is startled from her dreams by a loud bang and starts to cry. She's afraid it's another bomb and thinks that they'll have to run into the bunker again. Her mother runs to her side but can hardly comfort her. The adults have just opened a bottle of champagne that miraculously made its way into their home. It's an unbelievable treasure in a city where one can hardly even find bread.

At the beginning of April, Soviet troops take over the city. The bombings do not let up, the city continues to burn, and there is a biting smoke everywhere. Kitty's mother wants to take her to the Baltic Sea. But there is no way out anymore, no trains, no buses. Wherever they look, there are exasperated people seeking a way out of the inferno. German soldiers send them home again and give them this piece of advice: 'The Russians will soon be here. You must find shelter.'

In time, they find an air raid bunker. Kitty is paralysed with fear and takes in all that she sees as if there is a veil over her eyes. When the Red Army finally does arrive in the city, soldiers come to their bunker, escort the people out and march them along the train tracks back to Ponarth. Through smoke and fog, the dour procession marches on. No one knows what will become of them.

Refugees on the icy pier fleeing East Prussia, Pillau port, 26 January 1945.

Lothar's family is together for the last time for Christmas 1944. His father has returned from the front for these few days. There is a looming premonition of upcoming hard times, and just after New Year, things begin to feel dire. His mother can sense this. Cut off from the mainland of Germany, foodstuffs are scarce. Several neighbours decide to make their way to Pillau, where there should be ships to evacuate them to the West. Yet these are easy targets for the Soviet Air Force. It's a dangerous game and one in which her mother is not willing to participate.

Gerhard Gudovius's grandparents' basement is housing more and more people. Many are families that have been bombed out. Others are simply too afraid to return to their homes. The year 1945 starts off as one of terror for Gerhard. Königsberg has been besieged. The Germans, not willing to surrender, are holed up in the city and declare it their fortress. There is barely anything to eat. Their basement is only a place to hide out in. It's dirty inside and cold, and everyone is filled with despair. Gerhard keeps himself to himself. Outside he hears artillery shooting constantly, and when he goes out, he sees nothing but dead people. Some corpses are charred so badly, they are beyond recognition. Some have no heads; others have no limbs.

He climbs into a ruined building, searching for food. The odour of decay is unbearable. He struggles as he steps over dead bodies and represses the thoughts that these were living humans until only a short time ago, people just like him. Now they are but a soft mass over which he must creep. The little food he finds, at least briefly, compensates for the terrible things he sees and hears and smells around him.

It is 10 April 1945, the fortress of Königsberg has fallen to the Russians. A radio broadcast reports:

> After weeks of bloody fighting, the East Prussian Citadel has finally capitulated to the enemy. As of last night at eight o'clock, the roughly 30,000 people who are still living in the Königsberger region are now in enemy hands. Half an hour later, at 8.30, the city commander, General Lasch, gave the orders to his men to 'cease the needless resistance'.

It is the news everyone has been waiting for. The war is finally over.

Königsberg in ruins, April 1945.

The Red Army captures Pillau, 25 April 1945.

Chapter 4

The *Stunde Null*

The *Stunde Null*, 'the Hour Zero', was more than just the end of war for East Prussia. What the Hour Zero brought with it was a full-on economic and social collapse. But for most Wolf Children, May 1945 meant nothing at all. For them, there was no significant break whatsoever. Their suffering had begun much earlier on and continued relentlessly without letting up. Many of them only remember the Hour Zero—a moment that meant so much to the rest of the world, the moment that brought freedom from the oppression of the Nazis—only in vague terms. The end of the war was just one more episode of many of trying to escape the Red Army, or of fighting to stay alive in the now Soviet-controlled lands. For the Wolf Children, whether their first encounter with the 'Russians' was before or after the war, it made no difference to their already traumatised lives.

Even before the fighting came to an end, the revenge of the Russian victors had begun; revenge that was to be retaliation for the suffering that had been inflicted upon them earlier by the Germans. This meant it was primarily women who paid for Hitler's war crimes—rape and murder were on daily order. It wasn't Germany's defeat, but Hitler's tyranny and his world war that were to blame for the endless fleeing, hunger, abandonment and death. But how was a child to understand all this?

Twelve-year-old Eva Briskorn first experiences the war, and all the terrors associated with it, when it arrives in Königsberg in January 1945. With only minutes to spare, her mother packs the few things she's able to gather and rushes her and her six younger siblings, Manfred, Reinhard, Siegfried, Gisela, Rudi and Sabine, out of the door. They must run—now. Her mother pulls a sled carrying their belongings through ice and snow. The roads are choked with thousands of other fleeing people. Over and over, they need to jump to the side to make room for military vehicles that have the legal right of way. They too are having a difficult time manoeuvring around this endless stream of humanity.

Eva cannot feel her feet anymore and limps alongside her mother, who is trying her best to keep her children by her side. She doesn't have enough hands for all her young ones, and so she allows each one a short turn to hold on, then the next is in line. Never in her life has Eva walked this far. Sometimes she's freezing, sometimes she's hot, but there is never a time when she's not weary or hungry.

They don't get far. Within two days' walk from Königsberg, Soviet soldiers take them prisoner and direct this small group of refugees to march ahead of them. Suddenly, it happens. A Russian military vehicle tries to pass them. Five-year-old Siegfried loses his balance and slips underneath. He is killed instantly. The family stands over him, speechless. The truck drives on. No one stops to help the distraught mother and her children. Eva is the first to recover from shock. She wraps her little brother in a blanket and lays him on the sled—it all happens quickly because they must march on. To bury him here is impossible anyway. The earth is frozen, and the snow is much too deep.

A deafening sound of artillery fire pounds in the distance, and the wailing of low-flying aeroplanes drones through the air. Time and time again, soldiers chase the family off the road and out into the fields of this frozen winter land. There's a time when none of the children have shoes on their feet anymore.

After several days, they arrive in a village where the refugees are told they can bed down on the hay inside a barn. Eva's siblings cry themselves to sleep, while Eva and her mother go out and find a shallow trench in a clearing where they can lay the little Siegfried in his final resting place. With no spade, no shovel, no anything that can substitute for a tool, they use their bare hands to cover his body with snow and dirt. Seventy years later, Eva cannot talk about this moment without weeping.

One night the group is herded like cattle into a barn. It no longer has a roof. The floor inside is covered with straw and the people try, as best they can, to bury themselves in it, hoping for some warmth. When Eva awakes the next morning, she momentarily thinks she has arrived in Heaven. It has snowed and they're all lying under a white blanket of splendour. She believes their suffering has finally come to an end. This is what Paradise must be like, Eva thinks. Did she, perhaps, die during the night and is now with the angels? Yet, quickly, and cruelly, reality reels her back in. The refugees are told to gather together immediately. The trek must continue.

Throughout this never-ending journey, they see corpses everywhere. Bodies hang from trees, dangling like marionettes in the wind. More bodies lie in the roadside ditches, most are covered in blood. Eva will never be able to get this scene out of her head.

Sometimes they see German soldiers off in the distance and desperately hope to be rescued. At one point, Eva unties her headscarf and waves it in the air, trying to get their attention. A Russian soldier grabs her arm and roughly yanks it down. Her mother runs to her side. She knows exactly the sort of fate she's saving her daughter from. By now, she has been raped a number of times by Russian soldiers and each time, once it's over, she drags herself back to her children and continues on, just as before. This time the soldier leaves Eva alone.

One day they're allowed to stay in an abandoned farmhouse. Here, Eva gathers frozen potatoes from the fields. They've turned black and are hard, so she tries to melt them on the potbelly stove in their tiny farm kitchen. Once they've become soft, she grates them. As she has no pan, she fries the potato bits, like fritters, on the stove's surface.

Rudi, who cannot understand why they always have to trudge on for hours every day through the cold, repeats the same phrase incessantly: 'I don't want to die. But I'm so tired I want to die. I don't want to die. But I'm so hungry I want to die.' Eva's mother is beside herself and often breaks down in tears. 'What am I to do?' she says over and over. 'There's nothing I can do. We can't buy anything, my darling. There is nothing to buy.'

One day, Rudi gives one last whimper and dies. To Eva, he looks as though he simply fell asleep, but when her little Manfred also 'simply falls asleep', Eva gives up on life. 'With Manfred's death, there was something inside me that died,' she says when she tells her story today. 'He lay there while I held his hand. Of course, I didn't want him to go, but famine and the frigid cold took the life right out of him. They were all still such young children … and I was the oldest.'

Eventually she will learn to bury the guilt she feels for having survived these dreadful times. But by the time Sabine dies from typhoid, Eva gives up all hope. Maybe death is, in fact, a salvation, and she prays for it to come. Soon.

How long this odyssey continues, Eva cannot recall. When they arrive in the East Prussian village of Powalken, they are told they'll be allowed to stay for a while. However, there's nothing to eat. Eva gathers thistles, leaves and bark, from which her mother cooks a thin broth over an open fire. By now, the family has been reduced to three—Eva, her 10-year-old sister, Gisela, and their mother.

Fleeing East Prussia, winter 1944/45.

Christel Nitsch, from Gross Schönau in Gerdauen district, is 9 years old and the youngest of eleven children. Two of her sisters are married. The oldest brother, Albert, was killed in Russia in 1944. Her father, who works for the railroad in Pillau, is a heavy drinker and one weekend deserts the family. Her mother, left on her own, cannot believe what has happened and, as if paralysed, does nothing when the Red Army arrives.

The first to prepare to leave the village with his family is their neighbour. This enterprising young farmer harnesses his best horses to a sled and heaves his few belongings onto it. But an unexpected turn of events keeps him here. His elderly mother will not even consider leaving the farm where she has lived her entire life. Right up to the very end, he tries—in vain—to persuade her to join. Besides his mother, all that will stay on the farm are two old and sickly horses, and a rickety old wagon.

For a few families, including Christel's mother and her young siblings, the neighbour and his sled provide the only option to flee. In the final count, there are fifteen people who join him, and together they set out for the unknown. The adults walk, as the horses are too weak to carry anyone on the wagon. Christel, however, the youngest in the group, is allowed to sit up on top. Like all the children, she is dressed in several layers of clothing and can hardly move. For her, though, this is a wonderful adventure.

After a day's journey, they come upon an abandoned farm. The horses are tired and need a rest. It appears the farm was recently deserted, and it happened in a great hurry. Cows and pigs are still in their stalls; the pantry is full of food. Their small community of co-travellers is provided for, at least for the night. But their comfort is short-lived. Morning arrives and, again, they must trudge on.

The road is jammed with fleeing people. Blankets, wagons and bicycles lie everywhere, abandoned in the ditches. Even dead horses lie alongside the road. Christel finally understands how dire their situation is. For how many days they continue to flee, she can no longer recall, but there is a moment when everyone is screaming in loud confusion all about something that baffles her: 'The Russians are here! The Russians are here!'—what could this possibly mean?

Soldiers approach them and they motion to separate the children from their mothers. The children all run from the soldiers, who only half-heartedly go after the youngest. They concentrate primarily on the older ones. Standing at a safe distance, 9-year-old Christel watches as other children, if they don't comply, are brutally dragged off and beaten. What she cannot know is that her siblings will end up in a labour camp in Siberia, and she will never see them again.

Her mother tries to protect the rest of her children as best she can. She tells the Russians they all have typhoid. The lie seems to work, and the family is left in peace for the most part, even though they are kept hostage and are not allowed to travel on.

Their supplies are soon exhausted, and the children go out into the fields to gather everything they can find, including snails and frogs. Even cats and dogs are not out of the question. Half a year after they began their flight, Christel's mother has died from hunger and exhaustion.

Nine-year-old Lothar Wegner's parents do not want to flee. It's much too dangerous, they believe, so they decide to wait it out in Königsberg. The family comes together for one last Christmas in 1944. Horst, his older brother, who, at 16 years of age, was drafted into the German army as an anti-aircraft gunner, cannot attend. But his father returns home from the front for these few days. As if the adults have a premonition of what is to come, a family photo is taken.

It is the beginning of 1945, and the situation in Königsberg is critical. Even Lothar can see this. Neighbours, they learn, try to escape by boarding a refugee ship, but they eventually abandon their plan. The Soviet Air Force is bombing anything they see on the water, including civilian vessels.

No one knows where death will appear next. Will it be in the occupied city of Königsberg? Or out on the Baltic Sea? Lothar's mother believes the family will be safest if they hide inside one of the city's air raid shelters. There are a few other women, children and old people who do the same. The rest of Königsberg has been deserted, and the city looks like a ghost town.

It is April 1945 and Lothar, his mother and his younger sister, Ingrid, along with their remaining neighbours, are sitting in the air raid shelter once again. They are all terrified. The women and girls do what they can to make themselves ugly. They smear mud into their hair and rub soot on their faces, anything to look hideous. Lothar cannot understand why they're doing this. Out in the

German refugees fleeing East Prussia, February 1945.

street, he hears machine-gun fire, the detonation of grenades, and a constant barrage of artillery fire. The rattling of the chain links on the tanks as they roll by is deafening.

Suddenly, the door to the shelter is thrown open. Russian soldiers, just young boys carrying guns, storm in and order them out into the daylight. The soldiers look frightening. The dreadful anticipation the women had warned of seems to be abated for the time being, though. Slowly and with seeming propriety, the people are helped, one by one, out into the open. Some of the boys are asked to stand to the side, but Lothar is allowed to stay with his mother and sister. They will be escorted out of the city because heavy battles are about to take place, it is explained.

In formation, they walk into the countryside until, at dusk, they are allowed to enter the barn of a large estate. Lothar is exhausted. Even his mother and his sister Ingrid can hardly move any longer. His mother tries to cheer her children, but with each word, Lothar becomes ever more fearful. He worries the Russians will shoot them. But then, he wonders, why didn't they do so right away? He had vowed to his father to be a brave boy; it's what he promised when Papa left for war. His mother and sister need him, he knows, and so even with all these dreadful thoughts, he suppresses the tears that continue to well up.

The next night, Lothar has the fright of his life. It's something he's never experienced before: complete helplessness. He must stand by and watch as soldiers rip the clothes right off the bodies of the women and girls, and he must look on as they throw them to the ground and force themselves between their legs. He must listen to his mother's anguish as she pleads for mercy. But he cannot help her. This is the night Lothar's childhood comes to an end.

It is unusually quiet in the morning. No more battles, no more artillery fire. Only a few soldiers remain hanging about the barn. They motion to the shamed women that they are free to go. But there is nowhere to go.

When they reach the outskirts of the city, Lothar can see that all the houses have been destroyed. Windows, everywhere, are broken, torn curtains waft from ghostlike houses, furniture and broken china are scattered in the yards. His mother wanders silently stunned through the streets, holding her children by the hand. The picture of devastation is everywhere. Nothing was left untouched. When they arrive at their home, Lothar cries out. Everything has been destroyed; their home has been ransacked. Duvets slit wide open. Their feathers dance in the wind like falling snowflakes.

Within a few months, only one family member will remain alive—Lothar.

In October 1944, Liesbeth Dejok's family is told that they need to evacuate immediately. Liesbeth first realises the gravity of their situation when she sees her mother and father and the neighbouring farmers slaughter the pigs and quickly pack their belongings in preparation for the flight. The cattle are let out to pasture. But when she asks who will milk them, the 13-year-old receives only her father's frown as an answer. Liesbeth can see how it breaks his heart to have to leave the cows, the chickens, and the dogs and cats behind. It was only last week that they pulled the potatoes out of the ground and stacked them into their cone-shaped piles. And the wheat hasn't even been threshed!

That they must hurry is evident, as the road out front has become a sea of humanity, horses and wagons, as far as the eye can see. And there is an immense tension that permeates the air. Where are they to go?

After walking for many days, Liesbeth and her family arrive in the Samland, the Sambia Peninsula, once again—this time on the coast near Neukuhren (now Russian Pionersky). Some of the people on the trek attempt to run across the frozen lagoon, but many fall through the ice, and every day the Dejoks hear more horrifying accounts of refugees coming to a tragic end. These are stories they hear from other refugees—their only source of news.

Liesbeth's family comes upon an empty cottage. It's apparent the family had left for the unknown long ago. They decide to stay here through the new year of 1944/45—her father, her mother, her sisters and the youngest one, her brother. Liesbeth's father feels he's too old to flee. 'And if the Russians do arrive, what then? They are, after all, human beings, too,' he says over and over, trying to calm the rest of his family.

However, in February, the authorities warn them they must run once again. This time they should get to one of the harbours where, presumably, ships will be waiting to take them to the German mainland. Her father insists, though, under all circumstances, they will stay in East Prussia.

When the Red Army arrives, soldiers accost them and rob most villagers of everything they own. Liesbeth is horrified. Some of the soldiers have even filled their trouser pockets to overflowing with stolen goods. '*Uri, uri* …!' they shout incessantly, 'Watchy, watchy …!', and grab the men's watches and the women's jewellery. Miraculously, Liesbeth's family is spared. The only thing they lose is Liesbeth's sister's wedding band. Then they are free to go—and are sent back to the Elchniederung.

They begin their trek home, and fight their way through throngs of refugees moving in the opposite direction. All along the way, they talk to people who describe gruesome stories that took place at the hands of the Russians. And yet, right to the end, the family stays hopeful they will come home and find it just as they had left it a few months earlier.

What awaits them, though, exceeds even their worst nightmares. Already from afar, Liesbeth can see the entire village is now underwater. The dam has broken, and the Memel River has washed into the Niederung. Furthermore, everything is in ruin. The Dejok's house has been destroyed and plundered right down to the bedding. The family's once well-stocked pantry, empty; even the last of the canning jars, gone.

The Red Army enters East Prussia, February 1945.

Of the local residents, only a few have returned, and they find that every home has soldiers quartered in it. When darkness settles over the Niederung, the soldiers grab the women—every night this drama plays out. All through the night, the sound of women screaming and pleading echoes through the village, while the Russians sing their drinking songs. In the background, a cacophony of victory cries.

Liesbeth and a few other women hide in the reeds on the banks of the Memel at night. Climbing into wooden rowboats they had hidden in the marsh, they pull off into the water to sleep, camouflaged by the tall grasses.

During the day, Liesbeth works for the Red Army, as do all the villagers. With wheelbarrows, they are to haul pitchforks, spades, axes and saws from abandoned farms and deliver them to the Red Army headquarters, located in the village square. For pay, they receive a piece of bread or a bowl of soup. Her father is too weak to help with the work and, accordingly, receives no rations whatsoever. Liesbeth, her sisters and mother share what little they have with him.

Under cover of night, her sister combs through the Soviets' garbage pit, looking for something to eat. During the day, Liesbeth gathers unripe berries, sorrel and thistles, from which they try to cook a broth. It doesn't take long before everyone falls ill. Her father has typhoid and the entire family contracts cholera from the filthy water they've been drinking. One month after their return to the Niederung, her father dies.

Whether the war is still being fought or peace has been reached, no one in the village knows for sure. But one day a strange event takes place. With great fanfare, the Russians shoot their guns into the air and shout, *'War kaput! War kaput!'*—the war is over.

Liesbeth has no reason to feel joy. Since no one in the family can work anymore, there's no food for them. She's deathly ill, the family is ill, and there's no foreseeable end to their hardships. Soon her mother falls into unconsciousness, and dies the next morning. Liesbeth is 14.

For some East Prussians, the attempt to flee to the West in the last year of war was a success, and by all definitions they should have escaped the worst. For many of them, though, to leave the motherland of East Prussia behind forever was unimaginable. For these people, the war coming to an end merely rekindled their hope to return home.

Very little research has been done regarding the return migration to East Prussia after war's end; very few reliable numbers exist. But it's certain that in the spring and summer of 1945, many families left their refugee housing in Thuringia, Saxony, Berlin and elsewhere in Germany to make their way back to the East, where they had left all their worldly possessions when they fled. In fact, the Allied occupying forces tolerated, and even encouraged, this plan. Records show that the last official transport to East Prussia left Langensalza in central Germany on 17 July 1945.

It's hardly a coincidence that the Potsdam Conference, in which the future of the defeated country, Germany, was to be determined, began on this very day.

The Potsdam Conference lasted two weeks, ending on 2 August 1945. Here, three of the four victorious powers of the Second World War agreed to five political principles that were to govern Germany: Demilitarisation, De-Nazification, Decentralisation, Dismantling, and Democratisation. France consented to all these decisions at a later date. Furthermore, an agreement was reached in which all the German territories east of the Oder River and its tributary, the Lusatian Neisse, were put under Polish and Soviet jurisdiction until a true peace treaty would be signed. All German people in the area, as well as those in the Czech Republic and Hungary, were to be 'resettled in an orderly and humane' fashion. Further decisions about Germany's future continued to be debated over the years. However, the annexations to the Soviet Union and to Poland were deemed permanent as compensation for their losses, and both countries were uncompromising in this decision.

For the people who returned to their motherland in the East in the summer of 1945, the *Stunde Null* was to be a time to rebuild. It represented a new beginning and a time to heal from the wounds of war. Little did they know that by returning, they were headed straight for their own doom.

This is how it happened for Gerhard Heim, Bernhard Kießling and Rita Elm. They were children who did not know each other, but they all came from the same picturesque town of Gerdauen—a settlement that had been established by the Teutonic Order, with over five centuries of history. In their early years, they all had played hide-and-seek in the shadows of the fourteenth-century church, the Ordenskirche. They fished in the lake, called the Banktinsee, and shared bashful secrets behind hawkers' stalls in the market square. When their families had to flee, this idyllic childhood vanished instantly, so it is no wonder that their yearning to return to this lost paradise was so strong.

Gerhard Heim is 9 years old when he and his mother and younger sister, Hilde, must flee their home in Gerdauen. It is autumn 1944, and the Allies have been bombing Königsberg since August. Gerhard's father has been gone since 1942, fighting the war. His grandfather, who works for the national railway system, organises a freight wagon to bring the family to safety in Berlin. But he must stay behind and continue to work. The things they cannot take with them, valuables like crystal and china, are buried in a pit behind the house. They will dig them up again when they return, they believe.

The train travels west for two days and then is suddenly ambushed by heavy strafing. In a panic, everyone jumps off the train and runs. In her hurry, Gerhard's mother grabs only one of the two suitcases they brought with them. Low-flying aircraft circle above while the three run for several miles across stubbled fields covered in hoar frost and finally arrive at a railway crossing.

They are in luck. A train is waiting, and it happens to be going to Berlin. Gerhard's mother lifts her children up onto a wagon. As for herself, she insists she must return to the derailed train for the one suitcase she left behind. It contains all the last belongings they still own. Gerhardt is much too tired to protest. Just as his mother returns, the train begins to roll. The children are frantic and scream and scream. In a last-minute attempt, two German soldiers bravely jump from the moving train and help the woman up.

The family arrives safely in Berlin and remains in the capital city until the war is over. The ceasefire has barely been declared before they plan their return to the motherland. Perhaps his father has managed to forge his way home and is waiting for them.

Because passenger trains no longer travel east, Gerhard's family, including his grandmother and auntie, go by foot. They bring very little with them, other than the clothes they are wearing. They are en route for several weeks.

When they finally arrive in Gerdauen, there's no trace of Gerhard's father. Instead, a Polish family has moved into their home and will not even let them in. Gerhard has only a vague memory of what happens next. The events of the following months are much too traumatic. First his grandmother dies, then his mother's sister, the aunt who had just turned 18. The famine during the winter of 1945/46 eventually takes his mother's life as well. Suddenly, Gerhard and his sister are all alone.

In January 1945, 7-year-old Bernhard Kießling and his sister, Ilse, two years younger, leave Gerdauen with their mother. The Red Army is already standing at the outskirts of the city, and yet the family somehow manages to escape in the eleventh hour.

As a precaution, his mother hangs cardboard signs around her children's necks. She has written their names and birthdates on them and glues a prayer with an image of the Saviour on the reverse. But where should they go? The only possibility, they believe, is to evacuate by boat over the Baltic Sea. And so, they, like so many others, make the treacherous trek to Pillau, where supposedly there are ships departing for Germany.

On 9 February, it is finally time to go. Jostled by a pressing crowd, Bernhard and his sister stand at the pier with their mother. They intend to get on the *General Steuben*, which is headed for Kiel. His mother holds their hands so tightly it hurts. But Bernhard doesn't complain. The throngs scare him and to be separated from her is worse than anything he can imagine. The massive white ship is so near he can almost touch it, and then a murmur circulates through the crowd. The gangplanks have been lifted; the ship is overfilled.

Ilse begins to cry, and even their mother looks like she's close to tears. But they're in luck. Not long after, an escort boat, equally filled to bursting, arrives. This boat does allow them to board and brings them to safety in Kiel. It will turn out to be a much different fate from that of the *General Steuben*—a ship that was sunk by Russian torpedoes on the night of 10 February, killing over 4,000 refugees.

Bernhard's family experiences the war coming to an end from the outskirts of Berlin. What they see is nothing but a nightmare. Night after night, the sky over the city glows red. Berlin is on fire.

In May 1945, Russian tanks arrive in this small town where Bernhard, Ilse and their mother have found refuge. The way peace is supposed to feel remains a mystery to Bernhard, but his mother soon seems to feel at ease. The idea that they'll soon be able to return to their home lifts her spirits. A long road lies ahead of them, to be sure, but return to Gerdauen is what they want to do—his mother does not hesitate in this decision, even for one moment.

The return proves to be more difficult than they had believed. Most of the land's infrastructure has been destroyed. There are no passenger trains, so they do what so many of the other homeward-bound people do—they jump onto freight trains and ride like vagrants, ever pushing eastward. But most oppressive is the famine. Bernhard can think of nothing but food.

When they finally get to Gerdauen, Bernhard is struck with horror. His beautiful home has been laid to waste. Nothing is in its place. The windows are broken. There are glass shards everywhere. In the yard he sees shattered mirrors, broken furniture, the cosy sofa from the living room, slit wide open.

Russians are now occupying their home and chase them away with vile language. Discouraged, Bernhard's mother takes her two children by the hand and walks on until they find shelter in an abandoned house.

To receive at least a small portion of bread and soup each day, his mother works for the Red Army on a farm. She shares her meagre food rations with her children. It's not long before she collapses from exhaustion. She is emaciated down to her bones; her stomach is bloated. With a tablespoon, the children feed her water. Yet she dies two days later.

Bernard doesn't know what to do with his dead mother. He lets her lie in the bed for days. His younger sister lies next to her and cries. She refuses to get up. Not long after, even she does not wake up again.

Twelve-year-old Ruth Deske, her mother and three younger siblings, Helga, Siegfried and Karl-Heinz, leave their home in Gerdauen with the hope of finding an evacuation ship to take them to the West when they get to Pillau. They arrive in the Samland where they want to pick up her grandmother. Their plans, however, quickly change. Her grandmother insists she cannot make that journey. It's February in 1945. She's old and frail and doesn't want to board a ship. Ruth's mother faces a difficult choice, but leaving her mother behind is not an option. Her husband has been missing in Russia since 1944, and Ruth's mother cannot fathom losing yet another family member. What the family decides to do instead is go back to Gerdauen, with Ruth's grandmother in tow. In May, they start their journey home.

The children take turns pulling the handcart they have found on the side of the road. It's piled high with their belongings; 2-year-old Karl-Heinz and their ill grandmother ride on top. They are en route for three weeks. Time and time again they come upon Soviet soldiers who brutally beat them and rape Ruth's mother. There's no food to eat. And yet they finally arrive.

They find their farm is occupied by Russians, but at least they're able to settle on the neighbour's land, and they begin by planting a garden. This is how they're able to live through the summer, and, despite all their hardships, they have faith in a new beginning. Their confidence is crushed, however, at the end of October.

Without warning, Russian soldiers come one day and drive all the residents out of the village and into a nearby town. The reason is a new border zone has been created between Poland and the Soviet Union, and they are no longer allowed to be here. The whole operation is so abrupt and brutal that they need to leave the bedridden grandmother behind.

The next day, Ruth, her mother and another woman return to fetch her grandmother and bring her back with them. What they see when they arrive at the house where they stayed until only just yesterday makes their blood run cold. Windows and doors have been thrown wide open. Glass shards are everywhere. Finally, they find the grandmother's corpse in the bedroom. She's still lying on the bed. On the floor next to her is her severed head.

There's nothing the two women and the young girl can do but suppress their horror. And get to work. They want to at least bury the mutilated body in the yard. Two young Russians arrive on horseback and go after the two women. With her cropped hair and ragged trousers, Ruth looks like a boy, and they leave her alone. However, Ruth must stand by and watch helplessly as her mother is raped, once again. When the men are finished with them, they chase the women and Ruth off. Her dead grandmother will be left behind, lying in the front yard, unburied.

It is autumn 1945, and 7-year-old Rita Elm has already lost the better part of her family. Her father was *gefallen*, 'killed in action'. Rita cannot understand why he can never come home again, when all he did was 'fall'. During the escape from East Prussia at the end of 1944, her two 8-month-old twin sisters died. Whether they froze to death or died from the famine is not clear. In Rita's memory they look like two porcelain dolls with two perfectly formed little faces, disfigured only by their blue lips.

But it's a time of peace again, and the horrors of war finally seem to belong to the past. Rita and her mother return to her grandparents' small farm near Gerdauen, the farm from which they hurriedly fled a year ago.

Nothing is how it once was. Destitute from the plundering, and poor in health, her grandparents look alarmingly frail. Food is hard to come by. Not even the basics can be found. Rita's mother knows no alternative but to make a 'hamster-run' to Lithuania.

In Lithuania, she will find not only bread, but cake as well, Rita's mother tells her—a sentence that will stay with Rita for the rest of her life. Lithuania appears to be their castle in the sky. Rita bravely stays home to care for her grandparents. In Lithuania, just the other side of the border, her mother trades their last possessions for food on the black market. Three times she ventures out on this dangerous expedition. From the third, she never returns.

It's now January 1946. Rita waits with her grandparents, week after week. She boils water with frozen branches in it, making a broth that she feeds the old ones. First her grandfather dies. Her grandmother wakes only occasionally, acts confused, then no longer answers Rita's persistent questions, her begging and pleading, when might Mummy return. In time, even her beloved grandmother dies. Rita pulls a sheet over the two and makes her way to Lithuania. She wants to find her mother.

Chapter 5

Abandoned

In the minutes of the Potsdam Conference, held near Berlin in July 1945, the following dialogue was recorded:

Churchill: I want to raise only one question. I note that the word 'Germany' is being used here. What is now the meaning of 'Germany'? Is it to be understood in the same sense as before the war? …

Truman: Actually, Germany no longer exists …

Stalin: I find it very hard to say what Germany is just now. It is a country without a government, without any definite borders. Germany has no troops and no border patrol. She is broken up into occupation zones. Take this and define what Germany is. It is a broken country.

With this break-up of the entire country of Germany, life for the Germans in East Prussia most certainly came to an end. For the Soviet Union, on the other hand, it marked a new beginning. Stalin held high hopes for his war spoils, and the acquisition of the territory of East Prussia now guaranteed Russia would have access to the Baltic Sea year round. Furthermore, the rich land that was once the breadbasket of Germany would be an added, if not lucrative, asset to its economy.

The strategic plans that developed over the two weeks of the Potsdam Conference did little to quell the catastrophe that was descending upon the East Prussian people, a catastrophe fanned all the more by the hate propaganda that had been planted in the heads of the Soviet soldiers from the early days of war in 1943.

Prussia had been the alleged Nazi hotbed, and even the name Königsberg was, for most Russians, synonymous with the word fascism, and its spin-off, militarism.

For the 1.67 million Soviet troops who were deployed to East Prussia, the sentiment of their General Zhukov echoed in their heads: 'Woe to the land of the murderers. We will get our terrible revenge for everything. On German soil there is but one master—the Soviet soldier. He be both the judge and the punisher for the torments of his fathers and mothers, for the destroyed cities and villages.'

The revenge, however, landed less on those guilty of war—the Nazi administration, their SS minions and political bigwigs who had fled the land

Rally of the 8th company of the Red Army after having entered East Prussia, August 1944.

long before the Russians even arrived. Rather, it descended upon those civilians who were least able to run—old men, women and children. For them, the neverending time of 'post-war' was only just beginning.

Military communications from Moscow to the Russian front never conveyed that the Republic intended to keep this vast region intact. As a consequence, the Red Army never ceased destroying everything in sight—every home, the supporting infrastructure and the countless engineering achievements that had taken generations to build. And all this took place within a few short weeks and with it, they destroyed the very basis for a civilised life.

The Russian government intended to establish a new identity for this territory as well as create a new social structure. But plans for how this was to be implemented were never concrete and proceeded slowly and only incrementally. Long after the war was over, corpses were still lying in the streets of the destroyed city Königsberg, left to rot. Roaming through the midst of this human carnage were the few surviving German people, crazed by want of food. They ate the dirt off the streets; they ate thistles and dandelions, single kernels of wheat, carrion—anything they could find. Begging, robbing and black marketeering were the everyday norm. The violinist Michael Wieck mentions cannibalism in his memoir: 'Doctors recognised that the meat sold on the black market was in fact human flesh. Likewise, meatballs sold in the streets were made with human flesh. Russians, too, reported an ongoing slaughter of humans. People would coax others into alleyways, kill them, and profit from their flesh, lungs and heart.'

Even the Russian authorities documented these gruesome deeds after war's end. In Bledau, for example, a 40-year-old mother and her oldest daughter were arrested. The mother had fried the hearts, livers and lungs of two of her daughters, thereby feeding a few more people, saving them from starvation for another five days. Officials recorded dozens of similar cases throughout the territory.

In the first year following the war, the Soviet military was commissioned with the reconstruction of the territory's infrastructure, saying that they intended to provide for all people, regardless of nationality. However, another, more pressing, question bothered the Russian authorities stationed in Königsberg. Shouldn't the Germans, who now also needed to be fed and sheltered, simply be deported? There were still tens of thousands of them living in unimaginable conditions, burrowed inside caves, ruined buildings and cellars around the city, and although the farmers of East Prussia had harvested record crops in 1944, plundering and indiscriminate destruction turned it all to nought.

The roughly 36,000 remaining Königsbergers were now made available to the Red Army, whom they were to help clean up the destruction. They were paid for their work, but only very little. For twelve hours' work, they received 400 grams—about eight slices—of bread, and a bowl of gruel. And only those who had work received food. For the remaining 74,000 women, children, old men and disabled war veterans who were unable to work, this meant there was nothing to eat.

'Broad sectors of the German population are extremely undernourished and are in desperate need of all foodstuffs,' the Russian chief of police, Trofimov, reported to the Secretary of State Molotov in Moscow from his station in Königsberg. Even the Russian troops did not have enough to eat.

On 4 July 1946, Königsberg was renamed Kaliningrad. Further name changes followed. The harbour city, Memel, became Klaipėda, Insterburg was now called Chernjachovsk and Tilsit was Sowjetsk. Even the Memel River got a new name. The word 'Memel' was a name so German that it was part of her heritage going back to the 1800s, but in 1946, the river, too, received a new name: Neman.

After the 'Great Patriotic War', as it is known to the Soviets, new traditions were to be established for this annexed territory, and with them a new narrative was to be told. The 'liberation of Königsberg' is only one example, becoming part of the Russian legend when recounting the events of that war.

But even Russian settlers who first came to this new territory found it difficult to feel at home here. The situation was too uncertain, and provisions were too precarious. Many turned back, leaving Kaliningrad again to return to where they had come from. Too little had been invested in its reconstruction. With their own eyes, they too watched as industrial plants were dismantled, farmers' drainage ditches were blown up, and bricks, by the ton, were hauled off to Moscow.

In this new world, there certainly was no room for the children of East Prussia, especially since the Soviets did not even want them to remember their German heritage. For the Wolf Children, life was less distinguished between 'the time of war' and 'the time after war', as it was between 'the time with my family' and 'the time without any relatives at all'. For some, losing the security of one's family happened abruptly—through sudden, unanticipated separation, or a violent death. Others witnessed the death of their parents and siblings as an excruciating and slow progression of starvation or disease and illness. Either way, they eventually found themselves alone, the last of the family still alive.

The predominant experience these children remember between the years 1945 and 1947 was a deep and relentless feeling of abandonment. Since they couldn't rely on the new authorities to give them help, their predicament was made all that much worse in that they rarely received help from even their own people, the Germans.

This peculiar indifference, and even apathy, by the German people after the war—not only towards one another but also regarding themselves—has been studied in modern-day research. The philosopher Hannah Arendt had this to say about it:

> Amid the ruins, Germans mail each other picture postcards still showing the cathedrals and market places, the public buildings and bridges that no longer exist. A lack of response is evident everywhere and it is difficult to say whether this signifies a half-conscious refusal to yield to grief or a genuine inability to feel.

When the Wolf Children today talk about what they went through, they seem to condense their stories to four or five sentences without revealing any emotions. But it's true, for most people, it is too much to hear and absorb such tragic stories. After so many years of suppressing their memories, it is surprising for a Wolf Child to meet someone who really wants to dig deeper into the buried layers of their past. To go there, to remember and recount, and to listen, requires a tremendous amount of patience and compassion from both sides.

When I went to Lithuania to research this project, I was grateful to have the Dutch photographer Claudia Heinermann, an empathetic colleague and travelling companion, along with me. While I concentrated on documenting the Wolf Children stories, she captured their emotions, their body language and their environments. With her camera she was able to show how history has etched itself into the lines of their, now quite old, faces. Throughout our many interviews, we both could feel the painful loneliness and the lingering fear that continues to live within each of these victims even to this day. Claudia and I would often sit in the car afterwards for a long period of time before we could drive on, or even speak.

This is how it was for us after our visit with Hilde Horn, who now lives in Tauragė, the former German Tauroggen. She lives in the attic of a tiny farmer's cottage that is painted yellow and once belonged to her Lithuanian foster parents. Her overwhelming sense of abandonment is ever-present, even to this day. Her husband, a Wolf Child just like she, died several months ago. He was the only person who ever really understood what she had been through.

Hilde is from Gerdauen. She is 4 years old when her mama, after a heavy attack of typhoid, 'goes to Heaven' in 1940. Why it's supposed to be beautiful there, as the priest always tells her, is incomprehensible to Hilde. She only knows that she

Hilde Horn.

misses her mama desperately. Hilde is the youngest of four children, of whom only Helmut, who is two years older than she, will still be alive at war's end.

Not long after her mother's death, Hilde's father takes up with other women and barely concerns himself with his two grieving children. One day, Hilde has a new mother. At least, this is how her father introduces her, and then he takes off for the war. In truth, this woman does not fulfill her new role in the least. And not once is this 'new mother' true to her husband. Young Hilde sees strange men come and go as soon as he's out of the door.

Then her stepmother disappears, and along with her, her brother, Helmut. Hilde learns from a neighbour that the young woman took off for Germany with a Wehrmacht soldier. Why she didn't take Hilde with her is something she can only surmise. Maybe she was just too young or too wild or too impulsive. But now she is a 9-year-old, all alone in the world.

When the Soviets arrive to occupy Gerdauen in January 1945, soldiers ransack every home. They even come to Hilde's apartment. She stands by, terrified, watching, as they take the last of the valuables, leaving her standing alone inside her destroyed home. For days, she doesn't dare leave, and no one comes to look in on her.

Twelve-year-old Eva Briskorn, her mother, and her younger sister, Gisela, have been staying in a small village in West Prussia. The will to live has all but left her. All three of them have contracted typhus and they barely cling to life. *Lieber Gott mach mich fromm, dass ich in den Himmel komm* ... ('Dear God, make me devout, so that I will get to Heaven') is the prayer that she has prayed every night since she can remember. She hopes it will keep her safe throughout the silence of the night. Hunger is now the norm. Eva experiences life as nothing but a fever-plagued drudgery of weariness and fatigue. Her body hurts everywhere; the unbearable stomach cramps and persistent colic leave her in a state of dull listlessness. One morning, her mother is lying lifeless next to her in the bed. Eva needs a moment before she realises that her mother died in the night. Now she must also take on the role of mother for her little sister, Gisela, and try to find a way out of this hopeless situation for both of them.

With the Soviet occupation and the lack of hygiene during the war, epidemics—cholera, malaria and typhus, diseases that had once been effectively eradicated—now flourished throughout the region.

Thirteen-year-old Gerhard Gudovius falls ill with typhus in 1946. He spends several weeks in a military hospital in Königsberg, where patients lay two, even three, to a bed inside a large dormitory. The patients, including Gerhard—who also contracted pleurisy while in the hospital—freeze and shiver day and night. Icy winds blow in through broken windows that have been haphazardly stuffed with rags and wetted cardboard. Often enough, it snows right into the rooms and onto the beds. The potbelly stoves heat only to just above the freezing point, and anyway, firewood and coal are rare to come by. Even the doctors and nurses complain of the freezing temperatures. Frostbitten feet and black frozen fingers are a common occurrence. Water has to be hauled in from the outside as the pipes froze long ago and many of them have burst. Often the only way to get water is to melt snow. Soap has not been available in a long time. A saving grace is that Gerhard's grandparents look in on him as often as possible.

The food rations are just enough to stay alive. A slice of moistened bread sprinkled with a pinch of sugar in the morning. When bread or sugar are not available, breakfast consists of two pieces of hard candy. At noon and in the evening, a thin broth is served. Gerhard is deathly ill, but his grandparents don't give up on their darling. When he's finally released from the hospital, he can hardly stand on his own. He has to hook arms with his two grandparents in order to walk, but they are nearly as weak as he. Together they walk the long road home, holding one another up, since streetcars have not been working in this destroyed city for a long time.

Hunger torments all three members of this little family. Gerhard searches the streets for food and finds a small bag of powdered coffee substitute, *Ersatzkaffee*, in a neighbour's cellar. They boil it with water, drink the brew and then eat the grounds. His grandfather is not able to tolerate this concoction. He finally dies from starvation. Gerhard and his grandmother hold on to life a bit longer. He takes the few potato peels that he finds while digging through garbage pits out in the city and slaps them on the sides of the potbelly stove in their kitchen. When they have fallen off, they are considered done, and this is what the two of them have to eat.

Bruno Klein with three of his younger siblings.

Fifteen-year-old Bruno Klein from Königsberg wakes from unconsciousness one morning in 1945 with an aching body, a black eye and numerous contusions on his head. He is lying in a cold, damp cell inside Soviet headquarters. He doesn't know where he is. He doesn't recall at first how he even got here. Little by little, though, his memory returns.

He and an older Lithuanian gentleman had found temporary shelter inside a ruined building. Shortly after they fell asleep, they were awakened by Soviet soldiers and, with deafening screams and gun barrels pointed at their backs, they were marched out and taken in for interrogation. A young Russian boy is missing—what might they know about this? Bruno knows nothing, saw nothing, and is terrified. The Lithuanian man, too, does not know anything but tries to persuade the soldiers to at least let Bruno go. His pleading, however, is fruitless.

For several more days, the Lithuanian man and the young German boy, Bruno, are brutally beaten with rifle butts and interrogated again and again. When Bruno returns to consciousness, he is inside his cell and is bleeding from his ear. Half his face is numb, and he cannot hear. Long after the war, a poorly healed fractured skull will be diagnosed, and for the rest of his life he will be deaf in his right ear.

The Russian boy was found, and Bruno, still gravely injured, is set free. But where to go? He was separated from his mother when Russian soldiers stormed the bunker where they and several other women and children had been hiding. He's alone now.

And he will never hear from his mother again.

Nine-year-old Ursula Haak and her family from a village near Tilsit are among the first to evacuate East Prussia. Their journey of escape takes over a year.

Ursula, her mother and her two younger brothers, Horst and Willy, prepare to leave their home with an elderly field worker from a neighbouring farm in July 1944. The farmer has harnessed a horse to a wooden cart and the two young boys are allowed to take turns sitting on top of the wagon. They hear the sound of bombs and artillery shelling off in the distance, and, to the east at night, they can see the red glow of fire on the horizon—Tilsit is burning.

All around them, ditches are piled high with dead bodies. In the snow-covered fields, people's carts that had run off the road are now lying buried in the snow. Time and again, their cart, too, gets stuck and they're barely able to move forward. People on the trek constantly push to pass one another. There are many accidents, and often and inconsiderately, soldiers press the trekkers to the side so that they may pass first. At times the march comes to a complete standstill. What's worse, the Wehrmacht has barred fleeing civilians from using any of the main roads or railway lines. One hundred thousand German soldiers are now also fleeing the Red Army, forcing the people to use lesser travelled roads and impassable fields to escape—this, instead of helping the mothers, children and elderly people who

Ursula's mother.

are also on the run. Low-flying Russian aircraft fire at the helpless people. For Ursula, the journey has turned into the worst of nightmares. To top it all, Soviet tanks regularly roll right through the running crowds, pulling humans, horses, and carts underneath their slow, churning links.

On a warm spring day in 1945, their trek comes to a halt. The Soviets have decided the evacuees should return to their homes. Now, not only does hunger plague little Ursula and her family, but lice, eczema and oedema have turned this never-ending march into an excruciating agony. They spend the nights in abandoned barns, houses that stand in ruin and, when there is nothing else, out in an open field.

One night they find refuge in an empty farmhouse. As they are bedding down to sleep, suddenly Soviet soldiers burst in through the door. They grab Ursula's mother and tear the clothes from her body in front of her children. They are terrified and scream and plead with the soldiers to leave their mother alone. Finally, a soldier takes them and, without further ado, throws them out of the house. The soldiers continue to go at Ursula's mother all through the night. The children can hear their mother fight back; they can hear her kicking and screaming, until the soldiers finally silence her by stabbing her. When they've finished, they allow the children back into the house, but their mother is already lying unconscious. Surrounded by her 9-year-old daughter and her two younger brothers, Ursula's mother bleeds to death during the wee hours of the morning.

The traumatised children have no idea how they will manage now. Ursula, who has an open wound on her leg and can barely even hobble around, tries to comfort her brothers, but there is no alternative other than to leave their dead mother behind. As a way of saying goodbye, they pick wild flowers from the fields and lay them upon her body.

Then Ursula closes the door, takes both little ones by the hand, and they walk onward towards Tilsit, in the direction of home.

Dora Müller is raised by her grandparents and lives in Königsberg. This is not unusual for an illegitimate child. She does not know her father, and her mother works as a field labourer on farms in the countryside nearby. Her grandparents do their best to shelter their little girl from the horrors that are going on around them. They try hard to hide the increasing food shortages and give most of the little they receive in food rations to their grandchild. By January 1945, the meagre rations are no longer enough to feed them all. 'You still need to grow, big and strong,' her grandfather says, as he once again offers his single slice of bread to the hungry 10-year-old.

Dora finally understands why her grandparents are becoming increasingly frail. Her grandmother, who was always an optimistic and cheerful woman, hardly speaks anymore. One day, she no longer gets up from her bed. It's cold in the room, as there's no firewood. Her grandfather can barely drag himself with great effort around the room that the two old ones have shared all these years with their granddaughter. Dora cries softly to herself. She's scared and doesn't know what to do. When she wakes the next morning, both grandparents are dead.

For two days, she waits by their side, tucks herself under the covers next to them and prays for a miracle. But they do not wake up. On the third day, a neighbour woman finds Dora alone in the house. She's so cold, even her tears have frozen to her cheeks.

A few days later, the neighbour returns and takes Dora to her mother, who still lives on a farm out in the countryside, a mother who has seen her daughter on only a few occasions. This 30-year-old woman takes the news of her parents' death without much emotion and seems helplessly overwhelmed at the arrival of her daughter. For a while, Dora works by her mother's side on the farm, but soon her mother becomes ill with tuberculosis and dies. Dora is now definitively an orphan.

During the winter of 1946/47, Gerhard Gudovius's grandmother has become so weak she has lost all her strength. It is the beginning of January and the Red Army is preparing to celebrate their Orthodox Christmas. They slaughter a few geese. Gerhard watches the festivities from afar, hoping to bring home a few scraps that they might leave behind. When they notice him, a couple of the soldiers urinate demonstratively onto their garbage pile behind the barracks. Regardless, Gerhard sneaks over to the pit after the men have returned to their banquet. Hurriedly he tries to salvage a few discarded bones, wanting to share them with his grandmother.

Despite all his efforts to find food for her, his grandmother dies a few weeks later. The advice she repeatedly told him in the days before her death stays with him: 'Make your way to Lithuania. There you will be saved.' He has no idea where Lithuania is, nor does he know how he will get there, but this boy, just turned 14, has a strong will to live out these desperate times regardless of the circumstances. He is determined not to die.

When the motherless Ursula Haak and her younger siblings return to the farm near Tilsit where she once lived, she finds new Russian settlers have taken it over. The Russians give them food, and in exchange the children are to work. There are other German refugees who have returned as well, many of whom are adults. The women milk the cows, and the children herd the livestock. Ursula is at least happy they have a roof over their heads, and a little something to eat.

In the autumn, she and her two brothers are taken to one of the few Russian orphanages in the Elchniederung. Here they are temporarily cared for. For Ursula, though, these are not happy memories. The Elchniederung—a lowland where over centuries, farmers have worked to contain the imminent annual floods from the snowmelt—is disastrously flooded in the spring of 1946. As it does each year, the Memel had frozen over during the winter. Now, due to an especially large ice jam in the upper delta, a tremendous flood occurs, endangering all of life—humans and animals alike.

The deluge of water hits the orphanage where Ursula and her brothers are housed. The children, however, are not evacuated. Instead, the orphanage is simply given up to the flood, and the children are told to figure out for themselves where to go. Russian planes had tried to break up the ice jam by bombing it. In the end, it caused even the levees to break, allowing the river to rush unimpeded throughout the entire Niederung.

Ursula watches as the water rises steadily and is terrified by what she sees. There are no adults to help, but one thing is certain—she will not let the flood take her two little brothers. She manages to get the three of them onto a sand spit and, from there, tries to draw attention to her tiny huddled family. A local farmer arrives with a rowboat and brings them to safety, but he is there merely to rescue them from the flooding waters, nothing more. Ursula asks if he possibly has accommodation for them, but he shrugs her off. 'Go on to Lithuania. There you will surely find help.' This is his terse, and only, advice.

Ursula is 10 years old now and feels fully responsible for her two younger brothers, Willy and Horst. She returns to Tilsit with them, and from there she hopes to travel on to Lithuania. But Horst is too loud and too fidgety to cross the border safely. They must keep a low profile. He whines incessantly, saying he can't walk any longer, and Ursula and Willy are too weak to carry him anymore. She decides to leave him on a park bench in the city and tells him, unequivocally, he should not leave this spot until she and Willy return. How many days they are gone, Ursula cannot remember. Too many, though, for the little Horst, who is gone when they finally return. It's as if the earth had swallowed him whole. Their guilt plagues Ursula and Willy. What else could they have done? Ursula asks herself this over and over. But Horst will remain missing.

Chapter 6

The Land of Bread and Cake

As 1945 was coming to an end, East Prussians who were still trying to stay in the land their ancestors had occupied for generations clung to a small thread of hope—perhaps they could settle in Lithuania. Their beloved East Prussia no longer existed, and to stay in this now Russian territory gave them only two choices: death by starvation or death by disease. Most East Prussian families had shrunk in size from many to only one or two survivors. Lithuania, on the other hand, had been much less affected by the war, and its rural infrastructure was, for the most part, still intact. In their imaginations, East Prussian children believed that Lithuania, the promised land of milk and honey, was also the land of bread and cake. And the border of Lithuania was not that far away.

Before Gerhard Gudovius takes off for Lithuania, he gathers all the necessary things he believes he will need. It is winter in the early months of 1947. To protect himself from the bitter cold, he puts on several pairs of long underwear, one on top of another, a Russian dog-hair ushanka-hat with ear flaps, and something to barter with—a bag of salt. He doesn't want to arrive in Lithuania as a mere beggar. Rather, he intends to trade for help, as meagre as his possessions are.

    A freight train is standing at the station when Gerhard arrives and he jumps aboard, hanging tightly to the buffer between two of the railcars. Although he remains undiscovered, the journey is torturous. 'There is no end in sight, I kept thinking, and God only knew where I even was. When I first heard people speaking a new language, I realised I must have arrived in Lithuania, so I jumped off the train. It was in the middle of the night, and I had no idea where to go next.'

    Gerhard has a literal nose for luck. He happens to have jumped off directly in front of a bakery.

As easily as it came to Gerhard, the survival artist, a safe arrival in Lithuania was not a given. In fact, it was the exception, not the rule.

Six-year-old Dieter Gröning, while on his family's escape from the Red Army, watches as his mother and all four siblings, three sisters and one brother, die—likely the victims of a typhus outbreak. He is alone now and joins a group of about a dozen other orphaned children whose only goal is to reach Lithuania. When they arrive at the German side of the Memel River near Tilsit, they believe they have reached their destination. No one in their little gang knows how to read the sun, and they cannot reach 'the land of bread and cake'. They continue to wander the countryside for two more years, plagued by hunger, cold and 'the evil Russians'.

One day they meet another group of begging children. They are older and by now have managed to cross over to Lithuania several times. They tell Dieter's little band that in fact Lithuania is on the other side of the river. But they can't find a way to cross the Memel, and there's no one to show them how. They find shelter in an abandoned apartment building in Tilsit, a town that has been renamed Sovetsk in the meantime and has become occupied by new Russia settlers who are also fighting hunger.

The country of Lithuania is just a stone's throw from Tilsit, right on the opposite bank of the river. The Queen Louise Bridge, which once spanned the Memel, was destroyed during the war. In 1946 it was repaired, but as it is now on the border, the bridge is heavily guarded. It's their only means to get across, but to attempt it is just too dangerous. They never do make it to Lithuania.

Heinz and Arnold Willuweit are two brothers who have been orphaned ever since the Red Army invaded Königsberg. Heinz is 12 and Arnold, nicknamed Arno, is 10 when they leave the city in search of food, driven by their agonising hunger pangs. They leave their infant sister, Gisela, in the care of their grandmother.

The two boys have heard that there's supposed to be 'bread and cake' in Lithuania. To their ears, it sounds heavenly, and it is absolutely where they want to go. First, though, they decide to travel to the village where their other grandparents live. Perhaps they can rest a bit and maybe even find some food out in the country. At least this is what they hope. Yet, when they arrive, they are sadly disappointed. Several Russian families have moved into the house. Of their grandparents, there's no trace. The Russians curse at them, and the two boys are chased off. They spend several more weeks sleeping in animal stalls and farm sheds, which they enter only after dark in order to remain undetected.

Heinz and Arno continue to wander the forests, sometimes finding nothing for shelter, and so they simply bed down in the undergrowth. They feed themselves on grass, bark and frogs. Finally, they get to the border city of Tilsit. They see that a makeshift ferryboat is taking people across the river and over the border into Lithuania. The two boys have no official papers, nor do they have money, so they sneak aboard as stowaways, secretly elated at their good luck as the boat pulls away. Before the ferry even makes it halfway across, however, they're discovered. There's a lot of commotion and the captain threatens to throw them overboard. But in the end, they're spared their lives. Perhaps he has a moment of compassion, because he takes them to the Lithuanian side after all and lets them run off. There, they are discovered once again. And once again, they manage to run away.

It's now spring of 1946. But the boys have finally set foot on Lithuanian soil. Literally. They are barefoot. By now, they have experienced the death of so many. They've seen children as well as adults die of starvation. They've witnessed people collapse from exhaustion or freeze to death—all this before their very eyes.

The two little beggars wander from farm to farm, and from village to village, along the Memel River. Most of the farmers don't have much themselves. Nevertheless, when they can, they share what little they have with the children—a small bowl of soup, some bread, an egg, a rind of sausage.

For the Wolf Children who were too young to understand geography and for whom the border river was nothing but a name, there was an alternative mode of transportation that could take them north—the train. Whether travelling as stowaways under a seat bench or hidden behind baggage, whether standing on the running boards or lying flat on the roof, whether hanging onto the buffers between railcars, passenger and freight trains alike were equally considered a viable means of transportation. All it took was to jump up, hold on, and ride along to wherever the train might take them.

Local railway station in Groß Brittanien, Elchniederung, *c*.1930.

Some of the children wanted to leave the destroyed East Prussia behind forever. For others this was not an option. For them, Lithuania was merely a means to an end, a place to find food for younger siblings or a sick mother who had stayed behind. These young border-wanderers, like Ruth Deske, took unimaginable risks. Whether by train or on a boat crossing the Memel, both presented dangers that often proved fatal.

Ruth, who is from Ellernbruch in the district of Gerdauen, is 13 years old when she makes her first journey to Lithuania in 1946. Up until the Russians invaded, her family had owned a large farm with nearly 35 acres of land. Now they live as destitute refugees in the settlement of Karpauen.

In the autumn of 1946, Ruth and a neighbour woman take off on their journey north. It's their first expedition to Lithuania. At a railway station, they jump up onto a freight train, but they don't get far. Time and time again they are discovered, thrown off, and chased away. But they are not discouraged, and at some point, they reach their destination. Here they go on a begging tour for several days and then decide to return home, experiencing equally the same dangers as before, only this time they are carrying a sack full of potatoes, bread and flour.

In January, on a return trip from Lithuania, Ruth spends the night in the Tilsit railway station. She uses her most precious possession, her begging sack, as a pillow and, wrapping her arms around it, falls asleep. She is weary to the bone and falls into a deep sleep. In the morning when she awakes, she has the fright of her life. Someone has taken her sack with all the food she had begged for! She knows crying won't do her any good. Her mother and siblings are depending on the food she was to bring them, so she goes back to Lithuania to beg all over again.

It is now 7 March, and she is on her way home. She runs into a friend of the family from Karpauen who's on her way to Lithuania with her children. She tells Ruth her mother is dying and that she should return as quickly as possible. 'Hurry. You may still find her alive.' By the time Ruth gets home, her 35-year-old mother is already in delirium from starvation and dies before her children's eyes. The last words she whispers to Ruth are, 'Bread, bread'. And she is dead.

As soon as the sun rises the next morning, Ruth puts her siblings on a sled and they make their way to the graveyard. There are rats in the house where they are living and Ruth fears her mother's corpse will be eaten. She wants to bury her, but because the ground is frozen, this is not possible. They lay their mother on the ground next to all the other corpses and cover her with snow.

Ruth must now care for her siblings on her own. She's 14, Helga is 9, Siegfried, 8, and Karl-Heinz is 4 years old. How she's to do this is not clear to her just yet, but it's something her mother would have expected of her. This is something she understands unequivocally.

She takes the two older ones by the hand and goes out to look for food. They leave the youngest with relatives who live in the area. Ruth promises that they will come back every week with food from Lithuania. Riding on the roofs and the running boards of freight trains, they reach a village not far from the Lithuanian city of Kelmė. Here Ruth finds a compassionate farm couple who offer to take Siegfried in. It's not long before she finds a home for Helga as well.

One day, after one of her many hamster-runs, she is arrested by the Russian police while on a train going to Gerdauen. This young girl, barely a teenager, lands in a jail cell for several days, because Gerdauen has become a restricted area. But she learns the border to Poland is not far off. Even the northern country of Latvia looks promising, and this is where Ruth goes in search of food once she is let out. 'This went on for a year and a half,' she tells me. 'We Wolf Children would beat each other up just to secure a seat in a railway carriage, all the while on the lookout for the police, who could quickly end it all.'

Ruth often joins other children on these begging expeditions. It's especially dangerous in the winter, when it's cold, wet and icy. In these conditions, holding onto the carriages is nearly impossible, and often there are accidents. Children fall under the train and are run over. For this reason, Ruth sometimes decides to make the journey on foot.

The temporary wooden bridge near Tilsit is especially dangerous in the spring because of the rising waters of the snowmelt and the large ice floats. The Wolf Children are afraid to use the bridge and instead try to attempt to cross the Memel on rafts they make themselves. These are seldom more than a scavenged board or a scrapped door on which they try to balance while guiding themselves slowly forward with long poles. Time and time again, Ruth sees children who fail in their attempts to cross the river. They drown or freeze to death before they can reach the other side. 'It must have been hundreds of them who died like this,' she says. Only those who have money—in other words, Russians and Lithuanians—can pay for a ride to the other shore on one of the small fishing boats.

When Ruth returns to the farm where she had left her little sister, Helga, with the farmer's family, she finds the place deserted. Ruth's heart stops. Was the family deported to Siberia and Helga along with them? She has heard about such a fate many times by now. But Helga was lucky, as she later learns. She had hidden herself in the barn and watched as the secret police took the family into custody. It didn't take her long to find another home with another family in a neighbouring village. It's a heavy weight that has been lifted from Ruth's heart when she finds her sister is still alive and well.

By March 1948, the relative who was caring for her younger brother, Karl-Heinz, in Karpauen has become too weak to continue doing so much longer and gives him back to Ruth. 'I just ran off with my very sick little Karl-Heinz in my arms. For 18 kilometers we ran through the night to get to the railway station, hoping to cross the border. He was just skin and bones and could barely even walk without my help.'

As Ruth is running, carrying her little brother, it occurs to her how desperate her situation has become. By the time she reaches the Masurian Canal, she is at the end of her rope and thinks the best thing to do is to jump into the water with her little Karl-Heinz, finishing it off for both of them. She is unbearably tired and beyond hungry. To this day she cannot tell you what kept her from doing it. 'We just had to go on somehow—if only for Mother's sake. I felt obligated to her.'

When Ruth finally boards a train and hides with her brother, their hiatus is short-lived. They are soon discovered and thrown off the train in Tilsit. From there they try to make their way on foot to Pogegen on the other bank of the Memel. Again, she attempts to travel onwards by train. This time she succeeds and arrives in Tauroggen with little Karl-Heinz. She continues to wander for days, most often holding her brother in her arms. They travel for nearly 100 kilometers and finally come to Šiauliai. She believes this is where her other siblings are, and this, she decides, will be her new home. There's no longer a reason to return to East Prussia.

Lithuania was not the ultimate longed-for destination for all the Wolf Children. Some arrived by accident as they were in fact trying to get to Germany.

After the death of Eva Briskorn's mother in West Prussia, 14-year-old Eva has but one goal. She wants to get to Germany. But her sister, Gisela, who's two years younger, is not at all happy with this plan. She has neither the energy nor the desire to try to go that far. Eva doesn't have a plan yet herself, but she begins to ask around. A German couple in the village offers to take them in for the time being. At least for the interim, it's a relief to Eva. The couple's only daughter had died, and Gisela resembles her so much that they don't hesitate to welcome her. Gisela seems to thrive here, and in time the girls manage to put the memories of their siblings' and their mother's fateful deaths behind them. But even here, there's not enough food to feed them both, and Eva must eventually take off again on her own.

As she wanders the countryside, Eva sometimes hears the stone mill in the village grinding grain for bread. When she does, she sneaks to the mill to wipe a finger across the flour dust—this is how hungry and desperate she is for something to eat. One day Eva runs into Gisela and her new family who came to grind their own grains at the gristmill. But Gisela pretends she doesn't know her anymore and brushes her off as if she were nothing more than a pesky insect. Eva, to this day, feels deeply hurt by this.

Over time, Eva learns there are trains heading to Germany. Without saying goodbye to Gisela, she takes off for Königsberg, from where these trains supposedly leave. Eva runs for days over more than 200 kilometers in a north-easterly direction, hoping to reach the city. Unbeknownst to her, she is, unfortunately, running in the wrong direction. Whenever she's tired, she looks for a hole in the ground or a small ditch in which she can make a bed to sleep for a few hours. At some point, she finally does reach Königsberg.

Everything in the city has been destroyed. Even the railway station is difficult to find. Very few people are in the streets. No one looks trustworthy enough for Eva to ask for directions. She senses an atmosphere of hostility, and she's afraid to be singled out by the police as a German. She wanders the city streets for

Königsberg port with railway bridge in the background.

several more days until, one day, she hears the whistle of a train in the distance and makes her way in that direction. She soon finds the train tracks, and in an opportune moment, a train happens to roll by. She jumps on and hides. Now all she needs to do is stay undetected until she arrives in Germany, or so she believes. Yet when the train comes to a stop, Eva is discovered and is thrown off.

What a horror! She has no idea where she is. Even the language sounds foreign. There's a sign in large letters on the railway station platform, saying 'Kaunas'. Well, I'm not in Germany yet, she thinks, and jumps back onto another rolling train. A few hours later, this train comes to a full stop only to give her the ultimate disappointment. She's not one bit closer to where she wanted to go. In fact, she has travelled quite in the opposite direction. She's in Vilnius, the capital city of Lithuania.

Since her mother died, 10-year-old Christel Nitsch from the Gerdauen district has lived with her older sister, Gertrud, who has a 2-year-old son. Gertrud doesn't want to make the journey to Lithuania with her little boy. Rather, she wants to go to Germany. One evening, early in 1946, Gertrud straps a rucksack onto her younger sister's back, does it quickly, and takes little Klaus in one hand and Christel in the other. It all takes place on a foggy night, but Gertrud has decided it must be now and runs with both her charges to the railway station in Gerdauen—none of them have shoes; socks are all they have on their feet to protect them from the cold. The rucksack is so heavy that Christel thinks she will collapse at any moment.

When they arrive at the railway station hours later, there are Russian soldiers everywhere. Anyone who is German is chased off. Gertrud tells Christel to hide behind the train embankment until the next train arrives, which she does. Then everything happens very quickly. A train arrives, and all three of them jump on from the side opposite the platform. Until now, they've been undetected. Christel manages to find a spot on a running board. There's a knob on the car that she grabs onto. Shortly thereafter, the train takes off. She looks back and is horrified to see a group of military police rip Gertrud and her little son, Klaus, off the train, which is moving so fast that Christel doesn't trust herself to jump. How long she rides the train, she can no longer remember, nor can she remember where it went. She only knows that after travelling for a long time, the train finally comes to a stop. It's most likely at the Lithuanian/Polish border.

To this day, Christel does not know for sure where it was that she finally climbed down from the train. Yet this end station marks the end of the life she once knew, and the end of her childhood. A whole new life full of fear and dread, deprivation and misery starts to take hold—something that becomes clear to her within the first few hours. She has lost everything—her homeland, her siblings, her nephew, and her mother. She has arrived in a foreign world where she doesn't even understand the language. But Christel has an innocent trust in God and tells herself, have courage, have courage. She has faith she will be protected by the Almighty in Heaven.

She's stiff from the long journey and moves awkwardly as she walks into the station. Even though the waiting room is quite full she finds an open spot on a bench where she sinks, exhausted, wanting to sleep. But she finds no rest. The building isn't heated, and an icy wind blows in from the door through which there is a constant flow of people. Besides that, she's terribly hungry. She continues to lie on the bench, freezing and with a growling stomach, and waits until daylight.

In the wee hours of the morning, she gets up and goes outside, where a woman approaches and speaks to her. But Christel doesn't understand a word. Is it Polish? Using her hands and feet, the woman tries to make herself understood. She wants to know if Christel wouldn't want to come with her to help herd her cows. For Christel, it is a ray of hope. Once they arrive at the farm, the woman gives her food to eat and something to drink, and then she takes Christel to her cows. Christel is frightened when she sees how many cows there are—to her, it's a gigantic herd. But the woman motions that this is where she should work and, in the evening, she should return to the house. Then she turns to leave, leaving Christel alone with the animals.

The pasture is nothing but a stubble field, and the ground is frozen. Christel is barefoot and has developed large chilblains on both her feet. She tries her best to keep the cows from straying too far from the herd. Tears roll down her cheeks, and out of desperation she screams out in pain. She cries for her mother until she can cry no longer, and her voice has become hoarse. But no one hears her or comes to console her; no one takes her into their arms. When she returns to the farm woman's house, her resolve is clear—she wants only her bag, and to leave. But the woman doesn't return her things, nor does she let her go. She must stay a full week. That's what she had promised. Christel stays until morning and pretends to return to the cows. As soon as she's out of sight of the house, she runs as fast as she can and ducks into the thicket. Here, she hides until nightfall. Then she hobbles onwards as far as her bleeding feet will take her. Above all, she doesn't ever want to return to those cows!

The next day she comes to a small village. Hunger tortures her to no end. She travels from house to house, begging. She's thankful to receive the small piece of bread that people often give her, even unsolicited—it seems the farmers have pity on this ragged child. 'Every time it felt like a miracle to me. I was infinitely grateful.'

The 11-year-old girl has not been able to feel her feet in a long time. Her clothes are stiff with dirt and they stink, even in the bitter cold. Yet there's nowhere where she can wash or clean her clothes; no one asks her to come in to warm herself. And so, she sleeps under the open sky or sneaks into a vacant stall and buries herself in the straw.

Once in a while, a kind farmer will show compassion and give her not only something to eat but offer her a warm place to sleep in the barn. Once, Christel is even allowed to spend the night in a sauna out in the garden. It is, however, by no means warm inside, and there's no mat to lie on, and no blanket. She has dysentery and everything flows out of her body in a constant stream, like water. She doesn't know what to do; the floor and the walls have been sprayed with excrement, and her only thought is of these people who had been so kind to take her in. How angry will they be when they discover what happened?

At dawn, she sneaks away with a bad conscience and is worried she'll be caught. She spends the day alone in the forest once again. She still has one small piece of bread, and she eats it very slowly. But by the evening her hunger is unbearable, and she carefully approaches a farmstead at the edge of the forest.

At first, she doesn't dare go to the door and waits a while. But at some point, her hunger overpowers her fear, and she walks cautiously in the direction of the house. Sometimes these farmers have dogs that they let run free at night, or they are even ordered to attack wandering children. She's especially afraid of this. But this time, there's no dog. Instead, a friendly woman comes to the door and looks at her with kindness. Christel is in wretched condition—full of lice, oozing pus and blood on her dirt-crusted legs, not to mention her filthy clothes. The farm woman takes the poor child into her house, gives her something to eat, washes her in a tub of warm water, and gives her some clean clothes. Slowly, Christel begins to feel human again.

Christel is allowed to sleep on a bench inside a closet. It's been a long time since she's felt warm at night. On the sideboard in the kitchen there's a freshly baked loaf of bread. The aroma is so wonderful that Christel gets up in the middle of the night and breaks off a piece. She can't eat much because her stomach is painfully bloated. Like so many children from this era, she also suffers from rickets and is unusually small for her age. At 11 years of age, she looks more like a 6-year-old.

The next morning the woman wakes her up and gently tells Christel that she would like to take her to a doctor. Together they walk through the forest to the next village. She's dropped off in an overfilled waiting room, and here the child is supposed to stay seated and wait for the farmwoman to return. A long time goes by and eventually Christel gets a bad premonition that the woman just left her here and returned home without her, just when Christel had hoped that she might be able to stay with this family. In a panic, Christel jumps up and runs out of the door and back through the woods. But the woman is not at her farm. Just her children are there, who are frightened by this mad-looking girl with eyes swollen nearly shut from crying. They cannot understand why Christel came back alone.

A short time later, the woman returns. She's terribly angry, screams and scolds, then shows her the door. Christel understands nothing anymore and runs, crying, out into the fields. There's only one thought left in her mind: she wants to get to Germany.

What the route to Germany was that Gertrude had wanted to take her and Klaus on, she doesn't know anymore. The name 'Wehlau' comes to mind. This is where she should go, she decides, and from there she can eventually make her way to Germany.

Christel wanders to the next village and finds the railway station. Here she asks a man which train goes to Wehlau. He points to a train and Christel steps up on the running board, hangs onto the door grip and rides the train as it rolls on. It doesn't take long before the conductor, a woman, discovers the little girl and invites her into the seating compartment. 'Where are you off to?' she asks Christel. 'Wehlau,' she informs her. Then she should just stay seated, she's told, because the train is going in that direction and in fact it is the end station. Little Christel is relieved, not only for this bit of news, but because she doesn't need to show a ticket, and she's warm.

When the train finally comes to a stop, Christel sees that the sign does not read Wehlau but 'Vilnius/Wilna'. The conductor woman must have misunderstood her. Now she's further away than ever from her destination. Christel only wants to go home, to a land where the people speak her language and a place where she can pour her heart out.

But, once again, hunger has the last word, and Christel knows the only way to get something to eat is to beg. She doesn't dare go out into this unfamiliar city. She walks along the railroad tracks, on and on, until she finally arrives at a small railway station. A train arrives, stops momentarily, and then moves on again. While Christel tries to jump on, she slips and falls to the ground. She sees the last wagon grow smaller and smaller in the distance, and she begins to sob. She no longer knows what's what and cannot see her way out of her situation anymore.

A man walks up and asks her something that Christel doesn't understand. She begins to cry even harder. His wife rushes over. She's the ticket saleswoman and can speak a little German. Christel explains through her tears that she wants to get to Germany but didn't make it onto the train. The couple laugh and they tell her that she should be so glad, because this train was on its way to Russia. Christel isn't even able to laugh; she's so bereft, she can do nothing but cry. The adults invite her to join them. Christel looks at them with disbelief. But Sofia and Josef are sincere.

Sofia's sister, Nadja, lives with them and she, too, affectionately cares for the little one. Both women wash her and doctor her wounds. Josef takes the rags that hang from her body and burns them in the yard. She's given clean clothes. Then they eat dinner. Christel is impossibly hungry, but Sofia puts only a small portion on her plate. At first Christel thinks she's trying to torture her, but then she realises that these people mean well and only fear she won't be able to digest a full meal.

They arrange a place for the exhausted girl to sleep. Christel has barely laid her head down before she is deep in dreams. As if in a coma, she sleeps for two days and two nights. It's the first time in two years that she's not filled with fear, and she begins to relax. She counts her blessings. She's no longer plagued by lice and other vermin; she no longer needs to run barefoot through snow, ice and rain; she's warm, and her belly is full. When she finally awakes, Sofia is standing over her, beaming. 'You slept like a little puppy.'

Again, she's given a bite to eat and notices how warm and good it feels inside her stomach. The women try to ask more about her. Does she have relatives anywhere? But Christel's answers are evasive. She's afraid she might be sent back to the street, so she tells them she's all alone in the world. Whether her sister is alive is something she really doesn't know for sure, anyway. Josef, Sofia and Nadja leave her in peace. Christel has a roof over her head, she's not hungry anymore, and eventually, even her wounds heal.

Sometimes it was pure coincidence that brought the Wolf Children to Lithuania. This is how it happened for Dora Müller.

One night, 12-year-old Dora climbs up onto the roof of a stationed freight train. The cars' sliding doors are locked, and at least on the roof she's safe from wandering animals and freeloading tramps who could do her harm. She finds a narrow depression where she makes herself as comfortable as possible and, exhausted, she falls asleep. When she awakes, the train is moving. An icy wind blows into her face. Nevertheless, she clings to an iron bar and holds on for dear life. Her only hope is that the train will bring her to a safe place. But the journey turns into a nightmare. Dora cannot hold on much longer; she becomes nauseous and dizzy from fatigue. At the very next station, she jumps off. She doesn't know where she is. People are conversing in a foreign language, and she surmises that the train has taken her far into the east, to Lithuania.

It's been only a week since Dora's mother died, and only two days since she was chased off by the cruel farm woman, in whose family Dora was just an extra mouth to feed.

Since then, she's been living in the woods, abandoned barns, or in graveyards. One day she meets other children who, like her, wander through the forests, and through life, on their own. Together they camp at night and go begging or steal feed from troughs during the day. When, one day by chance, Dora sees her reflection in a mirror shard that she finds in the hayloft, she's shocked. She's become a wild-looking little thing. Her long hair hangs straggly in her face, her eyes have sunk deep into their sockets. She looks down at herself and sees how tattered her clothes have become, the holes in her torn shoes that she had stuffed with straw.

Dora breaks down and cries bitterly. 'What have I done?' she asks herself over and over, and blames herself for the death of her grandparents, who had raised her as a child while her mother was gone working on the farm. 'I allowed them to starve to death, and now the dear Lord is punishing me.' In her hysteria, she becomes a risk to the other children in the little gang. They finally walk away, leaving her behind in the farmyard. The next morning, a farmwoman finds her. The kind-hearted woman first bathes her in warm water, and then she gives her warm milk to drink and nurses her back to health. But Dora is not allowed to stay.

And so, she must make her way, once again, into the Nowhere.

Wild boars in the Lithuanian forests.

Chapter 7
Wolf Children and Forest Brothers

The Red Army was a feared enemy presence, not just in East Prussia, but equally so in the neighbouring country of Lithuania. This small country that had won its independence from the Russian Empire in 1918 was once again incorporated into the Soviet Union only months after Hitler's invasion of Poland in the autumn of 1939. Two years later, in July 1941, Lithuania was invaded again, this time by the Wehrmacht. For a short while it was referred to as 'the General District of Lithuania' of the Reich's Ostland, or 'East Land'. Three years later, in the summer of 1944, Russia recaptured the land as it took back all of the newly formed German-occupied territories, including Lithuania. For the people of Lithuania, it was just one occupier replacing the next—and they responded with their own resistance. This new Soviet government was no different and they fought back in whichever way they could.

Now, after the war's end, it was not only the Wolf Children who roamed its immense forests, took cover in empty farmsteads, and hid from Soviet soldiers. There was also an organised resistance movement, a group of Lithuanian partisan fighters called the 'Forest Brothers', who also inhabited these woods, fighting against the mandated integration into Stalin's Soviet empire. To these partisans, however, the Red Army was not the only enemy. The Germans, they felt, were equally to blame, as they were the first to rob Lithuania of her independence. But the war was over, and to these Lithuanians, helping the roaming German children was considered an act of subversion against their new rulers. It was no surprise, then, that in the early post-war years, two otherwise complete strangers made unwilling—and at times perilous—friendships: the wild, bedraggled Wolf Children and the lawless Lithuanian desperados.

Nearly every Wolf Child has a story of encounters with the Forest Brothers. Ruth Deske is one whose path crossed that of the insurgents, time and again, most often as she and the band of beggar children she roamed with were bedding down in the woods for the night. Each time she is frightened out of her wits when armed men suddenly step out from behind a tree or bush. Most often, these men are friendly towards her and her companions and, as a rule, usually give them a little to eat.

Gerhard Gudovius often spends his nights in empty farmhouses. When he comes to farmers' doors, begging, they usually point out an abandoned farm nearby where he can find shelter, a place where it might be safe. At first, he doesn't really wonder why these places are always deserted. But gradually it dawns on him that the people who no longer live here were probably taken away to the Gulag. He's been told that merely the *suspicion* of being a resistance fighter is enough for an entire family to be deported to Siberia.

Sometimes he meets bands of other begging Germans, women and children, who have moved into the abandoned farmsteads. Then he moves on; he'd rather keep to himself. He feels he'll have greater success finding food or work that way. One day, he wants to overnight as usual in an empty farmhouse. Just as he begins to make himself comfortable, partisans wielding machine guns storm the house. They had been watching him and mistook him for a Nazi spy. On closer look, however, it becomes clear that Gerhard is simply a *vokietukai*, a 'little German'. Realising their mistake, they take off again. Gerhard is safe, but not without having had the scare of his life.

At first glance, it was never easy for the Wolf Children to recognise who the armed men, the Forest Brothers, were who they encountered in the forests or on isolated farms. But those men were equally afraid of the Soviet soldiers, whose sole assignment was to eliminate the enemy. Whether this meant German children or Lithuanian rebels, it was all the same.

Konrad Fischer, from a village near Königsberg, made his acquaintance with the Red Army when he got into trouble with them while he was still in East Prussia, before the war was over. He is a farm boy, born in 1931. He and his family, of whom there are nine siblings, flee at the last minute when the front is already in hearing distance.

They don't get far. Soviet soldiers, arriving from across the frozen Baltic Sea, march towards their home. When they arrive, they take all the horses. Then the family's carriages are destroyed. And—most traumatic for the family—Konrad's father is badly beaten in front of his eyes. He falls to the ground and, when they have finished, he's hauled away.

The rest of the family are thrown out of the house and driven into the midlands along with other fleeing refugees. They have nothing to eat. They gather branches, bark and frozen potatoes that they sometimes find in the fields and, in make-do fashion, try to feed themselves. Konrad's youngest brothers, Helmut and Gerhard, soon die. The family buries them in the bushes—without a casket and without a ceremony.

One night during a heavy snowstorm, Konrad and his brother Hugo, who is two years younger, crawl into an empty barn and bed down in the straw, while the other refugees spend the night at a campfire in an open field. When the two boys awake in the morning, they're all alone. The others, including their mother and the rest of their siblings, have disappeared without a trace.

Fourteen-year-old Konrad and his brother cannot believe their eyes. Yet, no matter how much they wail and call out to the Nothing, they realise they're now on their own. The high snowdrifts and the bitter cold don't make it any easier for them to find their way, but the two trudge onwards, for days on end, with seemingly no purpose. Over and again, they encounter Soviet soldiers who show no mercy; rather, they chase them off, shooting bullets into the air that zing past their heads, and they poke fun at these frightened and hungry boys. As days go by, the two become weaker and more and more lethargic, and finally they lose their will to live. But in one last-ditch effort, the brothers manage to cross over to Lithuania.

Agota, a devout Christian farmwoman, who lives in a village near Marijampolė, has pity and takes them in. But she insists she cannot care for both boys. Hugo is sent off to fend for himself. She instructs Konrad, who can hardly speak a word of Lithuanian, to act as if he were a mute if soldiers should ever come to the door. And surely, Soviet soldiers do arrive. Konrad stands by, trying not to show emotion, as his foster mother is insulted, beaten and robbed. Her uncle was a general in the Lithuanian army and is surmised to have joined the Forest Brothers. Agota is afraid that, because of Konrad, both of them could be sent to Siberia. She's heard many stories of such cases.

Bernhard Keusling is 9 years old when he loses his mother and younger sister in 1947. He watches them both die from starvation while he can do nothing to help them. Upon their deaths, he lays a linen cloth over both bodies, closes the door behind him and goes on his way. But where to? Tormented by hunger and grief, he drifts, alone, for many days.

On his search for food one day, he finds half a rotted sweed that had been intended for livestock feed—nearly a delicacy to him—and some pork rind, both of which he eats in desperation.

He soon meets a few other boys and together they take off in search of horse carcasses, wanting the meat. The Russians tend to throw their dead horses into bomb craters. The two boys climb down into the ditches and, with pocketknives, cut themselves a few pieces of flesh, eating them on the spot. At first the Soviets make fun of them as they slide around clumsily in the mud and flesh, looking like wild animals devouring the rotting meat. One day the soldiers decide to end their activities by pouring lime over the horses. Did they do it to protect the children? Or was it to take away their last hope of food? How were they to know?

The other boys, whom Bernard only barely knows, tell him that in a few days they plan to travel with some women across the border to Lithuania. Bernard wants to join them. They make it as far as Tilsit by train, and here they spend the night in the railway station. The next day, they continue their journey and end up in Kibarten, where Bernard takes off on his own. He knows no Lithuanian, and often the people brush him off because he cannot make himself understood. In time, he learns enough of the language to be able to beg for a bit of bread here, or some soup there.

One day he arrives at a small homestead in which a German couple from the Memelland lives. Bernhard can hardly believe his good luck. Finally, someone who can understand him! All evening and nearly all night long, Bernhard tells them what all has happened to him. He's so happy to finally have found someone with whom he can share his sorrows.

Mikas is already an old man, yet he offers Bernard a place to stay, for which Bernhard is eternally grateful. The man's wife feels sorry for the poor boy, too. He's very weak, and she wants to nurse him back to health. She feeds him a most unpalatable cod liver oil and some snake schnapps. Both are supposed to make him stronger. It does seem to work, though, as, after some time, he recovers. But to this day, Bernhard remembers one thing above all else—the snake schnapps made him drunk.

He's given the job of herding cows on a neighbour's farm, so now he's got not only a roof over his head and something to eat, he's also able to make himself useful. But herding cows is not an easy job. The pastures are small and are not fenced in. Bernhard must make sure that not only the farmer's three cows graze on his small strip of land, but there are horses and a handful of headstrong lambs as well. One day, Bernhard falls asleep. When he awakes, the cows have wandered off in all directions and none are grazing where they should be. He needs to corral them back in, but doesn't know how he's to manage this on his own. A few farm labourers who happen to be walking by come to help him, so he avoids the otherwise imminent wrath of the farmer.

Mikas's farm sits at the edge of the woods. Often at night, groups of strange men show up at the door, and Mikas's wife always offers them a warm meal. It turns out they are Forest Brothers. At first, Bernhard is still so weak that he doesn't quite catch on who they are. After several weeks, a time during which he begins to gain his strength, he wakes one night to hear the men speaking Lithuanian in the kitchen. Bernhard, by now, has figured out who they are and is afraid he'll be discovered, as it seems they're talking about him—he's learned this much of the language. His thoughts race and he ponders how to escape if they should actually come after him. Very carefully and silently, he opens a window.

But then he hears Mikas's wife's voice. She sounds indignant and speaks up in his defence. 'If you even do the slightest bit of harm to the little one, you can be sure never to receive any help from us again,' she says. It goes on a while longer, back and forth, until the Forest Brothers leave and never lay a hand on Bernhard.

The next morning, he asks Mikas who those men were. Mikas is evasive but tells him that he should have no fear. He's safe with them. Slowly Bernhard begins to understand why he always needed to go to bed so early, right after dinner. He barely lays his head on the pillow when a knock comes at the door

Forest Brothers of the Vytis district, Lithuania, *c.*1947.

and a group of men enter. The farmer's wife always hosts them by giving them the leftovers from the day's meal.

It's not long before their secret activities are discovered. One day in the summer of 1949, the NKVD surround the farmhouse just as the Forest Brothers are sitting down to eat. Everything goes really fast from that moment on. The men are taken into custody; one of them tries to run and is shot in the back. Bernhard hides and, in an opportune moment, runs into the woods. His foster parents are arrested and Mikas is sentenced to ten years in the Gulag for the crime of helping the Forest Brothers. The USSR's 'People's Commissariat for Internal Affairs' shows mercy to no one.

Some of the Wolf Children were not only confidants of the Forest Brothers but accomplices as well. Joachim Pose from Tilsit crosses the border into Lithuania soon after his parents are arrested by Soviet soldiers for no given reason in 1947. He's 12 years old and has been working on a farm as a shepherd boy for over half a year when, on a late afternoon while sitting with his herd, he hears some curious noises. As he turns to look, he jumps with fright. Several men dressed in peculiar clothing and carrying machine guns step out from behind a bush. They're wearing an assortment of uniforms, some German, some Soviet, with yellow, green and red armbands on their forearms and cartridge belts criss-crossing their chests. Although they look frightening, Joachim sees right away that they're merely partisans. He feels he's got nothing to fear. Instead, the men now give him a task to fulfill. He's to find a particular farmer in the neighbouring village and let him know that they are about to arrive. Then, he's to say one sentence and one sentence only: *'We're coming tonight.'* Nothing more. After that, he's to return immediately, because his mission is secret, and it is dangerous. Under no circumstance is anyone to know about this. In the meantime, they'll watch over the herd.

Joachim takes a horse and rides like the wind to the village, as he had been instructed, and returns soon thereafter. The Forest Brothers see him coming and quickly disappear just as he dismounts from his horse. Although his task leaves him feeling unsettled and anxious, he's rather proud of himself to have been a courier for these men. It's but a small token of revenge against the Soviets for the terrible loss of his family.

Over and over again, Joachim encounters the so-called *stribai*, the Soviet military, who are on the lookout for the Forest Brothers. He sees how cruel they can be when, one day on a whim, they take aim at a farm cat and shoot it—for one reason alone: because no one is there to stop them. He sees that the farmers in the area don't dare say anything either. They know all too well how they can be threatened, punished and, for the smallest reason, get hauled off to the Gulag.

At times, Joachim hears shooting in the distant woods that surround the pasture where he herds his animals. Sometimes it comes from other groves; at other times the battles are so near, the bullets whistle right past his ears. He prays that the *stribai* will be caught in an ambush one day and that the partisan will, in the end, defeat them. A prayer that, of course, never comes true.

Wherever there's an opportunity, the brothers Heinz and Arno Willuweit work at whatever jobs they can find in Lithuania. Ever since their arrival in the spring of 1946, they've been working for farmers in need of labourers like them. One day they meet a farmer who offers to take one of them to be his full-time shepherd and even offers to raise him as his foster son. But there's no way that he can take both brothers; the risk is just too great that the two 'little Germans' would be discovered, and he would put his own life in peril. The Russians, he tells them, do not hesitate in the least to promptly deport anyone to Siberia. It's decided that the 12-year old Heinz should stay on the farm while the 10-year-old Arno must move on alone. They'll not see each other again for eight more years.

Heinz comes to this new home hungry and full of lice. The first thing the farm family does is burn his clothes, and then they put him to bed, where he sleeps for two days. Although they don't have much, the family is quickly endeared to Heinz, and they gladly share all they have with him.

But, from this point onwards, Heinz is not allowed to speak German. With only three years of schooling in East Prussia, he would like to attend school again, even here in Lithuania, for at least a few more years, but the farmer overrules this idea. It would be much too dangerous. In time, Heinz forgets his mother tongue. He's intelligent and the Lithuanian language comes to him easily.

His foster father is a supporter of the Forest Brothers. In time, one of Heinz's chores is to take care of these men in the woods. One night, as he is bringing them milk, Soviet soldiers grab him. But he's learned to keep his mouth shut. Under no circumstance is he to reveal anything. He stays true to his promise, even as they torture him by cutting open his arms with the intent of letting him slowly bleed to death. When the soldiers finally leave him alone, with the last of his strength, Heinz crawls back to the farmhouse. His foster parents never forget his undying loyalty and, up until their deaths in the 1970s, they keep a loving relationship with their German foster son.

The conflict between the Soviet forces and the Forest Brothers lasted a decade and cost both sides tens of thousands of lives. The resistance was best organised in the heavily wooded regions in southern Lithuania where partisan groups were better able to control large tracts of this rural land. Their intent was, of course, to free their homeland from the Soviet occupation. In retaliation, to deprive the insurgents of their logistical foothold, the Red Army would often deport entire villages, replacing them with Russian settlers. Furthermore, whole forests were razed in order to destroy the partisans' hiding places. Traces of this clear cutting can still be seen in rural Lithuania to this day.

By the early 1950s, the Soviet troops had taken the upper hand in the conflict against the Forest Brothers and, for all intents and purposes, won. Intelligence gathered by Soviet spies in the West and NKVD agents within the resistance movement led to large-scale purges and the elimination of most of the remaining partisan groups. The few remaining Forest Brothers finally laid down their weapons in 1953, when, upon Josef Stalin's death, they were promised amnesty by the Soviets. There were still a few individual partisans who remained underground well into the 1970s, eluding arrest for many more years. To this day, many of the surviving former Forest Brothers hold a bitter attitude towards the West, who, despite the unlawful Russian occupation of the Baltic States, shied away from a confrontation with the Soviets.

Wayside cross, with Lithuanian farmhouse in the background.

Chapter 8

Shelter and Kindness

Dora Müller, emaciated from lack of food, wanders aimlessly through the streets of a small town. The 12-year-old has no idea anymore where she is, after she accidentally arrived in Lithuania by train in the spring of 1947. Destitute and fatigued, she sits down under an archway of the city wall. A boy walks up to her who's not much older than she. 'Are you alone?' he asks. 'What's your name? Mine's Arthur.' The boy reaches out his hand and looks at her with compassion in his eyes. Not knowing what just happened, Dora throws her arms around the shoulders of this stranger. Her words catch in her throat. Unable to speak, she sobs uncontrollably. 'Just calm down,' Arthur mumbles, embarrassed.

He tells her that the endless search for food has driven him, his sister, and a few other children, to this place. 'It's not easy, but up until now we've managed quite well. It's because we've stuck together,' he says encouragingly. She follows him through the city gates to a makeshift shelter the children have built inside a destroyed barn that sits in the middle of an open field.

Over the following days, Dora is introduced to the art of begging. The children go out in groups of two. The first time she knocks at a stranger's door, it takes all the willpower she can muster, but in the end, it's easier than she thought. A kindly farm woman answers the door as if she were expecting them and invites them to come in. Although it's evident that she can't understand a single word, the woman knows what these beggar children need. The two step into her tiny farmhouse, which is nothing but a single room with a packed dirt floor and a large wood-burning stove. Otherwise, it is bare, with hardly a bit of furniture. Dora's ashamed that she, someone who's from a well-to-do family, should beg from such a poor person. The children each get a plate of warm soup. When Dora and her friend have finished eating, they receive a few extra provisions. In this way, they spend the day travelling from farm to farm and eventually have filled their begging sacks. Two raw potatoes here, a dry crust of bread there. For Dora, every small bit of food is a treasured gift.

Arthur tells her that in the larger cities there are often altercations between bands of children who try to steal each other's sacks of goods. It comes down to the survival of the fittest. Here in the countryside, the rewards are smaller, but not as difficult to come by. Past and future no longer mean anything to the children. They simply live in the here and now.

Within a few weeks, Dora's become well accepted into Arthur's little community of eight Wolf Children and spends the next several months travelling with them. Their need to find food is not the only thing that occupies their days, though. There are times when they play games of pretend, which help them forget the misery and the incessant hunger that plagues them, at least for the time being. But only when they believe they are safe.

In a small hollow near a forest road, the children have taken tree limbs, branches and leaves to build a shelter. It's half an hour to the nearest village. One child always sits guard near the forest road, making sure they stay undiscovered. In pairs they go out each day to beg at the surrounding farmhouses, and from time to time they also steal pig feed from their troughs. Dora's an especially gifted egg thief. In the wee hours of dawn, she sneaks into the chicken coops to find eggs, but she always leaves the hens alone. So that no one will discover the theft, she always takes only two or three eggs. Back at their fort, she hides them in a hole in the ground and leaves them there until evening. Only then can the children safely make a fire, where they fry the eggs on a metal plate they've found. Sometimes it's the only warm meal the children will have in many weeks. Less than half an egg for each child.

Johanna Erlach was born in Gumbinnen in East Prussia in 1934. She too lost her entire family in the turmoil after the war. The group she joins at the beginning of 1947 to make hamster-runs to Lithuania is made up of six or eight children. They first walk to Insterburg, where trains depart regularly for Lithuania. Hunger is a constant companion, and food is often nothing more than a few crushed grains mixed with leaves and grass. To ease the hunger pangs, in a pinch, they put pebbles in their mouths.

In Insterburg, they wait at the railway station until dusk. Protected by the dark, they jump onto slow-rolling freight trains. If one of them is ever discovered by a soldier and pushed off the train, they all jump off together. They've learned that sticking together helps to ensure survival.

They've successfully made the trip to Lithuania many times. Once there, they separate into pairs. Johanna usually goes with her little sister, and together they go begging from house to house. Most often they are given a little something, but sometimes they are also asked to help in the household or as a field hand as compensation. Sometimes one of them is even taken in for a day or two.

Before the children go their separate ways, they decide first on which day they want to meet up again. Coming back together always brings great joy. They all have experiences to tell, 'treasures' to share, and the too-big, or too-small, clothing they've been given, to trade—here a pair of pants too large, there two shoes that don't match.

In the summer the children usually sleep out in the open. All of them are plagued with lice and scabies. They treat the scabies with their own urine as water isn't always available. Johanna also has problems with her teeth, which are slowly rotting away. It's extremely painful, and her breath stinks.

As a 13-year-old, she's the oldest and is therefore responsible for the younger ones. She tries her best to cheer the little ones when they're too sad to go on, but often she too has her own sorrows. Sorrows for which there is no adult to sooth her, sorrows she must come to grips with all on her own.

There are 10-year-old twin girls in her group, Maria and Hanna. Maria, the frailer of the two, gradually becomes listless and doesn't want to go on. When on a frosty day in the early autumn they stop to rest at the side of a forest road, she simply lies down and doesn't want to get up again, even though the children want to continue on because of the cold. Beautiful things appear before her eyes. The children look at each other, bewildered. What the girl is telling them with euphoria and in great detail, no one but she can see. The children plead for her to get up and keep going, but in no way does she want to leave. She wants to stay, forever, here in the most beautiful place she's ever seen.

An otherworldly bliss comes over the dying girl. She pulls the other children into her aura, and it gives them the feeling that dying must be something comforting. Up until the very end, the children sit by her side and pray all the simple children's prayers they know, and they say the Lord's Prayer, gently caressing her skin. Then Maria closes her eyes, never to open them again.

Six weeks later, when the children return to the same place, they are in awe. Maria is still lying, unchanged, underneath the tree where they had left her. She doesn't look dead at all, more like someone sleeping, who could, with just a little nudge, be easily brought back to life.

There's nothing the Wolf Children longed for more than to find a connection again, people to care for them and who would give them a home. While there were many humble Lithuanians who helped them in the short term, it was much more difficult to find a place where they were able to stay for good.

Ursula Hundrieser was born in Königsberg in 1933. Memories of her father fade fast after he left for the war, and her older brothers were all killed. Who's left of the family is Ursula, her mother and her younger brother.

When the Red Army invades East Prussia, soldiers burst into her home and rape her mother in front of the children's eyes. Life becomes unbearable; the family is plagued by typhus and famine. When her mother continues to decline, Ursula decides to bring her, a now fully incapacitated woman, to the army hospital. But the doctors don't give her much hope. Six days after she is admitted, her mother dies. Ursula is not even able to say goodbye. The doctors won't allow her into the room as they fear she could become infected. Ursula's little brother, just turned one, also soon dies of starvation. His dying is torturous, and it nearly drives Ursula mad. His little stomach is bloated from malnutrition, and the baby cries incessantly and fusses without end. When he's finally dead, Ursula is relieved. She buries the little one in a mass grave, and only then does it dawn on her that she's now all alone in the world.

Barely 12 years old, Ursula flees to the nearby forests of Lithuania, where she begs and, when necessary, steals. One day she's taken in by a farmer's family and she hopes that now everything will become better once again. Even though the work in the household is hard and cattle herding is difficult, she endures her new life without complaint.

Life feels whole again, and she's nearly forgotten what brought her to this land where she's a foreigner, when one day out in the pasture a horse rears up in front of her and kicks her hard with his hoof. Ursula is badly injured. In the hospital she's not regarded as a member of the Lithuanian family that brought her there, but rather as a German. Despite the farmer's ardent pleading, the Soviet military doctor refuses to treat this 'fascist child'. He even forbids the nurses, who are otherwise compassionate, to bandage her bleeding wound.

Because the scared farmer fears repercussions for his own family, he leaves Ursula by herself in the hospital. Even though she's in tremendous pain, she tries to find her way back to the farm, but she gets hopelessly lost. Her wound stays infected for many more months and does not heal well—Ursula still bears a deep scar that is visible to this day.

Only because she's taken in by a group of Wolf Children does she survive. She gets to the point where she's lost all faith in mankind when, out of the blue, a family takes her in as a milkmaid in the summer of 1947. Here she is well cared for—and here she will stay.

In contrast, Eva Briskorn experiences one of the happiest times of her life in a Lithuanian hospital. It is September 1947 when this 14-year-old arrives in Vilnius by mistake. She's hysterical when she realises she, indeed, did not make it to Germany, but instead has arrived in a foreign country, a place she does not even know where exactly it is. But, above anything else, she's hungry and must find something to eat. A covered market is nearby and wonderful aromas, which she has nearly forgotten exist, draw her in like magic. It smells of fruit, vegetables, freshly baked bread, coffee and spices. The brilliant red of the tomatoes, the luscious green of the cucumbers, it all has a surreal effect on Eva. But Eva has no money. So, all she can do is beg and hope that one or another merchant, one or another market woman, will give her a little something from their—in her eyes—fairytale-like bounty. Eva can only imagine how dreadful she looks. Her stomach is bloated, her eyes are sunken, her clothes hang off her body in threads.

An old woman seems to have pity on her and takes her by the hand. Eva doesn't understand what this old one wants of her, but she's too weak to protest. They enter a restaurant and the woman points to a table. Eva feels terribly ashamed, but she's so hungry that she can't worry about what she looks like and sits down. The woman comes back to the table a short time later holding a hot cup of tea and some bread with butter on it. Eva begins to cry. All her burdens seem to have fallen from her shoulders in that moment. She's grateful for the kind gesture and feels, for the first time since she fled her home with her mother, that she's come to a place where she feels welcomed. But suddenly she thinks maybe something's wrong. What if the woman has something evil in mind? Eva is so scared by this thought that in an opportune moment, she dashes out the door. She doesn't get far. Weak as she is, after only a few steps, she falls in the street, unconscious.

When she awakes she is lying in a hospital. The doctors try to find some things out about her, but Eva can't understand a single word. Eventually a doctor comes who speaks a little German. He asks where she's from and when she was born. Eva, still dazed and unable to think clearly, tells him the wrong birth date. What she cannot know: this will be the permanent date that will be indexed with the Child Tracing Service of the Red Cross. Her family, who do make it to West Germany, will thus never be able to find her.

The doctors and nurses become endeared to the German girl and they decide to keep her in the hospital for an indefinite period of time. When she has recovered, after being bedridden for so long, Eva finds it difficult to walk again. Yet she always finds help, and she always finds someone who's willing to teach her Lithuanian and who will practise the language with her. After eighteen months, she becomes fluent—and she's fully recovered. One day, the doctors let her know when and, most importantly, to whom Eva is to be released. But she doesn't want to leave the hospital. There's food here, and everyone is kind and takes good care of her.

Even though saying goodbye to her now familiar surroundings is hard for Eva, she understands that she can't stay forever. A medical student in her last semester of school takes her under her wing and brings her home. Her parents need help in the household and perhaps Eva, who's nearly 16 now, would be suitable for the job. But the offer ends badly. Eva can't please her hosts and, within short order, is beaten black and blue. When she finally can't take it any longer, she runs back to the hospital. To Eva's good fortune, a new opportunity quickly presents itself. An older gentleman wants to take her home to help his wife. The couple live just on the outskirts of the city. They're kind people and friendly and help Eva get her bearings in Lithuania. For five years she lives in this household, working as a maid and helping out on the farm. She has a good life and, above all, she always has enough food to eat.

Erika Riess, from a small village in the Samland, is sitting with her brother at the side of a road in February 1947, shivering with cold. The 10-year-old and her brother, Heinz, who is two years older, have arrived in a strange place somewhere in East Prussia without family and without direction or even any idea what they should do next. Two German women approach the forlorn children and take them to stay for the night in an abandoned farmhouse where they've taken up residence. The next day they take Erika and Heinz to the railway station and tell them they need to get to Lithuania at all costs if they want to survive. The two

Erika Riess.

children jump up on the first train that comes along and hide in one of the freight cars, but after a few stops they're discovered and thrown off. Time and again, the older Heinz encourages his sister to keep going. She's weak and resigned. With the help of a few other boys, he's finally able to lift Erika up onto a cattle car. It's only because of his undying will to keep going that they finally arrive in the lauded country of Lithuania. The train's end stop is Kibarten, and from here the two siblings begin to roam the countryside.

One of the first farms they come to is a godsend. They're given fried potatoes and milk. But Erika can't keep anything down. Her legs show signs of frostbite, and her toes are completely black and probably frozen off. She hasn't felt them in a long time. The farmer is adamant that she needs treatment, and eventually, against all her resistance, he takes her to the hospital. The doctors see only one solution—amputate both legs from the knee down. But Erika fights against this diagnosis with the last of her strength. She screams and fights back until the nurses finally leave her alone.

Erika is allowed to stay for a while, at least until she recovers, while her brother works on the farm. She stays in the hospital for two more months and then is released, able to at least stand upright on both feet. Even though it's not easy to hobble, she's happy to have avoided the two amputations. Without legs, no farmer would have taken her in, and now she's even able to be with her brother. She cannot handle the hard labour in the field, so the farmer's wife sends Erika off with a begging sack to the surrounding villages, allowing her to return for the night.

In the autumn of 1947, the two siblings must move on because they're no longer needed on the farm. They find new refuge with a family who work as foresters and who offer to take them in as foster children. Together, they walk several miles each morning into the forest to work and don't return home until it has turned dark. These are difficult days of drudgery, full of hard toil. Erika can no longer think clearly. Her only thought is to get through one more day—each day. The father is strict and scares the two children. If they don't obey his every word, he warns them they'll be deported or even shot, and if, in his eyes, they're not working hard enough, he beats them. When he beats Erika particularly badly one day, she can't take it any longer and runs away, leaving her brother behind. But where to? Even the next family that take her in mistreat her. Erika can't bear to always have to run and hide and not be able to defend herself. She moves on again and in time finally finds a foster family that has compassion on this girl, who's turned 12 by now.

Ten-year-old Christel Nitsch has been living with Sofia and her husband Josef for several months and has established a good relationship with both of them. She's pleased that she's not let on to her new family that she has siblings because, as can be expected, she's afraid that her foster parents might send her away if they knew. She misses the others terribly, though, and a deep homesickness seeps into her very being. Sometimes she imagines a blissful reunion with them, just like in a fairytale. She often cries herself to sleep at night, thinking about her mama and the wonderful early years when the whole family was still together. And no matter how well she's treated, the feeling that she's a foreigner in a foreign land never leaves her.

Christel is 11 years old but has little contact with other children her own age. The kids in the neighbourhood taunt her because she's a German, and they know very well how much it hurts her. It's not uncommon for the Russian Communists to be on the lookout for Germans. One day, Sofia and Josef tell her they must hide her. They've been informed that any Lithuanian who is found sheltering Germans will get sent away—either to prison or, much worse, to Siberia. This continuous threat is also the reason Christel is not allowed to go to school. Yet she wishes for nothing more than to finally learn to read and write.

Josef is like a father to her, even though her real father was rarely ever home. Then, in 1948, a fateful event takes place. Josef, who works as an engineering manager, is arrested for embezzlement. In the factory where he works, papers with his signature have been found with a forged signature. Although he insists he's innocent, his case comes before the court, and Josef is sentenced to twenty-five years in a Gulag and sent to Siberia. Once again, Christel's world falls apart. She's heartbroken, and even Sofia doesn't know how to console her foster daughter.

Once, she runs away but, unable to know what to do or where to go, she returns the same day. Several times she tries to take her own life—with vinegar, with detergent, with matchstick heads, with anything she can find with which she hopes to poison herself. Alas, although she has more than one severe stomach ache, her attempts come to nothing. Without really knowing where Germany is or how it even looks, she fixates on the idea that she wants to get there. Maybe, she thinks, there's a train leaving from Vilnius?

For the Wolf Children who were still young at the end of the 1940s, help was sometimes easier to come by than it was for the others. Some were, as they themselves describe, 'taken in as one of their own', in other words, adopted, or at least were allowed to stay on a farm to herd geese or other small livestock for a good long time. But, especially out in the countryside, it was more difficult for the older children, who had lost their cuteness to puberty, to get taken in. They could not count on the sympathy given to the younger ones, and the only way they had even a chance with the Lithuanian farmers was if they could show they were strong and demonstrate an ability to work hard alongside the adults.

After the badly beaten 15-year-old Bruno Klein is released from Soviet headquarters in Königsberg in the autumn of 1945, he avoids people altogether. He lives in the streets and spends his time searching for food in the garbage pits of the new Soviet settlements. Every now and again he receives a handout, but mostly he survives on what he finds in the rubbish. Often, military police chase him away as if he were nothing but a stray dog.

That winter he joins a group of women and children who are on their way to Lithuania. Bruno and his fellow travellers hide under train benches as stowaways. Over and again they're discovered and thrown off. It takes a good week before they get to Kaunas. At first, it looks like paradise to Bruno. Even here, he must beg, but the people are friendly, and they give him what they can. And not just food, but even clothing. Bruno's stomach is no longer used to regular meals and, in particular, fatty foods.

One day he loses consciousness. Passersby bring him to the hospital where a man working the furnace takes the boy under his wing and nurses him back to health. Bruno is touched by the generosity of this simple man who keeps him for several weeks and treats him as if he were his own son.

Of course, Bruno doesn't want to be a burden to the old man. When he's recovered well enough, he moves on to find work on the land. Bruno has heard that many of the farmers in the area need help. In his wanderings, he eventually arrives in a village near Jonava. It is spring 1946, and a farmer offers Bruno work as a shepherd boy and farmhand. Until the autumn of 1949, Bruno leads a rather peaceful existence with him. Slowly he forgets his last months in Königsberg, the famine and the horrible beatings from the Soviets. His family treat him as one of their own. Bruno receives clothing and always has enough to eat.

Yet one day, a village elder, a devoted Communist, begins to harass him. Bruno apparently is a huge thorn in his side, and because of him, the villager begins to bully the entire family. They should once and for all send the 'fascist' off, he tells them, or he'll report them to the authorities. The farmer is saddened by this and at a loss for what to do. It goes against his grain that his heartfelt generosity should be so brutally attacked by someone whom he doesn't even know. He and his wife weigh up their options, while week upon week, Bruno sneaks off to the neighbours, sleeps in barns or simply under the open sky, trying to stay away from any potential authorities. In time, the farmer's relatives hear about the fate of this German boy and offer to take him in. So Bruno, who's become a young adult by now, moves in with a new farmer in a village near Kaunas. The head of this family is a forester and takes Bruno with him into the woods, while his wife takes care of the household. They have no children and are thrilled to have this precocious young man living with them.

Fifteen-year-old Gerhard Gudovius is lucky that he at least keeps meeting friendly and helpful farmers. He's a bright boy and learns from early on how important it is, with a few snatches of Lithuanian, to be able to make himself understood. It's usually the same conversation anyway, and Gerhard becomes ever more fluent with his answers. 'What's your name?' 'How old are you?' 'Where do you come from?' are the three standard questions Lithuanians ask of him. Gerhard always ends by asking politely if it's possible for him to stay the night. Sometimes he scores big and is allowed to sleep in the kitchen on a bench by the fireplace. On other occasions he sleeps in a cow shed or in a barn. It's not all that bad, he thinks, especially in winter, when he has been given a lambskin to keep him warm. In the mornings he wakes early along with the farmers and washes himself at the well, even in the worst weather. He wants to at least give a halfway decent impression when he breakfasts with them, whenever it is offered, which is nearly always the case. Then he moves on. Gerhard is a loner and always goes begging by himself. Where he roams is one of the wealthier areas of Lithuania, and he seldom runs into other Wolf Children.

He travels for half a year until the nights become longer and colder. Gerhard needs to think about his future, in particular the very near future, the upcoming winter. Even now, good fortune is kind to him. A farmer's family, who live in the vicinity of Kalvarija, gladly take him in. They have other children and Gerhard easily assimilates into the tribe. It is not long before he wins the farmer's unequivocal trust. Gerhard has made a good impression, and he shows them that he's hard-working and can be trusted. He's given the job of driving the milk wagon to the dairy in Kalvarija each morning. His work is fun, and Gerhard is even a little proud of himself. He works from sunup to sundown without ever feeling like his work is burdensome or that he's being exploited. Like everyone on the farm, he carries his weight and is rewarded with food, a place to sleep and, whenever necessary, new clothes.

The following spring, Russian units come to the village. They sniff around and show no respect for the farmers. To demonstrate their absolute power over the people, the soldiers often throw glass bottles filled with carbide—which explodes on contact with water—into the farmers' ponds, thereby killing the fish. They're able to have their own next meal, but after that the water is dead. This senseless destruction angers Gerhard no end. But he must hold himself back in order not to be noticed—this is clear to him.

Sometimes Gerhard works the 'night shift'—at a moonshine distillery. Twice a week, the farmer illegally distills somewhere around 8 to 10 litres of alcohol. The resulting drink is strong, containing at least 50 per cent alcohol. Not to mention the potato schnapps he's familiar with, better known as 'the poor man's booze' in East Prussia to Gerhard's great astonishment, as good as unknown in Lithuania.

Gerhard's night duty has two tasks. He's to tend the fire by continuously feeding it with firewood, and he must also taste the distillate periodically to make sure it's strong enough. This takes a bit of intuition and a lot of experience, something Gerhard 'acquires' after several tastings. By the end of these night shifts, he's always rather tipsy, but he learns the art of holding his liquor. His drinking habit begins at way too early an age, even by Lithuanian standards. It's a dangerous game, yet many farmers frequently use children for this job.

Moonshine is strongly forbidden and is harshly punished by the Soviets. Therefore, after the distillation operation is finished, the filled bottles are hidden under straw or inside haystacks. Secret signs are left scattered around so that the bottles can later be found. Using a metal stick with a hook attached to it, they can be pulled back out at a later time.

Because Gerhard always knows where the bottles can be found, he occasionally helps himself to one or two and trades the liquor at the market for things like perfumed soap. In time, the family begins to wonder how Gerhard comes by these

In the southern Lithuanian forests.

rare commodities but, because he always takes extreme care to cover his tracks, his small thefts are never discovered. He doesn't really consider himself a thief, rather he's a 'merchant', and always generously shares his acquired goods with his family.

The older girls and young women who also have the Lithuanian farmers to thank for their survival, nearly always, even into old age, feel it's taboo to talk about how difficult it actually was for them in the early years in this new country. Abuse, including sexual abuse and rape, were not uncommon in these farm families that took them in. It was more the norm than the exception.

Christel Plonus was born in August 1930 in a small town in the district of Labiau. After two unimaginably difficult years under the Russian occupation in East Prussia, she flees to Lithuania in June 1947. By this time, she's already been raped many times by Russian soldiers, the first when she was only 14.

 Christel has become used to being called 'whore', 'fascist girl', or 'German pig'. When she arrives in Lithuania, things don't go any better for her. She looks too old to be pitied like the younger children. She's often accused of being a thief, even though she has stolen nothing. And even in Lithuania, she's sexually assaulted several times. Farmers, when they believe no one is watching, pull her into a stall or throw her in all her nakedness into a pasture and rape her.

 With these experiences in their past, even today, most of the victims never speak about it. The gratitude they owe those who helped them, without whom they would not be alive today, is too great. Yet they are memories that Wolf Children like Christel Plonus will never be able to forget. It's a high price to pay.

Chapter 9

The Decision

All through the autumn months of 1945, Hilde Horn prays for a miracle. Ever since the Red Army left this little girl standing solitary and frightened in her destroyed home in Gerdauen, the days have become endlessly long. She's never felt so alone. When she knocks at the neighbours' doors to beg for a little to eat, they mostly just shake their heads, no. There's not enough food for one's own family, and Hilde is just another mouth to feed, something everyone shies away from. There is no one left to care for Hilde. One day, two neighbour women, wanting to make the journey to Lithuania, offer to take her along, most likely in the hope of finding someone there who'll take her in. This is how this 9-year-old finds herself in Tauroggen in 1946. At first, begging in the marketplace is terribly embarrassing, but she soon understands it's her only chance of survival.

Hilde doesn't speak a word of Lithuanian and is therefore often taken to be nothing but a little thief. Weeks go by and no family takes her in, although she's heard from other children that this does happen. No one wants her, Hilde thinks, because she's so filthy and full of lice. Then, one day, a farmer offers to take this emaciated child home with him. He helps her become more presentable. He gives her a bath and some clean clothes. After that, he introduces her to a family who would like to have her as a nanny. Hilde is overjoyed. A few months later, a second family even offers to adopt this pretty blonde girl, as they themselves cannot have children.

She grows up with this family, and from this point on, she has a good life. The family lives in a small wooden hut at the edge of Tauroggen. Fearing arrest, however, they forbid her to go to school. And no one is to know she's German.

Instead of school, she spends her days caring for the bedridden grandmother while her parents go to the market to sell the small amount of produce they've harvested from their farm. Other than that, depending on the seasons, she also works on the farm wherever her help is needed. Hilde doesn't learn to read or write, nor does she learn her sums. But she is eternally grateful to her adopted family for having saved her. Hilde is absolutely certain that without them she would not have survived.

One day, her father pulls her to the side to give her some advice. 'You now belong to us. You should also have a real Lithuanian name. What do you say to that?' Apparently, he was not prepared for her adamant resistance. 'I am *Hildegard*, and I will remain Hildegard!' she retorts indignantly.

This was an absolute exception to the rule for the Wolf Children. Most of them, out of sheer practicality, took on new names and, along with them, new identities. It was the norm and often happened without them even being asked, as it made survival so much easier—not just for the children, but for their foster families as well. In these early post-war years, Lithuania had already become part of the Soviet Union, and to 'aid and abet' the enemy was punishable by law. Lithuanian names made it easier for the Wolf Children to no longer be hunted down as illegal foreigners.

This decision was most critical for the older children, the consequences of which they could not have foreseen, for whatever their choice was—to remain a German or assimilate into Lithuanian culture—it would govern the rest of their lives. It was a balancing act between the hope of an eventual return to Germany and the emersion into a completely new life, a life in which the old one had to be forgotten, or at least pushed way to the back of their minds. So it was that many of the Wolf Children not only took on Lithuanian names, but were even baptised into a new faith and converted to Catholicism. They learned new customs and traditions, especially during high holidays, making them their own, sometimes even donning the traditional Lithuanian costumes.

Gisela Launert doesn't know in which year she was born … 1939? 1940? And she doesn't know where in East Prussia her family is from. She has only fleeting memories of the flight, but she thinks that she arrived in Lithuania with her grandmother in early 1946. Her mother and grandfather had been killed when their trek was bombed.

Because her grandmother is not able to manage with both Gisela and her 1-year-old sister, Karin, the baby is left with another family in East Prussia, who agrees to take her into their fold. Now it is just the two of them.

Gisela and her grandmother leave East Prussia and arrive in Lithuania in an area near Pogegen on the north shore of the Memel. Here they find shelter in an old schoolhouse along with a few other refugees, but there's nothing to eat.

Over the following months, Gisela makes larger and larger circles around the villages in search of food, but at one point she gets lost in the midst of all the farmhouses that all look the same around the Memelland. The way back to Pogegen is as impossible to find as is the way back to her grandmother. At first, she's terribly frightened, but she realises it's now a matter of survival. 'I just knew that I needed to take care of myself and find food. Even my grandmother couldn't help me with that.'

Gisela eventually arrives in a village where she finds a family who has children she can look after. The children are only slightly younger than she is herself. A year later, a family takes Gisela in and adopts her as their daughter. Gisela, once a Protestant, is now baptised into the Catholic faith, and is given a Lithuanian name. 'Gisela Launert', as she says today, 'remained in the past.'

At 15, she moves to a town near Klaipėda, and gets work as a housemaid. Here she meets her husband-to-be, whom she marries three years later. The desire for true love and a family of her own is simply overwhelming.

Hans Gladstein, too, is much too young to be able to make the choice either for or against his German roots. At first, his new Lithuanian identity is just something he has fun with, and, in time, it becomes quite natural for him to say that he is, in fact, a Lithuanian. This even makes it possible for him to go to school—a rare stroke of luck, one that seldom plays out in the lives of most other Wolf Children.

Like Gisela Launert, Hans also doesn't know exactly in which year he was born. He estimates that he must have been about 5 years old when the war came to an end. Where he grew up in East Prussia, though, he cannot say. He's sure that his grandmother lived in Königsberg. And that he had a brother, about two years older, whose name was Alfred and who, like his mother, had blond hair.

Hans has only vague recollections of a forced march around Königsberg, the dead bodies in the streets and in the ditches, and a garden plot in which they lived for a period of time. And he remembers standing with his brother and grandmother while they watched helplessly as his mother was raped on several occasions by Russian soldiers. He remembers, too, that his mother became pregnant and gave birth to a little boy who soon died. He remembers the famine and the nettle soup that was hardly more than warm water that his mother cooked each day. He remembers the warmth of his mother, who held him and kissed him, and didn't want to let him go. Yet one day, it comes to this as their last resort: she sends Alfred and Hans to Lithuania to beg. She wants to stay behind with his dying grandmother. One last kiss from his mother, one last loving hug, and the two boys go on their way. Hans is probably 6; Alfred is 4.

They join a few older boys whom Hans greatly admires. They know how to get to Lithuania. The group of them jump onto freight trains, and with only a few delays, they soon reach Šiauliai. Here, Alfred briefly leaves his younger brother, Hans, in the care of some strangers. By the time they are reunited, Hans is barely alive. He can't walk anymore and Alfred is way too weak to carry him. Yet, with great difficulty, the two of them move on.

Months go by in which the two boys live out in the open. They are so plastered with dirt that they dare go into town only on rare occasions. At the farmhouses around Šiauliai, they occasionally receive a warm meal, sometimes a crust of bread or a piece of pork belly. Otherwise, they spend their nights in ditches, eat leaves from the trees and drink water from the creeks.

One day while begging, Hans is so weak that he falls into unconsciousness. A Lithuanian couple find him lying at the side of the road and they take the little wild one home with them. They nurse him back to health and … he's allowed to stay. When he has learned to speak Lithuanian a bit better, the family sends him to school and he's able to finish at least an elementary school education.

Christel Scheffler, nicknamed Kitty, is on her first hamster-run to Lithuania with a friend of her mother's when she's suddenly left behind. She wasn't able to jump up on the train back to Königsberg in time. A man notices her a short time later as she is relieving herself behind a bush and offers to take her home with him. He can speak a bit of German and asks a few questions, like where is she from. Then he takes her to a small farm near Jonava. As he says goodbye to Kitty, he adds, 'This will now be your new home. So, stay, and be a good girl.' Obedient as she is, she will never forget this last sentence. It becomes the motto by which she lives for the rest of her life.

However, the Lithuanian family that takes her in treats her like a serf. The woman is from Belarus. She beats Kitty, who often does not understand what is wanted of her. She beats her at every chance she gets, to the point that Kitty ends up falling unconscious.

But the couple want her to stay. They manage to secure papers for her, certifying that Kitty is their daughter. She's given a new name, a new birth date and a new identity. She will now be called Aldona. To speak German is strongly forbidden in this household, but there are few opportunities to do so anyway. Within a few years, Aldona forgets her mother tongue. On the other hand, she's able to go to school for four years.

Luise Quitsch, too, needs to make adjustments to fit in with her new life, although under completely different circumstances.

In 1945, Luise comes to live with a Russian military cook in the barracks in Kaunas. The cook is enamoured by this cute 5-year-old girl, whose only toys are a broken doll and a wooden stick, which she plays with near the fence while he works. There's a hole in the fence, and a young woman sometimes comes by and gives Luise candy, handing it to her through the hole. Little Luise is always thrilled to have her attention. One day, when the woman comes once again and lures Louise with a piece of candy, she slips through the hole in the fence and simply goes home with her. When she tells her story today, Luise always breaks out in a big grin. 'She snatched me,' she says. 'Either that, or I simply escaped. Anyhow, I was gone from there.'

The early days with her new family are a big adventure for her. During the first few months—most likely out of fear of the Russians—the woman hides her away in a nearby village. She is no longer allowed to go by Luise; her name is now Alfreda, and she's not, under any circumstance, allowed to speak German.

Less than a year later, she moves in with a family in Kaunas, and here she goes to school. She is not introduced as a German girl, but rather as 'the orphan child of a family that had lived in the Memelland and who died in the chaos of the war', as her family tells others. Her new Lithuanian father is a cobbler by trade and her mother is a schoolteacher. The couple have two grown children and now want to also be good parents to the little Alfreda, the 'baby of the family'.

Luise Quitsch, not long after her adoption by a Lithuanian family.

When Luise is alone, she often thinks about how it used to be, when she was not yet Alfreda. She's always painfully aware that she is, in fact, a German, and yet it's out of the question to talk about it. She knows this. She doesn't want to seem ungrateful, so she tries hard to suppress the few memories she still has of East Prussia. For years, she feels like she's leading a double life. But, of her true self, she must keep silent. 'As a child, I always felt like a stranger in Lithuania. Like I simply did not belong.'

Her parents want her to help in the household. She gives her mother a hand with the cleaning and cooking, which she does gladly. There's just one thing she hates profusely: sanding the parquet floor by hand. The steel wool she's supposed to use cuts her fingertips and they often bleed. Luise is not the only one; the entire family is recruited when it comes to the floors. Just the word 'floor' gives Luise a headache. Every time she comes in from outside, she hears her mother's sharp tongue. 'Feet!' She's to take off her shoes so the parquet floors won't be damaged.

Luise's Lithuanian parents hold a good education and a strict upbringing in high esteem. To them, a disciplined life during the formative years is the greatest achievement. And so, it's not just good grades in school that matter. For example, Luise is supposed to learn to play tennis. As she sees it, this is a pointless endeavour. She's to practise in the yard—true agony! Why, in the heat of the summer, must she always run from one corner to the other, chasing a ball? The whole thing makes little sense to her.

There's one other thing that bothers Luise throughout her childhood. Whenever she's accomplished something, the adults tend to talk about her in her presence as if she were nothing but air. And it's always the same conversation. 'What should we do now with the child?' her mother asks. In the same breath, she answers herself: 'We'll sew a sack for Alfreda, tie it around her neck, and send her out in the street to beg.' Luise sits next to them, numb, with a lump in her throat, and can hardly hold back her tears. It's the worst feeling of rejection, a deep sense that love is being withheld from her. It affects her for the rest of her life. So much so that it is difficult to ever trust anyone.

While most of the other German children in Lithuania rarely, if ever, go to school, Luise is an exception, although it's not always a pleasure. In the autumn of 1950, she's to begin the fifth grade. But her spelling is so bad that she needs to study with a tutor throughout the summer months. While she can hear the other children in the neighbourhood playing outdoors, Luise is supposed to sit with her instructor listening while she dictates the daily lessons. The young woman does eventually succeed in not only teaching Luise the Lithuanian language, but also inspiring an understanding of all its peculiarities. In the end, Luise is a good student in Lithuanian and can well appreciate 'the consequences' of not studying hard enough.

Luise's family are not without their own sorrows. In 1947, their adult son is arrested and deported to a Siberian prison camp for 'political activism'. Her parents make their adopted daughter, Luise, well aware that they, too, could get sent away. In case the worst should happen, they've already made preparations. There are sacks of dried bread and a few jars filled with lard in the pantry, ready for the long journey. Every time someone comes knocking at the door at night, Luise is petrified and hides in the closet behind the coats. The fear of being picked up rattles her to her bones. Whenever she sees soldiers in the street, she crosses to the other side. When she hears Russian being spoken, she runs as fast as she can back home. For many years these fears rule her life.

Between the autumn of 1948 and the spring of 1950, a number of transports left Lithuania for East Germany (the GDR). While the expulsion of Germans from the Kaliningrad area is well documented, barely anything is mentioned in their archives about Germans leaving Lithuania. The historian Ruth Leiserowitz believes that 'one hoped to resolve the East Prussian issue in Lithuania in quick order by simply providing a few freight trains to ship them off.'

Indeed, there were transports, but the Lithuanians greatly distrusted their purpose. This was a time when mass deportations to the interior of the Soviet Union and its Gulags were at their all-time high. To many, it was highly questionable that the ordered transports were actually going to the GDR. Especially out in the country, wild rumours circulated about deportations and even about entire trains that had been blown up. Many Wolf Children say their foster parents advised them against boarding such trains. Others, like Kitty, never even knew there was a chance of going to Germany.

Margot Dudas, who spent her first years of life in the Königsberg-Ponarth area, in the same borough as Kitty (although they didn't know each other then), is brutally separated from her parents when the Red Army marches in. Margot, who's only 10 years old when this happens, spends the next two years living with other children out in the open fields of East Prussia. In early 1947, she arrives in Lithuania by riding on the roof of a freight train whose end of the line is Kaunas.

For the first few weeks here, she begs—mostly alone, because she believes it will yield more food. After some time, a farmer's family shows compassion and takes her in as a milkmaid. Margot is happy. For the first time since she fled her home two years ago, she has a roof over her head.

Her respite lasts for nearly two more years, years that are filled with relatively hard field labour, but she doesn't complain. Anything is better than living under the open sky, better than the cold, better than the hunger.

When the news that all German children are to take the transport to Germany, Margot's foster family doesn't believe it one bit. 'They'll take you to Siberia,' the farmer warns her. At the same time, he also lets her know that she can no longer stay with them—it's become far too dangerous. Margot is shocked. Weeping, she sits at the side of the road, not knowing which way to turn. In time, two sisters who live in the same village invite her into their home. From this time on, Margot takes care of their household, while the two women work to obtain Lithuanian papers for her. And finally, she's officially a Lithuanian 'foundling' from Klaipėda.

Ruth Deske from Gerdauen is just 13 years old when she arrives in Lithuania with her youngest brother, Karl-Heinz. She's been walking, carrying the little one on her hip for several weeks, all the way to Šiauliai in northern Lithuania.

Both are taken in by a tenant farmer. He has only one leg and needs help on the farm. Ruth does the work of two labourers, always hoping to receive a little more than just the one bowl of potato soup to eat. On those days when she cooks root vegetables as fodder for the pigs, she takes some for herself and then brings a small bowl to her brother for whom she must also care. She doesn't know if he'll survive. On some days he looks more dead than alive. But the farmer and his wife barely have enough to live on themselves. A tiny plot of land and a single cow are all that this small community of families have to feed themselves. They've been thrown together as a consequence of the government-mandated collectivisation of small farms.

One Sunday when the farmer's wife is at church, Ruth, Karl-Heinz and the farmer are sitting at the table saying grace, when the dog out in the yard begins to bark. Suddenly soldiers storm in. Where has he hidden the Germans, they shout at the farmer. He only mutely points to the two children. For a long moment,

Ruth Deske's Lithuanian family tending the fields.

Ruth's heart stops beating. It's all over now. But little Karl-Heinz, who's but a shadow of himself, looks so pitiful that even the crude NKVD officer feels touched. With a few short words, he orders his men to retreat.

The wife of this family is a member of the Communist Party, and with the help of her connections, Ruth eventually receives proper papers in 1950. Her name is now Birutė.

When, in 1951, all of the Germans still living in Lithuania are ordered to leave for the GDR, Ruth and Karl-Heinz hide in the forest once again, and for several weeks. Terrifying rumours are circulating of firing squads and deportations to Siberia. Only years later do they find out that the transports actually did go to Germany. But even the rest of her siblings stayed in Lithuania; none of them trusted the trains.

It was not just the warnings the farmers gave them that kept some Wolf Children from leaving. It was the journey into the unknown, and the fact that the feared Soviet officials were to be in charge that rekindled memories of the war, as well as the flight from East Prussia. Nevertheless, some did grab at the opportunity, hoping for a better life in Germany. But these return transports to the GDR were not always voluntary and were often brutally carried out.

For Dieter Gröning, it will be the longest journey of his life, riding inside a freight train. In the autumn of 1947, soldiers pick him up in Tilsit, bring him to the nearest railway station and, along with a number of other children, lock him inside a cattle car. When the massive bolt clinks into its metal track, the door is locked from the outside. Dieter can see everything through a crack in the wooden planks. Inside they find a few jugs of milk and some salted meat to tide them over. How long they will be en route, the children do not know. In the end, it's ten long days that they are without fresh air, without water and without a toilet. When the door is finally opened in East Germany, the children are life-threateningly dehydrated. Like wild animals they run to a well to quench their thirst. Eight-year-old Dieter is sick with whooping cough and is immediately taken to a hospital. There, he is cared for, for two weeks, and is later brought to an orphanage.

Gerhard Gudovius has been well received by his Lithuanian family, where he's treated like a son. Only his looks belie his relationship to his foster family. While they are all dark-haired, Gerhard's hair is straw-blond, and he has blue eyes.

One day in the spring of 1950, while delivering milk to the creamery in Kalvarija, Russian officials are already waiting for him. As he's German, he should be ready to be picked up the very next day, he's told. By now, Germany no longer has any meaning to Gerhard, who has, in the meantime, taken on the name of Gerhardas. It suddenly hits him like a ton of bricks, though, what exactly is happening. Back at the farm he tells his family about his encounter with the officials. No one can believe their ears; the women weep. But Gerhard knows no other way around it but to make himself available the next morning.

Over the next several days, he travels by train to the GDR—to a town near Dresden. But he will never forget the formative years of his youth in a village with a family that loved him, in Lithuania.

According to the Lithuanian census taken in May 1950, 3,274 'Kaliningrader Germans' were living in the country at that time. Amongst these Germans, 770 children were catalogued as having at least one parent, and there were another 365 without. The actual figures could easily be much higher, as the experiences of most orphans as regards the Soviet officials were not always the best. In many cases, it was most sensible not to risk exposing the fact they had a new Lithuanian identity but were indeed German. For even the youngest of them, their new living situations pushed the years of war and the years after the war to the back of their minds. Although the Soviet Communist culture in their new home was foreign to them, it nevertheless gave them a sense of stability, something they just needed to come to terms with.

Ursula Haak is 10 years old when, after the death of her mother, she returns to the region of Tilsit with her two brothers, Horst and Willy. But nothing is how it once was. Ursula decides to go to Lithuania on a begging tour and, with a heavy heart, she leaves Horst behind in Tilsit. As much as she looks for him when they return, Horst remains missing forever. For Ursula there are many difficult months and years to come in which she cannot help but feel responsible for the death of her little brother, even though she never knows for sure what became of him.

Willy and Ursula turn their backs on Tilsit and travel a second time to Lithuania. This time they want to stay, for good. Willy immediately finds a farmer's family who take him in as a shepherd boy. For Ursula, the search for a home takes longer, but she too eventually finds a home near Tauroggen.

When they are told of the orders to depart for the GDR, Ursula discusses the matter with her foster family. They don't believe the trip to Germany is real. 'Germany doesn't even exist anymore,' her father says. 'Everything is now Soviet.' By that, he probably means East Prussia, and possibly even the GDR. But the truth is, he knows of too many people who were arrested and ended up in a labour camp in Siberia. Ursula would prefer to discuss it with Willy, but he's moved and Ursula no longer knows where he is. She decides not to take the risk and stays in Lithuania.

That the fears of the Lithuanian farmers were not completely pulled out of thin air is confirmed for Ursula when a few years later she tries once again to look for her two brothers. She finds out about only one of them, Willy. Through a contact at the Red Cross she learns that her brother, not even of legal age, was deported to a labour camp near Smolensk. There, in a mining accident sometime in the 1950s, he lost his life.

Bernhard Keusling is 11 when his caregiver, because of his allegiance to the Forest Brothers, is arrested in the summer of 1949 by NKVD officials. Bernhard is able to run away in time to find safety in the woods. As soon it feels safe, he returns to the farm. For a while he continues to work there while also taking care of the neighbour's cattle. Even the farmer's wife and two daughters return home, and there are no more investigations by the police.

But a man is desperately needed on the farm, and his foster mother, the woman in charge of the house now, begs Bernhard to stay to help replace her husband's work. Around this time, all the farms in the area have been ordered to collectivise. Those farmers who resist this government-mandated takeover are required to pay high fines. Almost all the butter they produce on the farm is to be handed over to the government. After a while, they can no longer hold out against the collective, and so, Bernhard, having just turned 12 in 1950, now works at this socialised collective farm. As he has no identification papers, his work is credited to the farm woman's pension fund, not to one in his name. It will still take a number of years, and through some connections, before Bernhard finally receives his Lithuanian papers. Fortunately, while military service is mandatory for all men, the Soviets don't want him. As a naturalised citizen of German heritage, they are suspicious of him.

At barely 20 years of age, Ruth Deske leaves the farm where she lives to work on a collective, while Karl-Heinz stays on as a farmhand. Like Bernhard Keusling, Ruth always has problems as she's a German holding a Lithuanian passport. For example, she's not allowed to work in the industrial sector, where the working conditions are somewhat better than in agriculture, or even in forestry.

Vacys Gorys, a man of simple means, begins to court Ruth in the spring of 1953. He's head over heels in love with this young woman who is not only pretty, but strong and appears to know how to get the work done. But there's one issue that stands in the way of their marriage—she's Protestant. So that they can be married in the church, Ruth decides to be baptised into the new faith and becomes a Catholic. She comforts herself with the thought, 'There's only one God in heaven anyway.'

The couple eke out an existence on the piece of land that they received from the collective, and within a year they're allowed to own a cow. Things are looking good. Their only sorrow during these years is that their daughter, Irene, is not well from the time she's born in 1954. At first there's no diagnosis. Only after years of uncertainty, it is established that she has multiple sclerosis.

The Soviets have not forgotten about Ruth, though. Every month she's to report to the authorities, who threaten her, telling her that she's not ever allowed to leave the area. To improve their meagre income, in 1958 the couple decide to work as foresters. For the next sixteen years, Ruth will toil in the forest, working a man's labour, often with only primitive tools to fell trees and split logs. Nevertheless, the small family stays together. When all is said and done, Ruth has found her foothold in Lithuania.

Christel Scheffler bravely endures her foster mother's evil moods during her younger years of life. Under no circumstances does she want to have to go begging again. She fears the hunger, keeps still, withdrawn, and faces whatever's imposed upon her. The main thing is that she has a roof over her head. Shortly after her eighteenth birthday, Christel falls in love with a young Lithuanian man, and it's not long before they are married.

But it's not a happy marriage. Christel, hoping her relationship might get her away from her foster mother's brutal beatings, goes from the pan into the fire. Her new husband is a drunk and beats her. Sometimes he beats her so badly she falls into unconsciousness, even while Christel is pregnant with their first child. The hope that, with this new baby, her husband will soften his temper and become a responsible father proves to be wrong. His abuse does not let up. Christel becomes pregnant a second time, but this time she leaves her husband soon after the birth, only to move into the home of her former abusive foster parents.

Whereas most of the Wolf Children become young adults in the 1950s and some even marry, Konrad Fischer experiences a completely different set of circumstances.

For a good two years he lives with his adopted mother, Agota. In 1949 she becomes severely ill with tuberculosis. She has only a few weeks to live, a time during which Konrad, just turned 18, lovingly cares for her. She saved his life, he knows, and now, too gladly, he wants to save hers. But in the end her illness wins out.

Her only sister arrives from Kaunas for Agota's funeral. Moved by Konrad's unwavering devotion, she takes him back to live with her in the city. She's married, and soon after Konrad's arrival, her husband is arrested in Kaunas on suspicion of 'collaborating with the enemy'.

Life in the city proves to be difficult for Konrad as he has no papers. Through friends, he finally receives the identification papers of a dead Lithuanian by the name of Jonas Laimonas. Jonas's birth certificate has disappeared, which is why Konrad is able to live under this assumed identity. But Konrad's age, because of the missing documents, must now be determined by a medical commission. Presumably he now was born in 1936. Instead of being an 18-year-old adult, he is suddenly a 13-year-old child again. He can work as 'Jonas', but without an education, and without an occupation, his possibilities are limited to manual labour only.

Horst Fischer's age is also determined by a medical commission. Horst, born in 1937 near Wehlau, witnesses the ravages of the Red Army at its worst when they march into East Prussia. The rapes, the executions, the pillaging, and the violent destruction of homes have planted fearful memories deep within his mind. When he sees the opportunity to flee to Lithuania with his 3-year-old brother, Manfred, he courageously grabs at it.

The two beg in the villages and at farms along the Memel River, sometimes with more, sometimes with less, success. Together they are en route for nearly a year, but a second winter without a roof over their heads is something Horst doesn't even want to imagine. Eventually, they come to a village where they meet a couple. When they first set eyes on the two abandoned little Germans, the couple immediately decide to take in one of them, Horst. Manfred ends up with another family, but unfortunately, the two brothers soon lose sight of one another. It's much too dangerous for the foster families to keep up a contact that could so easily give them away.

The couple treat Horst like their own son. They call him Kostas and give him their surname. He's even allowed to attend the seven-year Lithuanian elementary school.

In 1956, when he tries to get an identification card, a medical commission decides that he was born on 3 January 1939 in Lithuania—making him two years younger than he actually is. These two years make it mandatory that he sign up for military duty with the Red Army, the hated army that killed his family, destroyed his home and erased his past. But from 1961 to 1964, he becomes a part of them.

Günther Roscher from West Germany is 14 years old when he first travels to Lithuania with his mother to beg. As evacuees out of the Rhineland, they had landed in East Prussia shortly before the war ended, trapped between two fronts and unable to return to the West before the area became Soviet.

On a foggy and bitterly cold January night, the two of them arrive in Kibarten. There is much chaos going on at the railway station and Günther loses sight of his mother. Frantic, this little boy cannot believe that he's now all alone. He doesn't understand the foreign language and has no money. He, too, is taken in by a farmer. Here he learns the language, the customs and traditions, and eventually becomes a true Lithuanian. No one can distinguish him from other natives. Not until 1952, when Günther must register for the military, is the lie almost discovered, because Günther does not have Lithuanian papers. In the eleventh hour, his foster father helps him acquire forged documents with a Lithuanian name. Soon thereafter, he enlists as a Lithuanian in the Red Army in order to fulfill his three-year military duty.

A train in winter, Lithuania.

Arno Willuweit is also not able to get around his military obligations when he comes of age. He was taken in by a farmer and lives not far from his brother, Heinz, although they have no contact with one another. Arno works on this farm until 1953, and the farmer eventually helps him get a forged birth certificate with a Lithuanian name.

Now that he's a Lithuanian, he is drafted into the Red Army at the age of 19. He's a strong man, and knows that he'll only have a chance at life if he can survive these years. They are not easy years, but when Arno is released from the military, he pursues his dream and becomes a blacksmith.

Heinz manages to avoid his military duties altogether. That he survived the torture when his arms were slashed is close to a miracle. To his foster parents, Heinz is a hero, and they protect him like he's the apple of their eye. He thanks them daily with his undying commitment to work.

As he grows older, Heinz makes friends with Lithuanian boys from the neighbouring farms. Once, when he is just 20, he's invited to a wedding in Tauroggen. There, he meets a beautiful blonde girl with whom he immediately falls in love. She's from East Prussia, like he is, and has experienced a similar fate—the escape from Königsberg and the years of begging in Lithuania. The young woman is named Hilde Horn. She will marry him within a year.

Chapter 10

Captured and Deported

The newly formed Union of the Soviet Socialist Republics covered one-sixth of the Earth's land surface, about two and a half times the landmass of the United States, and spanned eleven time zones. The immense size of the new geographic regions of the Soviet Union was as unfathomable to the Lithuanian people as it was to the Wolf Children. In order to keep control of the people living across this massive land, Stalin's regime built a nationwide network of prison camps of varying sizes and purposes. It reached from the western border of the Ukraine to Eastern Siberia and from the Arctic Sea in the north to the border with China in the south. The Stalinist politics of the time and the totalitarian regime's efforts to control its populations were not the only reasons these camps were established. Equally as prevalent was the need to extract raw materials such as coal and timber. Also a new network of roads was to be built. Why not use free labour?

The Soviet camp system is also known as the GULAG from the Russian acronym, **Glavnoye Upravleniye Lagerej**, roughly translated as 'Chief Administration of Camps'. While the term GULAG was intended to signify a mere system of administration, it actually came to represent a massive institution of forced and cruel slave labour.

'One was not sent to the Gulag because one did something, it was because of who one was,' the American journalist Anne Applebaum reports in her Pulitzer Prize-winning book, *Gulag, a History*. Who one was could be defined by one's political affiliation as much as it could be defined by one's ethnicity, or simply one's usefulness in the workforce. In order to support this Soviet Socialist economic plan, each Soviet republic was required to provide its quota of manpower. In Lithuania alone, 111,400 people were deported between the years 1945 and 1953. About a quarter of that number were children.

The reasons for their incarcerations were often arbitrary and in part even absurd. 'Anti-Soviet Agitation' was one label. 'Suspected Spy' or simply 'Related to the Enemy of the People' could land you in one of these prisons for as much as twenty-five years. Countless people were sentenced solely because of their nationality, which included many of those Germans who had fled to Lithuania or came from the Memel Territory. How many Wolf Children were amongst them is unknown. Very few records exist, and only a very small number of children ever returned.

In the spring of 1946, 11-year-old Hans Joachim Petereit is loaded onto a cattle car with a number of other Germans from Königsberg—their destination unknown. They nevertheless have high hopes that they are going to Germany. They travel for days through wide-open landscapes, something the train passengers can see only by peering through thin cracks in the train walls. Otherwise, the train has been sealed shut from the outside. The longer they travel, the more desperate they become. It's especially clear to the adults that this train is not travelling to freedom, but into the innermost regions of the Soviet Union, and most likely to a prison camp. Even Hans Joachim finds the long ride unbearable.

In the chaos after the war, he lost his mother and sister in the siege of Königsberg. Now he is a child sitting amongst strangers en route to nowhere. When the train reaches its destination, they're told they have arrived in the Siberian district of Krasnoyarsk. The prisoners are to line up on the station platform. Hans Joachim finds a spot at the very back. The train engineer sees him standing there and, without much thought, pulls him to the side. He has pity on this little boy who looks so lost between all the adults and takes him into his cabin in the steam engine room. The engineer is a Lithuanian and will soon be driving back in the direction of home. This time he'll be carrying a stowaway in his cabin.

The least of the child prisoners have such luck.

Since Lieselotte Schulz from Königsberg watched her four younger siblings, her grandparents, her aunts and cousins die, one by one, in the famine, nothing in her life is as it once was. Of the large family of twelve, only three of them are still alive: Lieselotte, who is 12, her sister Hannelore, two years younger, and her mother. In the spring of 1947, the three of them arrive in Lithuania. Here, her mother at least hopes to save her two daughters. But within days they become separated when their mother is arrested by the Red Army. Was she deported to Russia? Was she murdered, or is she still alive? What became of her is something the two girls will not know for many more years.

At about the same time in 1947, Elfriede Müller comes to the Kaunas region with her mother and her brother, Gustav. Elfriede is nearly 13, Gustav is 15. They soon learn they will not be able to stay together. A farmer takes Elfriede in; Gustav and their mother are taken in with another family in a village nearby. Even though she must work hard and is separated from her mother and brother, she is grateful to be a part of the farmer's family. But only a few weeks later, she has the shock of her life. During the night a number of families were arbitrarily arrested and amongst them are Elfriede's mother and brother. The girl is frantic.

All the Germans living in Lithuania are suddenly required to register with the authorities, and no Lithuanian wants to make it known that they have Germans living with them. Everyone is scared. Even the family Elfriede lives with becomes nervous and the wife finally decides to take her to another family that lives farther away, in the outskirts of Kaunas. Elfriede begins to work for this family as a nanny, even though she is still a child herself. But it is her only hope of survival in this, to her, foreign land, where she has no family and no official papers. The new family is kind to her. There is only one thing that's out of the question. Under no circumstance is Elfriede allowed to speak German.

Elfriede has no idea to where her mother and brother were taken. The adults always speak of Siberia, a cold region way in the east in the Soviet Union. But why? What have they done and why were they taken to Siberia? These questions will percolate in Elfriede's mind for many more years. She doesn't understand, and she will never find an answer.

Ten years later, in the autumn of 1957, Elfriede gets a visit from the farm woman who once took her in in Kaunas. She has a letter for her. It's from Siberia. Elfriede looks at the envelope and recognises her mother's handwriting—her mother, who has yearned for her children all these years and is now finally allowed to write a letter for the first time. It is in Russian, and Elfriede needs help reading it. In short sentences, her mother writes that she was imprisoned until recently in a labour camp near Karaganda in the Soviet Republic of Kazakhstan. She's been released but is now working as forced labour on a collective farm. She is subject to a strict curfew and is neither allowed to travel nor move away. The letter includes a return coupon so that Elfriede can write back to her. This will be the first news she has received since they were separated over ten years ago. An acquaintance helps Elfriede write the Cyrillic letters, a time-consuming undertaking as Elfriede has never learned to read or write, let alone in Russian.

That same year, Elfriede receives her first news from the Red Cross. How this organisation finds her is, to this day, a mystery to her. Gustav wrote a short letter from a Siberian youth camp in which he asks the whereabouts of his sister and mother. Shortly after their arrest, he was separated from his mother, and has not seen her since. Elfriede is overjoyed that they are both still alive. Yet the more she learns about their fates, the more she is devastated.

Gustav sent a passport-size photo of himself. Elfriede can hardly recognise her brother, who's only two years older than she is. He appears haggard and sickly and looks like a 50-year-old man, even though he's only in his mid-twenties. In comparison, Elfriede's life now seems to have been a godsend. She works as a seamstress in a garment factory. Heavenly.

Waltraut Minnt is one of those who was taken directly from her home in 1945 and immediately deported to Siberia. This 9-year-old girl is numb with fear when Russian soldiers storm her house and run past her and her siblings, going straight through the open door to her mother. The children can hear only her screaming, while neighbours hold them back, trying to keep them from running into the house—and to their own demise.

Waltraut, centre, as a young woman during Lithuania's Saint Jonas', or 'midsummer', festival.

Her mother is gang-raped. Hours later, she comes out to her children, weeping and bloodied. She can hardly stand on her feet, stumbles and falls into the road, right in front of a moving tank. What happens next, like a film in slow motion, one hundredth of a second per one hundredth of a second, is an image that has burrowed itself deep inside Waltraut's memory: her mother is run over. At the same time, she hears gunshots. One of the soldiers has shot her mother in the legs. The look on her face is one of disbelief and anguish. Her eyes search for her children. Waltraut wants to run to her but she cannot move. She is in a state of shock and cannot put one foot in front of the other. A soldier brazenly throws her mother's body over his shoulder and motions for the children to follow him.

He takes them to the railway station, where, along with several other families, they're packed into a freight train which soon takes off. It's an endlessly long journey. Her mother is dazed and drifts in and out of consciousness. While she continues to bleed, Waltraut lies next to her on the wooden floor and caresses her face. She speaks softly to her, hoping she can keep her alive. But, en route, her mother succumbs to her wounds and dies.

The destination of the long journey is a labour camp in Siberia. Waltraut has lost all orientation. She is distraught and tries to repress everything that just happened. The children on the train, including Waltraut and her oldest sister, are taken to a so-called 'youth camp'. These are Waltraut's formative years, but they become years in which she loses all control of her life—and, in time, like so many others, she is broken.

Agathe Czajka and her brother, Bruno, who's a year younger than she, grow up in a Polish-German family in the Allenstein district. Her grandparents speak Polish at home, but both children attend a German school. Her parents, on the other hand, speak more German than Polish but with a heavy Prussian accent, the so-called *Ermländischen* dialect.

The war doesn't become a reality to 16-year-old Agathe until January 1945, when her father, Johann, is drafted in the last days of the conflict. But he doesn't get far. On 20 January, the Russians take all the men in his unit to Allenstein as prisoners, back to his home, where he and the others are shot by a firing squad within the grounds of the Protestant cemetery.

Allenstein surrenders to Soviet troops, January 1945.

One Sunday afternoon, Agathe and her mother go to visit an aunt. This visit ends in tragedy. Russian soldiers march into the small village where she lives and take most of the villagers prisoner. Amongst them is Agathe. The next day she sees eleven people gruesomely murdered. Of the women and girls who survive, many become victims of a mass gang rape. Agathe, for some reason, is lucky and is left alone. As it becomes night, the village is laid to waste and all the farms are burned to the ground. With this, the livelihoods of all of its people are destroyed as well.

The next morning, the prisoners are told they must march until they finally arrive, completely exhausted, in Insterburg, a journey of nearly 200 miles. Here they're told to board a freight train—destination unknown. Agathe and three other girls hide under a horse blanket, hoping to remain undetected. There are around fifty women in this freight wagon, which has a trough in the middle in which they can relieve themselves. There's no heat, so the urine and faeces freeze into hard piles that at least don't stink.

After a good week the train makes its first stop. A rumour goes around that they're in the vicinity of Moscow. The large sliding door is opened but only for a brief time. They can see that they're in the middle of a frozen 'Arctic' landscape that stretches all the way to the horizon. Soldiers shovel broken pieces of ice onto the floor and throw some hard crusts of bread after it. Then they close the door and soon the train takes off again.

How long they continue on, Agathe can no longer remember. More than a week, maybe even two or three. 'You lose all sense of time and space,' she says. The most valuable thing she still owns is her lined rubber boots. But one of the women has an eye for them and tears them from her feet one night while she's asleep. There's no allegiance amongst the prisoners; pure survival is all that matters. Agathe must go barefoot from now on.

Agathe no longer remembers the name of the camp in Siberia, only the town, Chelyabinsk. 'There were three or more camps there.' Here she is put to work in a coal mine. She lives in a barracks that she shares with roughly 100 other women. They sleep on wooden bunks, and there are no blankets. At minus 40-degree temperatures, the women get sick, and many die. In the summer, mosquitoes plague them, and a number of prisoners contract malaria. For two years, Agathe is without shoes, summers as well as winters, even while working in the coal mines. Calloused corns, blisters and boils develop on her feet. She uses dirty rags to wrap her wounds.

Food for even the hardest labour, working a punishing three-shift-system, is barely enough to sustain them, consisting of two cups of soup or barley porridge, served three times a day, plus a few slices of bread.

Agathe chips the ore away from the rocks with a pickaxe. Then, with bare hands, she throws the ore onto wheelbarrows, which others then push along a narrow track that's been mounted on wooden planks. Hauling these heavy rocks to their collection point is a nearly impossible endeavour. And then in the background is the overseer's constant shouting, harassing them with, 'Faster! Faster!', 'The ore should not be held up!' or, 'Carts! Where are the carts?' If the quota is not reached, there'll be no food. Fear is Agathe's constant companion.

Not until her second winter in Siberia, when another woman dies, does Agathe dare beg the other women if she could be allowed to have the dead woman's shoes. They allow her the shoes, and she will even be wearing them when she travels west in the summer of 1947. Agathe is released by the Russians. She's fully emaciated by now, and she's no longer of use to them. When, and only if, an inmate is too weak, they find mercy and send her back. But there are exceptions as well. Of the 3,000 women who arrived with Agathe in Chelyabinsk, only 300 returned to Poland.

Agathe is not sent to Poland, however, but to East Germany. This time the journey is bearable, the doors remain open throughout the trip. A warm summer breeze welcomes her 'back to life'. In East Germany, the Soviets group the inmates together who've come from all different camps. Agathe has only a vague idea where Hoyerswerda in Saxony is. She and a friend are temporarily held in a transition camp until her mother is able to find her through the Red Cross.

Agathe is finally returned home. But the home she grew up in has been burned to the ground. Her mother has moved to a small homestead where she has rented one tiny room. She earns the money to cover her rent by gathering berries and mushrooms in the summer and firewood in the winter.

Agathe will never see her brother, Bruno, again. Shortly after her arrest, he was captured and taken to Königsberg, where he died under unknown circumstances. Nothing is as it once was, and Agathe has a hard time readjusting to her old homeland; the memories of the suffering she has endured weigh too heavily upon her. Not to mention the fact that she lost herself along with her German identity back in Siberia.

Lieselotte and Hannelore Schulz spend many years begging in and around Tauroggen but are finally settled in the mid-1950s. Right about the same time, they receive news from the Red Cross that their mother was released from a labour camp in Siberia and has been transported to the GDR. There's a flurry of letter exchanges with their mother, who now lives near Leipzig. But suddenly the correspondence stops. After two years, Lieselotte finally learns in 1957 that her mother died from issues resulting from her life in the prison camp. She died only six months after her release from the Gulag.

Elfriede Müller's brother, Gustav, returns to Lithuania from Siberia in the late 1950s. He's very ill, has lung issues, and can hardly breathe. Gustav soon meets a woman and the two marry. But their happiness lasts only a short time before he finds out he has tuberculosis. His lungs no longer work, and in 1965, he dies from complications due to his disease.

In 1990, after forty-five years, Elfriede is finally able to bring her old mother from Siberia home to her in Lithuania to look after her. She has to take a train for five days to Karaganda to fetch her and her few belongings. Then the two travel the long journey back to Kaunas. They spend four happy years together during which Elfriede and her mother re-establish their relationship, which was so cruelly ripped from them when Elfriede was only a child.

After an exhausting railway journey back to Lithuania, in the care of his empathetic train engineer, Hans Joachim Petereit manages to stay in the country without official papers and learns to speak the language. As a German he has to report to the police every two months, and one day he receives a summons from the medical commission. They've decided that his birth year was 1936, a year later than in reality, but with this official 'birth certificate' he's finally able to get identification papers and is now allowed to work. He never loses sight of his one goal, though—to some day be able to return to Germany.

While her older sister does not survive the hardships of the Gulag, Waltraut Minnt is released from the camps in the early 1950s. She's deported to Lithuania—a country where she knows no one and whose language she cannot speak. She's afraid of the people and wants nothing more than to be left alone. She takes refuge in nature. In 1956, after months of wandering, she finds a farmer's family near Tauroggen who take her, a severely traumatised girl, in. Waltraut runs away over and over again. She doesn't trust this family. But she always returns. Then she helps with the gardening and in the fields. But Waltraut doesn't want to talk. This is how she lives her life for many decades.

The frozen Baltic Sea in winter.

Chapter 11
The Allure of the New Germany

On 20 June 1951, the widely circulated *East Prussian News*, a West German weekly for the East Prussian expatriates, featured this front-page headline: 'Königsbergers return from Lithuania'. The article describes the circumstances under which the last of the East Prussians finally return to post-war Germany. Although the news was a relief to the many relatives who had waited so long to hear about the fate of the East Prussians who had remained behind, it was also rather eye-opening.

> After many difficult years in which hopes and dreams remained unfulfilled, the last of our compatriots, some of whom have been missing for years and whose relatives had never heard word of their whereabouts, have now come from Lithuania and are at the Friedland transit camp near Göttingen. Twenty-two of them arrived on the 13th of June; another twenty-nine on the 14th; forty more on the 15th; forty-five on the 16th; and on the 18th, another sixty people. In the span of six days, roughly two hundred in all arrived. Most of them are East Prussians from the Königsberg area. Included amongst them are some of those German refugees who had been duped into leaving the West during the war, believing they would find refuge in East Prussia and ultimately found themselves in Königsberg in the early months of 1945.
>
> In the ensuing horrendous years of famine, 1946 and 1947, many of these desperate people from Königsberg and the surrounding Russian-occupied territories left for Lithuania in search of food. The generosity and the kindness with which they were received there is no secret.
>
> In early 1949, all East Prussian Germans living in Lithuania were required to register with the Soviet authorities. They were told they could immigrate to Germany only if they could produce proper residency papers. Many of them were distrustful of this mandate, but they registered all the same.
>
> Recently, 3,500 East Prussian Germans with such papers in hand boarded transports arranged in Lithuania and finally left the Soviet Union. They travelled through our East Prussian homeland in cattle cars, arriving in the GDR where they were held in one of the three major quarantine camps: Wolfen near Bitterfeld, Bischofswerda and Fürstenwalde. …
>
> Most of our people must however remain in Soviet-occupied East Germany. Many have no idea what happened to their relatives, and inquiring about them from inside a quarantine camp is next to impossible.

For others, however, applications for residency in West Germany were denied, citing insufficient information, or their applications were simply deemed unacceptable altogether. In particular the orphaned children and young people—nearly a thousand of them—are required to stay and have been taken to orphanages in Saxony and Thuringia.

This report alone made it clear how difficult this exodus back to the country of their origin was for these Germans. The transports out of Lithuania that the article referred to were not the first. As early as 1947, nearly 1,600 orphaned children were taken from Königsberg to Thuringia. In fact, the first child-transport to East Germany from the USSR was relatively well organised. However, transports that followed in 1947 and later happened under the most miserable of conditions, as records show:

> 2,386 children, ages 2 to 16, were transported in cattle cars with bare floors, not even a layer of straw. Only a few had stoves and heating materials. Many arrived without accompanying adults and were found to be in extremely undernourished and dehydrated condition. Toilet facilities were not available in any of the cars. The duration of the trip was typically four days and four nights.

Some of the transports took longer, and over and again, deaths were reported. In the seventh transport alone, there were fifteen dead children when it arrived. Those children who arrived alive were nothing but skin and bones and often so undernourished that they could not even withstand the urgently needed immunisations.

In all, about 100,000 Germans of all ages from the Königsberg area were resettled in East Germany during the years 1947 and 1948.

Joachim Pose is 14 years old when, in May 1951, he is loaded onto a child transport headed for the East German quarantine camp, Fürstenwalde. Once the children are registered, they are separated into groups: those who can verify they have relatives in West Germany, those who can verify they have relatives in the GDR, and those, like Joachim, who have no one.

The orphans who have no relatives are taken in two buses to the orphanage, a so-called 'Children's Village' in the town of Kyritz in Brandenburg, East Germany. Already while on the bus, they are instructed that they will now be raised as 'good Socialists'. To Joachim's ears, this announcement sounds rather peculiar. To be *more* socialist than in the USSR, he thinks, is impossible.

However, the children in this village do feel supported in that they have each other; they have comradeship and a sense of solidarity. The pedagogical concepts by which they are taught is a system that is far ahead of its time. The children live in so-called family-groups with ten children each of varying ages. Joachim is placed in such a family, and for the first time in a long while he has the feeling 'of belonging to a real home once again'.

The new arrivals are being tested to determine their respective knowledge and to be able to assign them to a grade. Joachim has not seen a school bench in six years, but he passes the entrance exam with flying colours and is the only one from his group who's admitted to the fourth grade. To help the older children catch up to their full grade level, an additional six months' worth of schoolwork is tacked on to each school year. The pressure to succeed is thus enormous; the homework seems to have no end. But teachers often reach out and offer additional tutoring for those stragglers who fall behind.

One day, Joachim receives a surprise visitor whose news brings both great joy and deep sadness. A round elderly woman in a nun's habit with a starched white cap introduces herself as Auntie Bertchen. She's his mother's oldest sister, she announces, a deaconess who runs a senior living centre on the Baltic Sea. As soon as she lays eyes on him, she takes him into her arms and embraces him with all her heart and soul.

Joachim's very first thought is that he's now no longer all alone in the world. Does Auntie Bertchen know anything about what became of his parents and his brother? From a radio broadcast listing missing children through the Child Tracing Service, Auntie Bertchen had learned that Joachim has been searching for his relations, but she gently skirts around what else she knows.

She has news about his mother, who had been put in a woman's prison camp somewhere in the vicinity of Solikamsk in the Russian oblast of Perm. His mother has written a short letter, a message that was handed on between prisoners and smuggled out to Bertchen. She writes that Peter, Joachim's favourite and older brother by ten years, was drafted into the German Wehrmacht shortly before the end of the war. He even took part in the Battle of Berlin.

Here he was taken into custody and placed in a British internment camp. Not the worst thing that could happen, but as he became ill with tuberculosis, he was soon released.

Without help, without money, and without knowing if he still had relatives or where they might be, he finally lost his battle against that insidious disease in 1947.

With this news, Joachim's world falls apart. The inner strength he had relied on so heavily during all those hours of loneliness and despair dissolve into nothing. And now he learns, too, that there's no news of his middle brother, Klaus. And absolutely nothing about his father.

In time, the Children's Village lets out for the summer holidays, and the children are taken to live in a castle near Neuruppin. Here Joachim and the other children lead a carefree summer life full of play, swimming and ball games.

When the summer holidays are over and they return to Kyritz, they find that life as they knew it has completely changed. All the families have been disbanded, and the children are now to live in new groups according to age and gender. The state has taken over the home and intends to run the children's lives based on strict Socialist ideals. At first the changes are difficult for Joachim, but he soon learns to adapt to this new set of rules. Having a real family, this now 16-year-old tells himself, was only an illusion anyway. Their biological families are gone for good, and nothing can ever replace them.

Joachim's new group in Kyritz turns out to be a supportive community that seems to have been brought together by fate. The young ones often talk about what they had gone through. Their teachers listen with compassion and understanding. This is how he lives out his teenage years, and here he tries as best he can to process his past.

Only the Socialist lessons don't go so well for him. The horrible experiences he underwent just after the war at the hands of the Stalinists of the Soviet Union are still much too vivid in his memories. The slogan 'To learn from the Soviet Union means to learn to triumph!' is, to Joachim, inseparably tied to the brutal violence and vodka-breath of the Russian soldiers he saw at the end of the war. To him, the soldiers of the Red Army disavowed any semblance of truth to these 'wonderful' Socialist ideals.

Solely due to the commitment and empathy shown to the children by the school administrators and the teachers at Kyritz, this children's home will always be known as a second home to many of the Wolf Children. For them, it was a home where they were able to recoup at least a piece of their lost childhoods, while at the same time it helped to lay the foundation for their future. Most of the Wolf Children from Kyritz hold a lifelong gratitude for the years they spent in the orphanage, a gratitude that, for many, also includes the GDR. Even as adults, many of them return again and again to Kyritz to spend their holidays caring for the new orphans at the children's home.

This is what happened to the Liedke siblings from Wehlau, whose life story is well documented in the book *Ostpreußen nach Kyritz* (*From East Prussia to Kyritz*), by Ruth Leiserowitz.

After their mother's death in the summer of 1947, the five children, ranging in age from 6 to 13, make their way to Lithuania, where in time they become separated from one another. Rudolf, the oldest, is taken in rather quickly as a farmhand. At a harvest festival, Irmgard meets a farmer who, that very day, takes her by horse and cart to his home, where she is invited to stay at least for the time being. The younger three children aren't even able to properly say goodbye to their sister, but they're happy she'll now be cared for. Not long after, 8-year-old Waltraud finds a home on a farm, while Sieglinde and the youngest brother, Ulrich, continue to wander the countryside for weeks, begging and hoping to, but never do, find a family to take them both.

The Allure of the New Germany 115

Martha Liedke with her children: Irmgard, Sieglinde, Peterchen and Rudolf.

Emaciated and feverish from typhus, looking more dead than alive, one day Ulrich stands at the door in front of his older sister, Waltraud. He's lost his sister Sieglinde, but with dreamlike instinct he remembers how to find where they had dropped the older Waltraud off. The kindly farm family takes Ulrich in as well and cares for both children, who are given the jobs of herding geese and looking after the infant baby of the family. In return they're given food and clothing. But this respite lasts only a few weeks—the Lithuanian family is suddenly ordered to give up their farm.

The two children must wander again, begging from village to village for months on end, until they finally arrive in a village where they find their brother Rudolf. He tells them to take a train to Königsberg. He believes there they'll be able to find transports leaving for Germany, and he promises to join them soon. Waltraud and Ulrich are able to smuggle themselves onto a train, and they get as far Insterburg. But here they're caught by Russian soldiers, although this time they're treated with kindness. When they are asked their names, Waltraud says, 'I'm called Schumpelchen [little Schumpel],' and Ulli declares, 'My name is Ullimatz [little Ulli-child].' This is what their parents had called them at home. They can't remember their real names, and they don't know their ages or their birth dates. The children end up in a Soviet orphanage in Königsberg, where they're tenderly looked after by German caregivers, who will also accompany them on the transport to the GDR.

At Eggesin, in an interim quarantine camp, Waltraud and Ulrich reunite with their brother Rudolf, who stayed true to his promise to join them. Now, only the whereabouts of their two sisters, Irmgard and Sieglinde, still remain an unknown.

After several more holding camps, the siblings eventually land in Kyritz. Besides the school, there's also a working farm with cows and horses, a woodworking shop, a shoemaker, a sewing studio and a library. The children are especially thrilled about the little zoo with wild boars, foxes and beavers. In the winter, a skating rink is poured for the children to skate on. Their recreational time is particularly unique. There are not only sports, painting and photo groups, but also dance groups, choirs, an orchestra and even lessons in glider flying. At Christmas and for their birthdays, the children receive gifts, something they can hardly remember having—a toy of their own.

Rudolf, the older brother, takes good care of the two younger ones. He makes sure they get good grades in school and that they learn good manners, and he tries to awaken an interest in cultural things. As for himself, he is a studious scholar. In his first year of school, he is one of the first to attend the newly built high school. Their only woe now is that they have no news of their two missing sisters, even though countless inquiries have been made at the Red Cross.

Then, in the summer of 1954, an inquiry arrives at the German Red Cross in Hamburg. It is from Sieglinde, who is finally able to locate her lost siblings in Kyritz. Sieglinde is now 19 years old. In 1947, she was taken in by a Russian family. When the couple decides to move back to Moscow, they offer to adopt Sieglinde, wanting to give her a fictitious Ukrainian identity. By now, Sieglinde has completely forgotten her German language and only speaks Russian. Even with all these disadvantages, she's determined to hold on to her German heritage and her German name, and she decides to stay behind in Lithuania.

Here she finds a job at a factory that manufactures pharmaceuticals. In fact, the manager is not really allowed to hire her, as she doesn't have valid work papers, but he covers up for her. What's more important to him is to have hard-working and talented employees. Now that she has a regular job and a little income, Sieglinde decides to break through all the red tape and try to legitimise her German roots. After several unsuccessful inquiries at the Red Cross in Vilnius and in Moscow, a Lithuanian colleague advises her to turn to Hamburg for help.

Inspired by the promising information she receives from Hamburg, Sieglinde uses her vacation time in the summer of 1955 to search for Irmgard. For weeks she rides buses through Lithuanian villages and asks farmers, pastors and mayors about a missing German girl. As she's just about to give up, she is given a critical piece of information. A girl named Irmgard has been living on a farm since 1947. But she's been kept there as a slave. She doesn't even have a bed to sleep in.

Sieglinde goes to the farm. She cannot believe that the young woman standing before her at the door is her sister. For Irmgard, the hope of ever seeing any of her siblings again is something she gave up long ago. The wolves killed them way back when, the farmer had told her. The communication between the two sisters is difficult. While Sieglinde only speaks Russian, Irmgard speaks only Lithuanian. Only after sharing family photos is Sieglinde convinced that this is her sister after all. The farmer, however, considers Irmgard to be his personal property and doesn't want to let her go. Not until the determined Sieglinde threatens to turn him in to the police does he finally give in.

Irmgard takes her sister to Kaunas, and a year later, in 1956, Sieglinde receives permission to immigrate to the GDR, where she's taken in at Kyritz. Another year later, Irmgard is allowed to follow her.

Sieglinde is now 20 years old and is given a furnished room at the Children's Village, which allows her to settle into her new life. Ulrich, her older brother, is still in school in Kyritz, and Waltraud and Rudolf are in the process of completing their vocational training. The siblings' reunion is moving and heartfelt, and they help each other wherever they can. In order to help Sieglinde acculturate, the principals at the orphanage enrol her into a number of classes, so that she can relearn the German language without the stigmatisation of being 'a Russian'. After only six months, she is able to start a distance learning programme to become a residential childcare worker.

At the Children's Village, Sieglinde meets a young man, Heinrich Kenzler, who had also come to East Germany from the Königsberger children's home where Waltraud and Ulrich were once kept. He had been Rudolf's roommate at the transition camp, Eggesin. The two Wolf Children, Heinrich and Sieglinde, become engaged, but marriage is not possible. Sieglinde took on Soviet citizenship and is not allowed to marry a German. Not until 1958 is this law reversed, and from this time on, nothing can stand in their way.

The orphanage at Kyritz was an anomaly. For most of the banished, orphaned and traumatised children, the reception in the new Germany was much less embracing.

After a tearful farewell, Gerhard Gudovius leaves his Lithuanian family and travels on 15 May 1951 to East Germany. As hard as the parting is, the adventures that await him are equally as enticing. Never in his life has he travelled this far. He is excited about Germany and about what awaits him there, although he has no concept of what it will be like. He can no sooner recognise the borders on a map than know how it will even look once he's there.

After travelling by train for several days, Gerhard arrives in Bischofswerda in Saxony, where his reception is a brutal one. Once he gets registered, he is to go through a number of medical examinations, all of which are done in a manner more like a meat inspection than anything humane. Once this is done, he and his fellow travellers must undergo a delousing procedure in which their naked bodies are sprayed down with a foul-smelling powder.

His arrival in Saxony makes it clear to Gerhard that he won't be going any further than the GDR, at least for now. As he has no relatives in West Germany, there is no one 'over there' who's waiting for him, so this is where he must stay. But Gerhard has no desire to live in another 'Russian zone'. He has witnessed all too often what this could mean when he was in East Prussia and Lithuania.

Gerhard has turned 19 and soon moves to Bitterfeld in Saxony-Anhalt in East Germany. There he is to be trained as a 'farm expert', so that in the future he can be employed in the government-run agricultural sector. Studying is difficult for him, as he had finished only four years of elementary school and learned rudimentary reading and writing.

But once again, even in East Germany, luck is on his side. It is the summer of 1951, and the Socialist Unity Party, the SED, plans to hold a huge Communist event in Berlin—the World Youth Festival—and Gerhard is invited to take part. It is being held in the capital, East Berlin.

Dressed in a smart-looking FDJ, the 'Free German Youth' uniform, Gerhard notices that the rest of the participants are mostly interested in things other than party doctrine. Mass rallies take place where the participants are called to pledge their allegiance to the Socialist Party and its government. Yet most of his comrades have their own ideas of what they want their future to look like. All the ceremonies, intended to further indoctrinate them with the Socialist ideals of the new East Germany, are taken in with scepticism after having been misled

Students carrying portraits of Stalin, Mao and Wilhelm Pieck, the East German president, during the opening ceremonies of the World Youth Festival for Peace in East Berlin, 5 August 1951.

by the Nazi government not that long ago. This propaganda cannot even hold a candle to all that West Berlin has to offer. Life pulsates there. The big city with all her enticements is calling.

While most of the participants sleep in tents or in barracks, Gerhard is blessed with good fortune. A family wants to host him in their home. It's his first personal contact with a real family since his arrival in Germany. He is received with open arms, compassion and heartfelt warmth. Although it's against the law to talk about his escape from Königsberg and his subsequent deportation from East Prussia, his hosts want to know everything. In fact, they even offer to adopt him. He's thrilled by their kindness but is reticent to accept their offer in good faith. He knows all too well how quickly a moment of altruism can turn into quite the opposite.

Despite the prevailing political atmosphere at the games, the athletes don't seem to want to talk much about politics. Instead, they discuss school, careers, girls and friendships. They tell jokes with one another and share stories and life experiences. They sing songs and play cards. And, last but not least, they take part in their required Party events. Everyone must do it, and Gerhard, too, enthusiastically participates. It's fine with him; he has come to a grand moment in life, a time of promise, of new beginnings and new adventures. And, anyway, all doors seem to be opening for him. It's up to him to decide how things will go from now on.

Even in 1951, one can still see traces of the war in East Berlin—piles of rubble and bombed-out houses that the war left behind. One day, without his FDJ uniform, Gerhard wants to venture into West Berlin. He had heard from friends that it's not all that difficult. You're just not allowed to get caught. Gerhard, by now, has become adept at the game of cat and mouse, of deceit and secrecy, and takes on the challenge with gusto. After so many years of hardship and a life deprived of almost everything, what he sees on his first outing to the west sector of the city is a wonderland. In West Berlin there are all kinds of things that he has not seen since his childhood days in Königsberg: beautiful wares on display, cakes and torts in the cake shop windows, and even delicacies like condensed milk! The flair of an international city is in the air; women are well dressed. For all he has to thank the GDR for what it offered him over the last several months, it cannot compare to the charm of the West. Just for this, participating in the festival games was worth it all, Gerhard thinks, who at the end of the day, once again stands proudly in his FDJ uniform along with the others, singing the words of the festival anthem: 'In August, in August, the roses bloom. In August, in August … in Berlin!'

After the festival has ended, Gerhard is allowed to stay with his host family for a few more days. With this bit of good luck, he now decides, unequivocally, to escape to the West. To return to Bitterfeld and become a 'farming expert' is not something he has any desire to do. But life in West Germany? Most definitely!

But it's not quite so easy. In order to gain entry into the West, Gerhard must first get a special travel visa stamped into his interzone pass. At the travel office he tells the pretty girl at the desk he wants to go to Hanover to visit relatives. She's quite taken by this young man's charm, and, without further ado, puts the proper stamp in the proper spot in his interzone pass. Gerhard is on his way.

Eva Rapp's family, who live in the Elbing district, have been planning to immigrate to the United States since 1939. Her father, Herbert, lived in the US for some time, has an American passport, and is in the process of organising the move for his wife and children. The first shipment of personal items is already on its way to Alabama when Hitler invades Poland in September. Within days, all the main roads in Germany are shut down; all German borders are closed. The family now sits with packed suitcases and is unable to go anywhere for an indefinite amount of time. Eva is the youngest of her siblings, Erwin, Vera, Douglas and Henry.

When, on 11 December 1941, Nazi Germany declares war on the USA, a series of unexpected events happen to the family. As an American citizen, Eva's well-travelled father is no longer seen by his fellow Germans as the eccentric he once was. Rather, he's now the enemy. With all diplomatic ties with the USA revoked, all protections for American citizens vanish, and he becomes an outlaw. The children are confronted in school with an open hatred against them, because they are now 'foreigners'. Douglas especially, because of his foreign-sounding name, is bullied and taunted, even by his teachers. He's a persona non grata. His fellow students simply call him the 'American Asshole'.

For two years, the family is harassed by the Gestapo, and then, in 1943, Eva's father is arrested. Eva is 8 years old by the time her father is

Eva Rapp.

finally released from prison at the end of 1944. Nevertheless, the family clings to the hope of a quick end to the war and of their immigration to the United States. 'It can't last forever' is the hope that keeps the family going. But in 1945 their longed-for freedom turns into something much different from what they had expected. Suddenly, salvation is nowhere in sight.

As thousands of others do, the Rapps attempt to flee, but they're apprehended by the Red Army and are forced to live under Soviet rule and all its atrocities for several weeks. One day, Russian soldiers come to the house and take Eva's father and brother Erwin away, telling them they need to register for work. But soon

Eva's mother learns the truth. Her husband and son, like all the men from the neighbouring villages, are on their way to the labour camps in Siberia.

Her mother soon becomes ill with typhus. Over the following weeks, the small community of neighbours that had been thrown together during the flight tries to bring Eva's mother back to life. But in the end, she succumbs to her disease and dies. Now Eva and her brother Henry are on their own. By the summer of 1945, the area comes under Polish rule, and a time of wandering and begging begins for the two children. In 1947, they finally arrive in Görlitz, in the GDR, on a transport carrying evacuees from East Prussia.

The days that follow are full of 'documentation'. Eva is 11 by now and doesn't have the answers to many of the questions that are asked of her. The girls are separated from the boys, and Henry, who's older and knows much more than she does, is registered independently of her. Her ward is an elderly woman who patiently reads back to her everything that Eva supposedly said. The authorities want to make certain that all the details match up. Making sure everything is correct is the only way to ensure that the family will find one another again. Eva is giddy with joy. Someone is looking for her! In her childish imagination everything will be all right—the older siblings and her father must be somewhere.

Barely half an hour later, she learns the shocking truth. A young nurse tells Eva to pack her things, she will be moving—into a barracks for children from where they'll be transported to an orphanage. But Eva doesn't want to move to an orphanage! She's sure she still has relatives, and she wants to wait for them. The nurse tries to calm the upset girl and explains that all children live in orphanages until their relatives are found. It's a small consolation for Eva, for whom time cannot move quickly enough now.

In the barracks, there's little to do during the day. But she meets a boy, who, according to the nurse, suffers from 'shell shock'. Eva can't imagine what this means, but the nurse explains that he startles easily and needs to whittle at a piece of wood all day long in order to calm himself. One day, Eva approaches the boy, very carefully. He's in the process of planing a rough piece of wood. 'What should I make with this?' he asks Eva without lifting his eyes from his work.

'Maybe a kitty?' Eva suggests, shyly.

'Well, let's see if a kitty is hiding inside,' he replies.

Eva watches his carving skills with fascination. Abruptly he jumps up. 'What're you staring at me for? Go away!'

Eva backs away, terrified, and weeping, she runs off. That night, when she goes to bed, she finds a little wooden kitty on her pillow. She goes to sleep holding her new kitty cat in her hands and dreams of Schnurrbart, 'little mustache', the family cat back home in East Prussia.

The day comes when she's relocated to the orphanage. Here, as in all holding camps, the children are first medically examined. The girls are to undress and stand in a line. Eva notices that some of them have extended stomachs, just like her. She's convinced a baby is hiding inside. Will the doctor cut it out? Eva learns that her stomach will shrink back again all on its own. Malnutrition, she learns, has caused it to swell, and by no means are any of the girls pregnant. Eva is very relieved.

Her bed neighbour is named Agnes. Already on the first night, Eva begins to feel just a little more at ease when Agnes wishes her a good night. Here is someone who knows her name and who, just like her, is waiting for someone to take her home.

The next day, Eva is introduced to daily life in the orphanage. Agnes's parents are both dead, Eva learns, and she's hoping to be adopted soon. 'Every Sunday is Adoption Day here,' Agnes tells the perplexed Eva. 'All kinds of couples come to choose a child to take home with them. I hope someone will choose me soon, too.' Eva begins to brood. Will she too be adopted before any of her relatives can even find her?

The nights in the dormitory are often noisy. Many of the children have nightmares, as does Agnes. Often Eva wakes up to hear Agnes wrestle and weep in her sleep. On the escape, her trek had been bombed. Agnes and her mother ran to hide in a ditch, but it was too late. A grenade struck them directly. Right in front of her eyes, her mother was blown to shreds. Agnes cannot get this image out of her head. Eva is a dear friend to her and listens as she tells her about all the horrible things that happened and holds her in her arms when she needs to cry. 'I want to go to my mummy …' Agnes sobs. In these moments, tears come to Eva's eyes as well. What would she give to also be able to bury herself in her own mummy's lap?

Two months have gone by when, one day, the administrator of the orphanage calls Eva and Henry to her side. She has a letter for them from a certain Elsbeth Rapp. It's an aunt, who has found her niece and nephew through the tracing services. She writes about her efforts to find them and that she's already prepared the needed applications for the family to reunite. As she lives in West Germany, however, it will take longer for the paperwork to be processed. But Eva and Henry are overjoyed. On that very day, they write to Tante Elsbeth, who they can still remember visiting them on weekends when they lived in East Prussia. Eva's answer is but two short sentences: 'Dear Tante Elsbeth, I have missed you very much. Please come and get us soon.'

A few more weeks go by, and it is finally time. The children should pack their things and be ready for the trip to the West. On the evening before their departure, Eva looks to the night sky, wanting to find the brightest star in the star-filled heavens over Bautzen. Up there, she's very sure, is where her mummy lives, who has watched over her all this time. And she now wants to leave it all behind, all that she experienced over the last two years—the loneliness, the hunger, and the suffering. Tomorrow she'll begin a new life and all that belongs to the past shall remain there. Shortly before Christmas in 1947, Eva and Henry arrive at their Tante Elsbeth's home in the longed-for West.

124   The Wolf Children of the Eastern Front

Eight-year-old Dieter Gröning arrives in the GDR on a children's transport in 1947. He's placed in an orphanage for children with behavioral issues as they have vacancies, and he is lovingly received. There's a lot of time for play, running around and singing. Amongst the children, though, there's often an unrelenting battle to be the first to get to the food, and for attention. And there's often way too little of either.

The orphanage's house mother, Tante Ursel, is well loved by all the children, but she has only one lap. And already an hour before the dining room door is unlocked, the children stand in a long line, waiting, because the one who gets to the table first, gets to grab the biggest piece of bread. Every crumb is scuffled over. When there is not enough food to go around, the house father plays a mandolin. Tante Ursel sings a song. And in this way, their hunger is 'sung away'.

In November 1948, Dieter receives news that he had long given up on: his father is alive. The boy is so emotional, he has a breakdown.

His father's letter is from a city in the British sector of Germany. It appears he has no idea what happened to the rest of the family. He writes:

My dear, dear Dieter,
I'm so very happy that I've found you. I hope you'll be with me soon. And bring along whomever is still with you. I can hardly wait for you to come to me and for you to tell me how things went for you. And do tell me, where have you left Gerhard, Brigitte, Elfriede, Gisela and Mutti?
   With loving kisses and blessings, your Papa.

Winter in southern Lithuania.

Dieter does not know how he should answer. It takes him several days, and he needs his house mother's encouragement before he can bring himself to write.

> My dear Papa, after such a long time we've finally found each other. Elfriede, Brigitte, Gisela, Gerhard and my Mutti are dead. My dear Papa, I had lost all hope that you were still alive. I'm so happy that you'll now come to get me. I want so much to be with you. Dear Papa, I didn't know when I was born. Because Mutti never told me when I was born. Because Mutti thought we would always stay together, but in the end we didn't.

Chapter 12

In the West

Joachim Pose finishes high school in East Germany in the early 1950s. At first, he lives with an aunt, but later he attends a boarding school. 'Of course, in comparison to the Wolf Children who stayed behind in Lithuania, things went much better for me,' says the now 75-year-old. 'I received a good education and was even able to pursue a few hobbies.' Yet, he carries a melancholy inside him that, over the years, has turned to bitterness. '1955 was a big year for me in every way. When Konrad Adenauer visited Moscow, suddenly so much changed. Nearly 10,000 German prisoners were released from the Soviet prison camps after that and my mother was one of them.'

After so many years of loneliness and uncertainty, Joachim finally learns what had happened to her and his father after their arrests in Tilsit in 1947. Both fell victim to a secret trial, entirely politically motivated, in Stalinist Russia. First, his father, a disabled veteran from the First World War, had his leg prostheses taken from him. He was tortured again and again and finally caved under the pressure, eventually pleading guilty to a harsh sentence: twenty-four years in a Russian Gulag. His crime—'spying for the papacy'. Joachim's mother's fate wasn't much better. She was sentenced to eight years' imprisonment for 'conspiracy'. The last thing she heard her husband say when they were torn apart will remain with her for the rest of her life: he, a man who never believed in God, had, as a result of the torture, found Christ. He told her that he could now well understand the suffering the Lord went through.

In 1953, Joachim's father died in a prison camp near Kuybyshev, the city known today as Samara, in south-eastern Russia. The cause of death: 'internal bleeding'. From a fellow inmate, Joachim will learn years later that right up to his death, his father never stopped blaming himself for the dreadful circumstances that befell his family back in East Prussia.

For the first five years of her detention, Joachim's mother was in a prison in Königsberg. Nearly every night, the prison director raped her. Only after she tried to kill herself, did a female Russian doctor put an end to her torment. She was temporarily sent to the infirmary and eventually to a prison camp near the Ural Mountains.

In light of what happened in his own life and given the suffering both his parents went through, Joachim finds it hard to comprehend why the Germans are the only ones who are blamed for the war and must carry the burden of their collective guilt, while other parties to the Second World War are let off scot-free. His mind is plagued with both historical and existential questions.

Joachim lives with his mother in a three-bedroom apartment in East Germany, and he feels a growing resentment that people like her are still being seen as war criminals in the GDR. Time and time again, he clashes with authorities. In school he often asks uncomfortable questions and makes the occasional brazen comment that gets him into trouble, all of which is recorded in his report card: 'Joachim's character and political stance do not always correspond to his otherwise good performance. He lacks self-control and a desire to improve upon himself.'

With regards to his 'Civic Engagement', it states that he's 'active in the FDJ [Free German Youth] and the GST [Sport and Technology Association]' with this caveat: 'able to help with national reconstruction, but lacks political maturity'. With such a politically charged diploma, the acceptance of Joachim's application to study civil engineering at the Technical University of Dresden does not stand a chance. Disillusioned, he flees to West Germany. He's now, once again, separated from his mother and his other relatives in the East, and possibly for good. Given the documented discrimination Joachim had faced in the GDR, he's eventually recognised as a refugee on political grounds and is welcomed into the West.

When he arrives in West Germany, Joachim starts to enjoy life to the fullest. He's enthusiastic and full of energy—whether it be political discussions, sports, or reading new authors whose work had been forbidden in the GDR or whose work was simply not available.

He takes a construction job in Hanover in order to fulfil his internship requirements for admission at the university. However, before he starts at the Hanover Technical University to study architecture, he wants to get to know a bit more of this new Germany. He and his friend Rudi sell newspaper subscriptions, and the two criss-cross the country as travelling salesmen. It doesn't take long to realise this form of capitalism doesn't do either the people they convince to buy the subscriptions, or themselves, any good. They're always broke, even though they work every day from early morning until late at night. One day they simply chuck the whole idea and close that chapter of their lives.

Joachim is 22 when he begins his studies at the Technical University in the autumn of 1958. He joins a fraternity, which becomes a second family to him. It's a close-knit community of young men, many of whom also have relatives in the GDR. The years he lives in the fraternity house are some of the happiest of his life.

In 1967, he completes his degree and starts working as an architect. He marries, has a son, and lives a rather comfortable life in West Germany. What still bothers him, though, is what he calls 'the bitter worm inside me'. He knows how lucky he is that he was able to leave East Prussia; he knows the luck he had coming to the orphanage in Kyritz during those early years just after the war; and he knows how lucky he is to have found his mother again. Even then, the loss of the beautiful world he once knew as a child weighs heavily on his mind.

His first marriage falls apart. Joachim gets a divorce and soon marries again. He has two more sons. After Germany's Reunification in 1990, he returns to eastern Germany to be near his mother, and there, he works again as an architect. But in 2006, he declares bankruptcy. 'I simply fell apart. I was already old enough to be able to retire. But then, I lost everything again—like all those years ago in Lithuania.'

He divorces his second wife and moves to Düsseldorf. He finally decides to write his memoirs, a look back on his life. In his book, he philosophises, 'Everything that happens and that continues to happen has a reason, but that reason is not always easy to understand. Doubt, even despair, can get the better of us. And in the end, you are simply paralysed.'

The Soviet-occupied zone that was later to become known as the GDR was difficult for most Wolf Children to accept as their new homeland. To try to integrate into this new political system required that they staunchly deny any of their own suffering or any of the circumstances under which they had to flee East Prussia. Even just saying the word 'expulsion' was illegal. Instead, you were to say 'resettlement', perhaps a fitting word in the context of the many German war crimes, but it completely erased all that had actually happened in their own lives. Their plight was to be spoken of as an 'inconvenience', something you had no right to complain about. Moreover, they were from the wrong side of history, and they should, by all means, bear the burden of their country's past. Some of the Wolf Children took on this guilt as their own, and did as they were supposed to do. They stayed silent. Some even agreed with this new ideology of the Socialist Unity Party of Germany, the SED, believing that all Germans deserved their fate. But others, for whom this stigma even further traumatised them, people

Searching for missing relatives in the Friedland transit camp, November 1955.

who were just children at the time, saw no way around it than to leave their newfound home once again.

In the village of Friedland, which literally translates to 'Peaceland', near Göttingen in Lower Saxony, the British military administration set up a transit camp right after war. To this day, it is a symbol of hope for refugees as well as ethnic Germans from countries of the former Soviet Bloc who come to Germany as immigrants. Friedland is located where the borders of the once British, Soviet and American-occupied zones butted up against each other. It was a natural choice. It was centrally located; it had a railway station; it was a major thoroughfare; and furthermore, the empty stables that had once been part of the adjacent Göttingen University could easily be converted to barracks. For the thousands of refugees, displaced persons and returning soldiers who were searching for relatives or looking for a new place to live, it soon became the largest transit camp in all of Germany. On any given day, one could see a mêlée of desperate people swarming the area. Many held signs in their hands with the names and photos of the missing persons, and all the while new transports continued to arrive. The walls of the barracks were plastered with one note after another from people seeking relatives. In the midst of all this, over and over again, there were indescribable moments when a relative was found, or worse, when it was confirmed the person they were looking for was dead.

Gerhard Gudovius arrives in Friedland in the autumn of 1951. Every day, he sees the turmoil and witnesses the many moments of anguish and joy. This emotional roller coaster of heartbreak and exultation overwhelm this young man. To him, the place looks like an endless, frenzied ant hill. 'There was a tremendous amount of activity and at first I felt completely lost in it all.'

He's happy when he's finally able to leave Friedland again. His journey takes him to southern Germany, and for two years he lives in a temporary shelter for new arrivals from the East in the Swabian town of Biberach. The housing is a simple barracks built of thin wooden slats that look more like summer cottages than homes. But for Gerhard, what's worse than the living conditions is the boredom, an irony in comparison to the chaos he just left behind in Friedland. 'There was nothing to do. We weren't allowed to work yet, and so what does one do the entire day?—Nothing. Boredom is hard to live with. Especially when one is a strong young man with way too much energy.'

In 1953, he moves to a holding camp where he stays for a short time, just until he's able to establish residency in the city of Reutlingen. 'I was able to find a job quickly, and work was something I was eager to finally do again.' He works at a book printer's in the neighbouring village of Hochdorf and loves what he does.

As a young refugee from East Prussia without family ties, Gerhard is once again in luck. He's able to move into a state-run boarding home.

There I received 20 Marks a week in pocket money and was otherwise completely provided for. I didn't need to pay for living expenses, food or laundry.

I met my wife Gerlinde in 1957. By that time, I had already been in Reutlingen for a few years. She was originally from Saxony. My parents-in-law warmly welcomed me. They understood me, as they, too, had lost everything. They, too, had to flee back then, and on short notice when my father-in-law was warned he could be arrested for his political views. They, too, had to leave everything behind.

The relationship with his fiancée's family does Gerhard good. They share a past over which few words need to be spoken, and yet they understand one another well. 'I realised then how much I wanted a family of my own. I needed the bond.'

At about the same time as he gets engaged, he decides to write to the Red Cross. He wants to find his mother's brother, the uncle who once took him and his grandmother to the synagogue in Königsberg on the morning after Kristallnacht to show them the magnitude of the destruction. Indeed, his uncle is alive and has made a home for himself in Kaiserslautern. This city has become the largest US military base outside the United States. In American lingo, it's often referred to as 'K-town', a term coined by the American military, who found the name otherwise difficult to pronounce. Here his uncle owns a popular barber shop for the GIs. His specialty is Afro-style haircuts, and his business is doing very well.

Nonetheless, his uncle wants nothing to do with him. This is a terrible blow to Gerhard, and it soon becomes clear why. It has to do with the reconstruction programmes Germany initiated after the Second World War to compensate those who needed to flee their homelands in the East, thereby losing their properties. It was a rather complicated scheme, but in short, enormous amounts of money were spent over a period of several decades, and can partly be credited for the German 'economic miracle' that came about in the early post-war era. Payments were made incrementally over time, sometimes as much as thirty years, at a rate of 50 per cent of the original value of property lost during the war.

'My grandparents had owned a plot of farmland of about 33 acres, and I needed to sign a statement confirming that this was true. After I did, my uncle received part of the compensation. But apparently, he thought that it wasn't enough.'

Angry letters begin to arrive from his uncle accusing Gerhard of taking too much. It comes as a shock to Gerhard, who can't believe what he's reading. 'And to think, he even owns a hair salon! I had nothing! I didn't even have a suitcase to my name when I arrived in the GDR.'

His uncle's lack of understanding for the suffering he had gone through as a child is something Gerhard cannot fathom. The contact with the only blood relative he has breaks off for good. 'Those were difficult times. When I came to the West, not a soul gave two hoots about me. No one was interested in where you came from or what you had been through.'

Everyone has a story, and everyone believes their own story is the worst that could have happened.

> To this day, I can't understand how my grandparents could have said, 'the Russian, too, is only human'. Of course, the Russian is only human, perhaps even a good human. But that is the civilian Russian. I have nothing against the people of Russia. But the Russian military? They inflicted the worst experiences of my entire life on me, and when I was just a child.

In his first years in the West, Gerhard often longingly thinks about Lithuania. 'It was a time when everything was in order. It was where I had a home, and I had a good life. I've asked myself over and over, throughout my entire adult life, what would have become of me had I stayed in Lithuania?'

Gerhard is a loyal employee and stays with the print shop until it closes. Evolving changes in the industry have made the business unprofitable. Gerhard, now a father, moves on and in turn finds work as a painter at a Reutlingen factory before getting a position at the Dacora-Kamerawerk, a well-known German camera manufacturer. Although the factory produces supplies for all the leading brands in the photo industry, it too closes its doors in 1972.

Once again, Gerhard needs to find a new job and looks for work at a supermarket. It's a new concept for grocery shopping in Germany. Modern times have arrived. When he applies for the job, he's asked whether he feels he has enough knowledge to do the work since he never received a formal education. But, by now, Gerhard is no stranger to challenges, and he's certain he'll succeed even here. It will be his longest stint—fourteen years as a grocer. Compared to his days as a Wolf Child in Lithuania, and without much schooling, by the time his career ends, he feels he has come a long way.

'When I received my retirement notice, the discharge papers read, "Department Head"! It had never been all that clear to me. There were three women and one man for whom I was responsible.'

With this acknowledgement, Gerhard feels a sense of appreciation, a feeling of self-worth for what he had achieved. 'It was the first time I felt like I belonged, even though an old East Prussian like me could never fully become a Swabian.' While the Prussians are known for their ethical code and conservative values, Swabians are commonly seen as the Scots of Germany, thrifty, overly tidy and a bit prudish—cultural peculiarities that Gerhard is referring to.

Gerhard's wife Gerlinde speaks with a strong Swabian accent, even though she wasn't born here. She remembers: 'When we first met, he told me very little about himself. It's only now in his old age that he's beginning to open up. Now I know more about his past. Back then, he suppressed it. It was all too painful for him.' Her husband always had been particularly lucky, she says. 'Ever since his mother died, someone was always there to take him by the hand.'

What, in fact, did she know of where he came from? Of his past? 'I knew he came from Königsberg and that he had been all alone in Lithuania. My parents took him in with open arms; he was conscientious and hard-working. My mother, in particular, considered him beyond reproach. In fact, she actually took to him more than to her own children.'

Gerlinde radiates an inner peace. Whenever Gerhard gets upset about anything, she stays calm. 'It wasn't always easy,' she admits frankly. 'I blamed it on the alcohol. Back in Lithuania he was at the tap for nights on end when the moonshine was being burned. I only recently learned about all this. In the early days when he drank, he wouldn't let up. Those were difficult times.'

But she never seriously thought about divorce. 'We always stuck it out. Every time we had problems, I thought, "He's all alone in the world, and he'll fall apart if we don't work this out." It just had to work. We have three children, and they love their father. We just hung in there together.' A short pause, then a kindly gaze comes over her face. Then she says, 'And now, in our old age, things are much more peaceful.'

Gerlinde is 72 years old. For thirty-five years they have lived in a tiny terraced house with a small backyard owned by their church congregation. Everything is well kept and lovingly cared for by Gerlinde. There's one thing, though, that's hard for both of them to understand. 'Our children,' Gerlinde says, 'I've often found fault with them, that they have no interest in their father's past. Perhaps it's because they're still too young, or they're too busy. We too didn't want to hear from our parents about what they went through during the First World War. On the other hand, their father's is such a special story.'

Gerhard adds, 'They can't even imagine how it was for me. Only our granddaughter, who's just finishing school, asks questions sometimes.' Something else bothers Gerhard. 'It's sad that so little is known in Germany about the role the Lithuanian people played in our survival after the war. How many thousands of children's lives were saved because of them?'

What have not disappeared are the memories, and the worst among them are those from right after the war, the dead and the badly wounded in the final months in Königsberg.

When I see wounded people on television today, I say to my wife, 'It doesn't affect me,' and she can't even fathom what I'm talking about. I crawled over charred corpses, over … I don't know how many there were, but I remember that it felt soft. They had all suffocated in the firestorms. I saw charred little children and adults, too, people with severed heads. This, inside the besieged city of Königsberg! The bombs fell from above, the artillery shot at us from all around. I could hear the tanks rolling through, and right in the midst of it all—there I was. But as a child, one just lives with this, one is hardened to it. Right after the war came the next horror, the famine. After that nothing could get to me anymore. If I were to recap my life, I would have to say that those childhood experiences have influenced every decision I've ever made.

Some of the Wolf Children were never able to feel at home in Germany. Many of them migrated further, to Switzerland, to England, Australia and the United States.

Eva Rapp lives in West Germany, where she goes to school until she's 16 years old. Her older siblings, from whom she's been separated since the end of the war, have moved to the United States in order to not lose their American citizenship. Eva and her brother Henry will follow after they graduate from high school.

The relatives who've been caring for Eva and Henry up until the time they can emigrate, do so because they feel an obligation to their parents. They make sure that both the children learn to speak English, and speak it well, so that they'll be able to feel confident in their new lives. Eva remembers her time in Germany as a time that gave her breathing space, even if the memories, the studying, and their paltry living conditions during the early post-war years are not easy. But she is loved and cared for, and, most importantly, she's being prepared to move on to the life her father had always wanted his family to have.

Eva stays in Germany until 1952 and then takes off for Chicago to be reunited with her siblings, only now her two older brothers are at war again, this time as soldiers for the US Army, fighting in Korea. She describes her departure from Germany:

> It was a strange feeling. I was on an ocean liner, travelling alone as an underage child. I was an American. I automatically received my citizenship when I was born through my father's naturalisation. But, to think: my father had been taken to a Russian prison camp. And there he lost his life.

Her luggage consists of a small overseas crate containing her books, a single suitcase with clothes, and 'an unbroken optimism that only the young are able to bring to the day'.

In Chicago she first lives with an elderly German couple, who essentially leave her to her own devices. But she accepts her life, finds a job, and is soon able to support herself. 'I didn't have time for self-pity,' she says today. 'To the contrary, I had the feeling I was really lucky. I had survived, and I could now make something of myself. I wanted to learn perfect English and integrate into

American society so that I would never be caught in such a crisis again or ever need help from anyone else, ever again.'

It may sound like the stereotypical American comment, but it was more than that. The experience of complete helplessness and then living at the mercy of others can have varying and even opposite effects on people. While for some the trauma pushed them into a deep depression, others worked to pull themselves out of their situation and did what they could to secure a better life for themselves.

Eva changes her name back to Evelyne when she arrives in the US, the name her father had given her when she was baptised. She marries young in the hope that starting a family would give her stability. Yet her memories haunt her, and, to the contrary, her marriage soon falls apart.

Not until her second marriage, many years later, does she begin to process what happened during her childhood. The Iron Curtain has fallen and her name is now Evelyne Tannehill. The memories of her past come back to her, but they are no longer as threatening as they once were.

'When my children were growing up, I never spoke about my past. It wasn't until they were adults that I realised I needed to take some time to write it all down. Otherwise, the experiences and the stories would be lost forever.'

Evelyne Tannehill travels with a few of her German friends to the village where she grew up in the former East Prussia. If she ever doubted her memories or wondered if she may have imagined them, this trip is a confirmation. 'I realised what I remembered was actually true, that my memories corresponded to real places and events. I knew then that I had to put my stories to paper. It was a long, difficult process, because it brought up so many painful memories, especially in my dreams. Or better said, my "nightmares".' It takes her six years to finish writing her memoirs, and for another four years she puts them aside to let them 'ripen', as she calls it.

Evelyne returns to East Prussia two more times and even meets the Polish family that lives in her family home today. What does she think of these people?

> I have no qualms with the Poles or even the Russians. All sides, and of course the Germans, too, committed horrible war crimes. I think that every human being is given the opportunity to do good or to do evil. It all depends on the circumstances in which one finds oneself. And the drive to survive can sometimes make people do things they would never have imagined themselves doing.

She doesn't consider Germany her homeland. 'I love visiting Germany, and I do it often. But America has become my new home, my new homeland—this is where I feel at ease, and this is where I belong.'

Evelyne's children are stunned when they first learn about their mother's life during the war.

We never used to speak about it and naturally it was a shock when they first read about the terrible things I went through. It was easier to create a new life and not always think about the past or get dragged down by sad memories. I certainly couldn't change my past, but I knew my future was in my own hands.

But there are things Evelyne cannot forget.

The strongest emotions are those I have when I visit my mother's grave in Poland. In my thoughts, I often speak to her: 'I want to tell you about my life. I loved you far more than I knew back then. It wasn't until you left us that I knew how much I loved you. And I will keep that memory of you in my heart forever …'

Early summer in the Lithuanian countryside.

Chapter 13
Strangers in a Strange Land

Erika Sauerbaum had always thought that there must be other Germans living in Jonava. But during the Soviet era, it just wasn't possible to act on such impulses. It was much too dangerous. Then, in 1993, while visiting the cemetery, the friend she is with points out a woman who's also there, and suggests she could possibly, too, have German roots. 'Just go ask her,' she

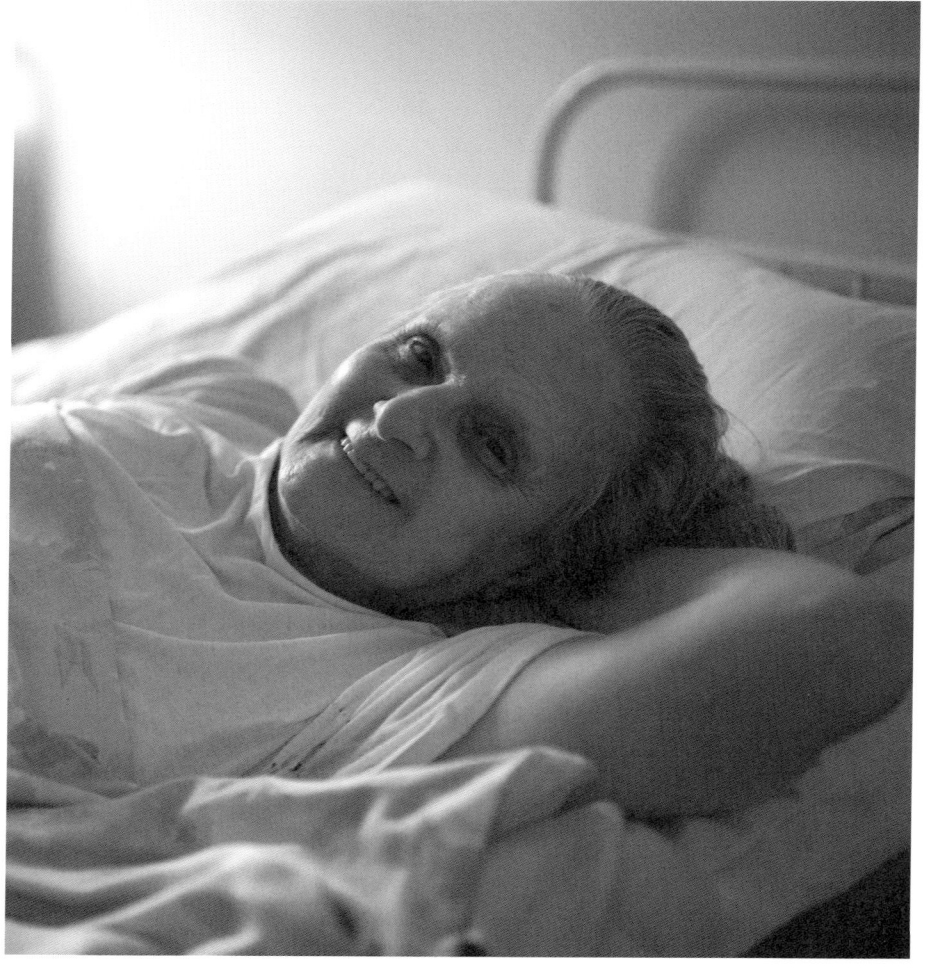

Erika Sauerbaum.

encourages Erika. Never shy to speak her mind, Erika approaches the woman and realises she recognises her. She's often seen her around town, and both come to visit the cemetery regularly.

'Excuse me, but might you be German?' she asks, not giving it much thought.

Without hesitation the woman retorts, 'Why? Do I look like one?'

Today, Erika and Christel Scheffler, who, at the time didn't even know her German name, laugh about these opening lines of introduction when they first met. Over the years they've become close friends, and they can no longer even imagine their lives without one another.

Erika is from Königsberg, as is Christel Scheffler. 'The advantage we older ones had was that our mother tongue was never quite lost. We never did quite forget our German,' the 83-year-old Erika tells us. Erika is one of the older Wolf Children and has been helping others in the area write letters to the Red Cross, to the German authorities, and to relatives ever since Lithuania's independence. She now does the same for Christel.

Christel is introduced to a whole new world after she meets Erika. 'Of course, I knew about the fall of the Iron Curtain and the independence of Lithuania, but I had no idea where I should turn to find out how to search for relatives or to even make myself known as a German.'

Erika is all too happy to help her. When they get together, she asks Christel about her life and those things she remembers from the past. Christel knows she lived in Königsberg, that she had either foster parents or adoptive parents, and that she may have once been called Käthe Wind. But how all this came about is an unknown to her. She was too young to remember. She knows her approximate birth year, and she remembers a home where there were trees and underground bunkers. She has memories of the nightly bombings, of the dead, the wounded, the wretchedness and hunger. These are the memories that haunt her. To even talk about them is incredibly difficult, and she cannot help but break out in tears.

Her new friend Erika encourages her to contact the German weekly *Ostpreußenblatt* and ask them to publish a search notice. Erika helps her write it.

> We are looking for relatives and acquaintances of Käthe Wind, now known as Aldona Žigmantienė. She was born around 1940 in East Prussia, possibly in Königsberg. She came to Lithuania as a young child in 1947. She doesn't know who her parents were, but it's possible she has an older brother.
>
> Käthe once had blonde, curly hair and her eyes are blue. Her face has a round shape and on the right side of her ribs is a birthmark. There's also an invisible birthmark between her eyebrows.

Although Erika has a number of friends who've found relatives in Germany using this same method, Christel cannot imagine that her request will amount to anything. Yet one day she receives a letter in the post. It's from Germany, but

The earliest photo Christel has of herself after arriving in Lithuania.

she can't understand a single word. She can hardly wait for Erika to translate it for her.

Erika tells her it's from a man who says he thinks he could be her brother and is asking for more information. His name is Gerhard Windt, and he lives near Stuttgart in southern Germany.

With Erika's help, Christel writes to him immediately. She tells him how things have gone for her all these years and then lists the few things she can still remember.

Indeed, not long after, she receives a long letter from Gerhard in response:

Hello and *Guten Tag*!
I received your letter yesterday and can't tell you how many times I've read it over.

First, I want to point out how well it is written—flawless. One could think that you 'immigrated' just yesterday! Where in Königsberg, dear Miss Erika, did you live? But now, let me address your burning questions.

I will try, as best I can, to reach into my past. How your name was changed from Kitty to Keti to Käthe Windt, as I wrote to you in my last letter. And why I think you could be Christel Scheffler, my parents' foster child.

So, how did you come to be named Windt? It was much easier for my parents to pass you off to the Russians as their own child at the end of the war in Königsberg, in the least to be able to get food rations for you.

It was such a terrible time! I've known for many years that East Prussians fled to Lithuania after the war, or at least tried. Their fate was so horrible, but what do we know? What purpose did it serve? Despite many inquiries with the Red Cross, my parents were never able to find out anything more about the woman who took you with her. They also never learned anything regarding the whereabouts of your biological mother. I met her twice, both times when she came to the house looking for you. Your mother was young. She wasn't married, but I don't know anything else about her, not even her name.

My parents were resettled in 1948, my father to Saxony in the spring, my mother to the island of Rügen [also in the GDR] a few months later. They found each other again through the Red Cross and lived their lives out on Rügen until their deaths. My father died in 1972/3; my mother died in 1974/5. Both were buried in Sassnitz. It wasn't until years later that I learned all this through some acquaintances.

Professionally, I worked as a repairman and travelled a lot, both domestically and abroad. Although I kept a home near Bremerhaven, I was rarely there. …

My parents never had official papers for you. All that was not destroyed by the British bombings in 1944, the Russians finished off in 1945, and our

East Prussian culture was systemically eradicated. Our people, who were driven out, had, for the most part, only that which they wore on their backs. And even that was often too much for the Russians.

So now, for those things you remember—for example, where we lived. You know we lived at the Fichteplatz, which was actually two squares: The Fichteplatz was an athletics field on one end and then there was a grassy patch that made up the other square. I hope this suffices for now, and when more questions arise, I'm at your disposal!

A regular correspondence develops between Gerhard and Christel. The two write to each other once a month, and for Christel, with each letter, there's always a new piece to the mosaic of her past to discover. She has no doubt now that Gerhard is in fact her older brother, the brother who so lovingly called her by her nickname, just as he did when she was a child.

11. April 1994

Dear Kitty!

Thank you for your kind Easter greetings. It was a surprise and, of course, I was delighted. But now I must ask a stupid question. Do you celebrate Easter again in Lithuania? Weren't these holidays forbidden during the Soviet era? The attitudes that your former rulers had towards the Church were of course well known.

It is nearly your birthday on 26 April. I beg for your understanding that I've not sent a card yet. Then again, it's probably a bit premature, as your true identity has not really been established yet, although for me, there is absolutely no doubt. Hopefully, it won't take much longer.

Rest assured that I'll be thinking about you on your day, as I do every day. I too had a birthday not long ago, my 69th. I celebrated it in all peacefulness and contentment with my lady friend. The Windts were an April-family, did you know that? Including you, Kitty, we had four birthdays in one month!

Well, what have you decided to do? Will you try to legalise your given name? Or are you content with the present situation? I would think that you now know who you really are. I have been looking at the photos from the past so many times. For me there's no doubt that this really is you.

Once as a child you fell and injured yourself at the corner of your mouth. Take a moment and run your finger from underneath your nose to the right corner of your lips. There, you should still be able to feel a scar.

I hope that this letter finds you well. I can imagine how impatient you will be for Miss Erika to have it translated. How long does it take for the post to reach you? And now I have a request of you … Please write a sentence for me, even if it's in Lithuanian. I would love to see your handwriting!

Best wishes, all the best, your Gerhard Windt

And, indeed, Christel has a barely visible scar in that very spot that Gerhard describes. On 27 April 1994, she finally has the courage to write a letter to the Office of the Registry, the *Standesamt 1* in Berlin, which logs the births of all Germans born abroad, as well as of those Germans who were displaced during the war.

> Most honorable Office of the Registry,
> I have a huge favour to ask of you. I am a German from Königsberg. In 1947, after the war, when the famine was so terrible in Königsberg, I fled to Lithuania with an unknown woman. I was a young child at the time, not even of school age. I was taken in by a family in Lithuania who raised me. I still live in Lithuania, am married, and am now called Aldona Žigmantienė. I only remember the names 'Kitty' and 'Windt'. There was an older boy in the family. I thought he was my brother. Now that Lithuania has become independent, I was able to write a letter to the *Ostpreußenblatt* in Germany to inquire about my family. I soon received a letter that contained a photo of a certain Gerhard Windt. Amongst other things, he wrote that I look much like the foster daughter his parents, Fritz and Gertrud Windt, took in to live with them in Königsberg-Ponarth in a neighbourhood near the Fichteplatz. My name would have been Christel Scheffler, and I would have been born on 26 April 1939 in Königsberg. Whether or not I was adopted by the Windt family, we don't know. It could be.
> I couldn't pronounce the name Christel and so always said 'Kitty', and this is the name that stayed. I can well remember 'Kitty Windt'. Also, there are several memories I have of Mister Gerhard Windt that have been confirmed by him. Now for the favour: Would you possibly have my birth certificate or otherwise my adoption papers? If so, could you please send me copies? I would be most grateful!
> Ponarth, to be clear, was in Region II.
> Most respectfully, Aldona Žigmantienė

Another letter arrives from Gerhard, dated 12 May 1994.

> *Grüß Gott!*
> When you receive this letter, it's possible that the weather where you are will be as beautiful as it is here. I started my letter today with the Southern German greeting, *Grüß Gott!* But no worries: While I eat the local bread and have taken on the local customs, I will never be anything other than an East Prussian.
> Dearest Kitty, your emotions on your birthday, on 26. April, must have been extra special this year. For me, after all the giddiness of having found you had passed, I thought about everything once more, and I know—there

is absolutely no doubt in my mind—that it is truly you. The other day I wrote about the scar on your face, but there's something more. Please take a close look at the thin line in your skin that runs from your nose around your mouth and down to your chin. I remember it from back then, and it looked just like it does today! I have wanted to write this to you for a long time, but I kept forgetting. And one more thing about the name Windt. It was extremely rare in Königsberg.

I am very curious to know if you have received any news from Berlin. The registry there is our only hope, as everything was destroyed in Königsberg.

So, the day will be here soon when the Russian troops will depart our land, soon to be known as the <u>former</u> GDR, once and for all. It could not come soon enough!

Last but not least, I don't want to forget to wish you a happy Pentecost. Live well, stay healthy, and my most heartfelt greetings to you,
Your Gerhard Windt

In the meantime, Christel receives a letter from the Office of the Registry in Berlin. There is unfortunately no documentation regarding her identity and no trace of her existence from the records in Königsberg. Christel is saddened by this news, for she would have been all too happy to finally have certainty about her identity. Now she'll probably never know who her parents were, or where she was born, or under what circumstances she became the child of Gerhard's parents.

2. July 1994
Good day, dear ones,
Once to you, Miss Kitty, and of course to you, dear writer, Miss Erika. I hope you are well and are not suffering in this heat the way we are here.

Thank you so much for the photo. I was so happy to receive it. You look well and your son looks like he has done well for himself, too. Am I just imagining this or do you look a bit solemn? Could it be because of circumstances not related to your work, other problems? I don't want to put you on the spot, but so many unfortunate things happened to you, through no fault of your own.

These last sentences move Christel to her very core. For the first time since she was a child, someone is asking about her, someone is actually interested in how she feels. 'Gerhard's letters were a gift from heaven for me. Even though hundreds of kilometers existed between us, I had a sense that he truly loved me, that he really cared.'

Indeed, it seems that Gerhard is genuinely taken by Kitty's stories, and so with each letter, he tries to help her link her memories to their shared past.

Dear Kitty,
I read your letters many times over and paid great attention to all of it. What became of us because of this war, especially in East Prussia? Everything was destroyed; our entire culture was annihilated, and much will never be made whole again.

Dear Kitty, there's another sweet story I want to tell you about your childhood. Our mother had learned two professions, cooking and tailoring. So, all the little dresses you wore when you were young were dresses she sewed for you with great devotion. You were to always look pretty, and, surely, you did. You were, without exaggeration, a very sweet and happy girl. You really had it good in our family. My parents loved you better than any of the rest of us!

For days on end, Christel cannot get over this letter. There were people in her life to whom she meant something. A mother who sewed clothes for her, and not out of necessity but out of love. Now in her mid-fifties, Christel, for the first time she can remember, feels that she was once truly loved.

26. July 1994
Dear Kitty!
Thank you so very much for your letter from 11th July. It arrived on the 20th and it was very informative—unfortunately, too, in a negative way. But I'll address that part later in this letter.

First, I would like to wish you both a *guten Tag* and hope that you are well and that this letter brings some joy into your house, or better said, into your home. Have you always had a proper home the way it is customary here, for example with a bath?

Now, with regard to your letter. I was quite surprised when I read that you wanted to go to Königsberg. Hopefully everything worked out well with the journey. Maybe someone was with you who knew his way around Ponarth. If you found the Fichteplatz, was the large Fichte school still there? And how did the athletics field and playground look? It was so lovely to have lived there when we were young!

And indeed, Christel went with a group of Wolf Children in a minibus to Königsberg. It was a memorable trip that they will talk about for years to come. 'The older ones who had lived in Königsberg in their teens wrote the German street names that they could still remember onto the Russian maps. This is how we found our way to Ponarth and also to the Fichteplatz,' Christel explains. The entrances to the bunkers were still there. Right away, Christel recognises the very place where she fell and injured her lip. 'It was overwhelming. And so lovely to have experienced it in the company of the other Wolf Children.'

They find the house where she once lived as Kitty Windt and ring the doorbell. A young Russian woman opens the door and, after a few words of explanation, she invites them in for tea. Christel is allowed to take her time to look around the house. Many images of her past flash through her mind as she takes her tour, stories she hopes to tell Gerhard.

The group also tries to find the former homes of the other Wolf Children. With each house, there's always suspense, wondering whether or not the street, the building or the home still exists. On the evening of their first day, Hannelore Weintke, the organiser of the tour, has an idea. 'We didn't have any money and could never have afforded an overnight in Kaliningrad, so we decided to sleep in the bus. Hannelore decided to ask the bus driver to park in front of the German Consulate,' Christel explains.

Once they've parked, and as the travellers begin to make themselves comfortable for the night, the consul walks out to ask what they're doing here. Hannelore answers him rather frankly: 'We're Germans. We're from Lithuania, and we have no accommodations in this city. We thought, of all places, this is where we belong.'

The consul and Hannelore exchange a few more friendly words and then he disappears into the residence. A few minutes later, the iron garden gate mysteriously swings open, and the caretaker waves them in. The bus is allowed to park inside the gates and this friendly gentleman even makes the guest bathroom available to them. 'It was much more elegant than anything we had expected our overnight to be,' Christel says with a mischievous grin. 'Some of us slept on the ground in the garden, like we were used to doing, in the grass. Others, like Hannelore, decided to spend the night inside the bus.'

Gerhard learns all about the Wolf Children's adventures in Königsberg in the next letter Christel writes to him, and he can't quite believe what he reads. It's always difficult for him to find the right words or to write them with the proper tone. At the end of July 1994, he writes:

> Do you know that it's not easy to write such personal letters when we've been forced into separation by nearly fifty years? And you were—I will write this anyway—I believe you were such a friendly, happy girl who loved to laugh. How does one reconcile that joyful time with all the suffering that came just after?
>
> What were the people like in Lithuania, the people who took you in? Were you able to enjoy some of your teenage years? Or were you simply used as a housemaid? All this interests me tremendously. I'm also very keen to know about your financial situation. If you no longer work, do you receive any sort of retirement compensation? Do you drink coffee, for example, can you still afford it after Lithuania devalued its money due to the subsequent

inflation? Especially with imported items like coffee, I can imagine things could be tight. Please do write about these things!

Well, dear Miss Kitty, for today I've come to the end of my letter. Hopefully you'll receive it soon, and please don't forget to give my regards to all those who've shown interest in your life, especially, of course, Miss Erika. It's so nice that she's there with you!

Stay healthy and stay strong. Your Gerhard

15. August 1994
Dear Kitty!
Many thanks for your recent letter in which you told me all the stories of your journey, although they left me rather shaken. The Kaliningrad of today is nothing like the Königsberg of the past!

My compliments to Erika, who remembered the street names so well. I used to ride the number 15 into the city from Ponarth-East. From the Barbara Street, I took the 8. It used to be the 11—but it took off later in the mornings. And often, to save the fare, I rode my bicycle via Rosenau-Speichersdorf to Ponarth.

We could write and write and dream on for hours about our old homeland, but there's not enough paper for that. I've heard that the underpass from the Dirschauer Street to the central train station no longer exists but that the East Prussian Exhibition Hall still stands. A nurse here at the local hospital told me so. As an ethnic German from Russia, she was resettled to Königsberg after the war and was later allowed to immigrate to West Germany. Oh, don't let me forget to tell you how happy I was that your trip to Königsberg was a success!

But even more so, it makes me so happy that there's no longer the least bit of doubt that you are Kitty, my sister. And for this reason, I would like to say we should go forward addressing each other with '*Du*'. It would have been that all along anyway, had the war and the post-war time not torn us apart and destroyed everything.

For Christel, these are no small words. She can feel Gerhard's heartfelt sincerity. She has a sense of belonging that she cannot remember ever feeling. She begins to trust Gerhard, and so she has one request: could he please put in writing—and have it notarised—that, in his opinion, she is who he says she is?

Dear Kitty, your postscripts asking me to validate your identity, I will do without hesitation. I'm sure there'll be some further legal documents that I'll need to sign, but that will be taken care of immediately as well. I'm writing to give you one small confirmation that those things you can remember are definitely true. Life is so short when one looks back, and at my age, anything could happen. So, with this letter, I hope to put at least something in your hands until that official document arrives.

I'm grateful that you told me how things are concerning your finances. I was worried that this was the case, and I would like to help you. I could send you money; that would be no problem. However, for that I would need your banking information.

Maybe you could just let me know what, for example, you could buy for 50 DM. I could support you with a small amount each month, and I would be happy to do so. Not the least because I have missed you so very much all these years.

And then, I have one more important question. Can you remember that our father was home for some time in 1944? He was injured and wore a huge bandage across his chest. He had been shot through the shoulder and was sent home to recuperate after he was released from the field hospital. It was a huge bandage that wrapped all the way around his shoulder and down to his hand, holding his arm very still. Perhaps Erika can better describe it to you.

In my last letter I asked you to write to me how it was with the people you lived with when you were in your teens. Were they good to you? Please write and tell me.

As we read through these letters, Christel tells us that it was difficult for her to fully open her heart to her brother.

I didn't want to write letters that only talked about the bad stuff. I worried that he would reject me if I sounded like all I did was complain. At the same time, I would have loved to have thrown myself into his arms and have told him everything, everything that I went through. He was the only person who ever asked me about those times.

17. 9. 1994
Dear Kitty!
Thank you so much for your letter from 30. August, which I was, once again, so happy to receive. Our father, by the way, would have had his birthday on 24. August. It would have been his 93rd—I fully understand that you can't remember him so well, because he was hardly ever home, just like me, while you were growing up.

I'm sorry that I'm just getting around to writing to you today. It's because of several doctor appointments. I've been to two banks and have, unfortunately, not been able to find out exactly how to transfer money to you. I will therefore write you again in a separate letter once I have the information.

I've read a lot about the difficulties former Germans have had in regaining their citizenship. It's a complicated process, but if such an opportunity should arise, you can count on my full support. Your Gerhard

In the autumn of 1994, a letter from Gerhard goes missing. Christel has not heard from him in a long time, and she begins to feel unsure of herself. Perhaps there was a miscommunication. But she decides to write to him anyway. In the letter that follows, Gerhard confirms that his last letter must have been lost in the mail. 'It was only one letter,' Christel says, 'but every letter meant the world to me. It was as if suddenly a link in our chain had been broken, and that upset me very much.'

There's an exchange of Christmas post, and then, in February 1995, Christel receives Gerhard's notarised letter certifying her identity. 'When that letter arrived, it was like a birthday for me. Finally, I had it in writing that I was, indeed, German.'

Most important to Christel are the small stories about her childhood, the tokens of love that stay with her as she carries on with her everyday life, like Gerhard's letter of February 1995 with this short paragraph directed at Erika: 'Tell Kitty she should keep a little of her sunny disposition. As a child she was always so sweet and affectionate.'

In mid-April 1995, a little over a year after her first contact with Gerhard, Christel receives two letters in a row. One is registered mail, marked for her birthday. The other one is not that easy to decipher. The penmanship has markedly changed.

> Hello dear ones,
> many thanks for your last three letters. My responses have taken some time, there was always something that came up, and health-wise, I'm not at my best.
>
> But first, I want to answer Kitty's question about photos from home. There are none. Everything that we had in 1945 sadly was lost. In fact, with best intentions, I had left several pictures at home when I went off to war at the end of 1944, hoping to be able to keep them safe. When I was in Kiel at the end of the war, in May 1945, I could just as easily have had them with me then. But who knew in advance how things would turn out?
>
> With regards to your papers, I hope that they will help you and that there will be no further questions as to who you are.
>
> Dear Kitty, I am also sending my kind regards to your scribe, Erika. What would you do without her? To write such letters is no small undertaking. I can tell she's been well schooled, and my compliments to that! How wonderful that she's not forgotten her German. On the other hand, for you, dear Kitty, you were so young that living with strangers in a strange land, you couldn't help but forget your mother tongue. But perhaps speaking with your fellow countrymen has helped you to understand some things a bit better now.
>
> Now I would like to thank you for your thoughtful gift for my seventieth birthday. It was a wonderful surprise! Of course, I immediately recognised

our 'East Prussian Gold'. I have the pendant hanging from my key ring, and it will stay there for as long as I live! Once again, thank you so very much. Now I have only one wish—that my greetings for your birthday, the registered letter of 11. April arrived safely.

   Your Gerhard

It is the last letter from her brother. Christel is inconsolable when a letter arrives not long after with the news that Gerhard had died. She is 55 years old and once again experiences loss, and she cannot get over it.

> For the longest time I just could not believe it, did not want to believe it. I had finally found him, the one person who knew me as a child. We had not even been able to meet one another, and only a year later he was dead. It fits so well with the story of my life. Never did good come to me. When it did, it was always a fleeting thing.

And with every loss, all her other losses return fresh, as if they happened just yesterday.

It is these letters that Christel pulls out right away when we visit her in Jonava. This small town, about 30 kilometers north of the city that was once Lithuanian's capital, Kaunas, is the hub for a number of surrounding villages. It is where the farmers come to market and where work was to be had during the Soviet era in the emerging industrial sector, including Lithuania's largest fertiliser factory. Yet something else is rarely mentioned today: a century ago, it was a city with a flourishing Jewish population. During the Second World War, it was invaded by the SS and in short order the Jews were gone.

   Christel lives in a Communist housing block that looks rather dilapidated. Everything looks sterile. There are no nameplates, postboxes or doorbells, only a house number with a lock having a combination we do not know. Behind some of the curtains we can see stirring. Most certainly Claudia and I, two young blonde women who look as if they really don't belong here, are being scrutinised.

   Fortunately, we are with another Wolf Child, Liesbeth, who is not shy and stops passersby to ask if they might know Christel. Other than the mother cat that has made herself comfortable underneath the front doorstep with her litter of tiny kittens, no one pays us much attention. Not knowing what to do next, we simply stand at the entrance to the building. Suddenly a woman good-naturedly calls down to us in Lithuanian from an upper floor and gives Liesbeth the access code to get in. On the ground floor we are to ring the bell at the middle door. As we do, the door immediately springs open. Christel is visibly moved. She remembers us from the Wolf Children visit in Germany but cannot believe we actually made good on our promise to come to her home to visit her. She is elated.

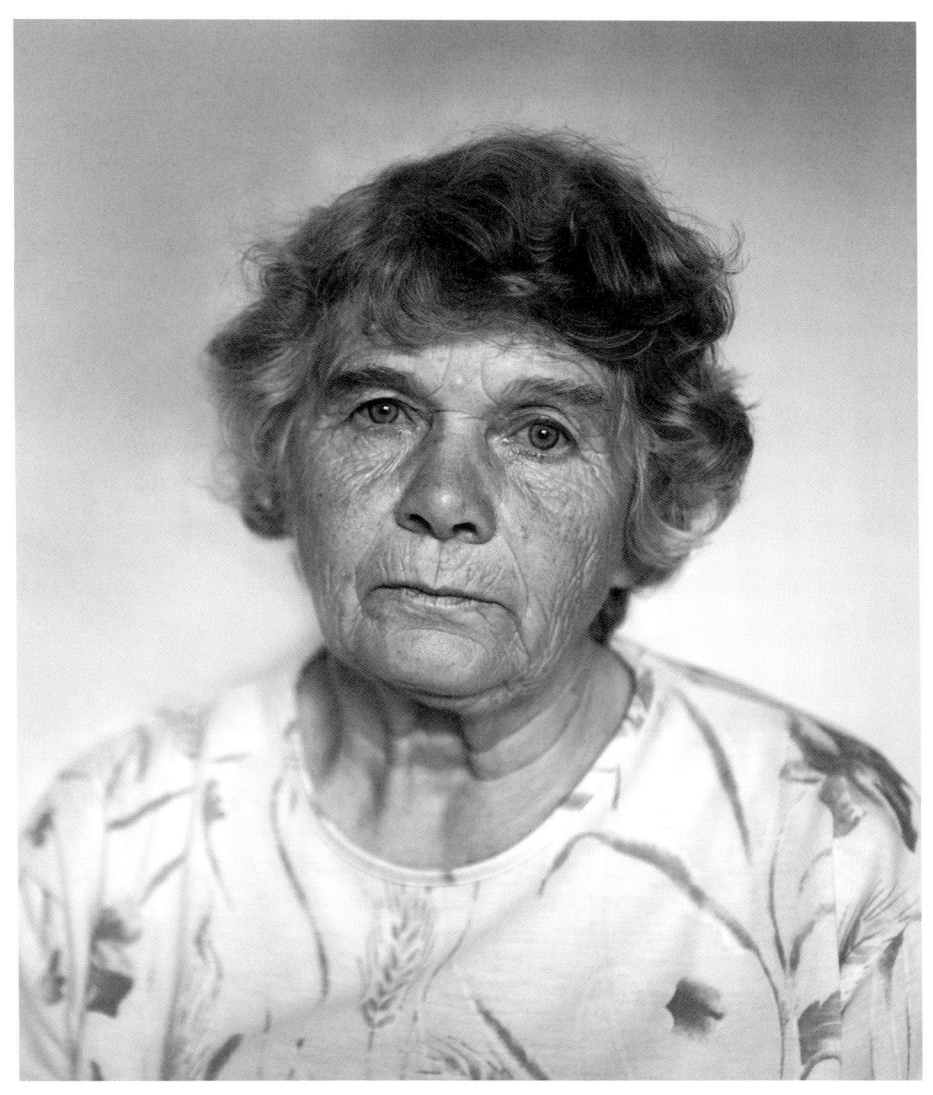

Christel Scheffler.

Christel lives alone in this two-room apartment, near the city centre. From time to time, her granddaughter also lives with her. 'It all depends on whether she's getting along with her mother or not,' Christel tells us, Liesbeth interpreting. She's proud of her granddaughter, who is studying veterinary medicine. But Christel is worried that she will not be able to find a good job that pays well in Lithuania. 'All the young people leave to go abroad,' she explains.

There's one other housemate, a fox terrier that looks much like the dog in *The Adventures of Tintin*. He's Christel's devoted companion, keeping her company during some of her loneliest hours.

Christel has fortified her home well. A thick upholstered double door muffles any noise coming in from the outside. In this ground level apartment, Christel doesn't seem to like opening her windows, either.

We sit in her living room. Christel keeps looking at us in disbelief, and then touches our arms, as if to assure herself that we are really here. She wants to tell her story. Her entire story from the beginning. She begins by bringing out the letters, then she tells us about her big brother, who she says she wishes were here right next to her, helping her feel safe. 'I actually never felt safe,' she muses.

She leaves her first husband right after their second son is born. 'He was an alcoholic, and a good-for-nothing. And, he beat me.' Christel moves back to the Lithuanian family that had once taken her in as a young Wolf Child. There she never felt safe either. She was often abused, both verbally and physically. Yet when she moves back in, she cares for her Lithuanian foster mother up until her death. I ask Christel if she felt responsible for her.

'No. But where else was I to go?'

Her two sons are named Peter and Paul. Her younger son, Paul, was drafted into the army in 1979 to fight in the invasion of Afghanistan. 'The war destroyed him. So many of his comrades died or were wounded or came home sick. He never wanted to tell me exactly what he went through, but when he came home, he was no longer the same.'

The war in Afghanistan was hated in the Soviet Union, but one was not allowed to say so in public. Thousands of young people from all over the country were drafted each year to fight in the Hindu Kush. Paul, a broken, badly traumatised man, died a few months after his return, from unknown causes.

Peter, the older son, was married and had a daughter, Christel's only grandchild. Ever since Lithuania's independence, he worked for a firm that had business contacts in Germany. Christel was thrilled her son was able to travel to Germany regularly and see a bit more of the world. Then, one day in 1999, two police officers rang at her door. They were bearers of sad news for Christel. Peter had been in a car accident in Thuringia and was killed.

A year later, Christel's new husband, also a drunk like the father of her children, dies. Pain and redemption seem to run hand in hand in Christel's life.

She brings out some photos. Some are of Christel as a young woman—even then she has an earnest, almost sad look to her face. Never does she smile in any of the pictures. Her eyes, cornflower blue and deep as a mountain lake, have a hard look to them. The happy little girl that her brother Gerhard remembered so fondly has disappeared.

Christel worked hard her whole life. For thirty-five years she was a factory worker doing a man's job, fabricating fiberglass. This meant she also handled asbestos. As for worker's compensation, no one seemed to care.

I'm curious if she remembers the explosion that happened at the chemical plant in Jonava in 1989, in which a considerable amount of ammonia had been released into the atmosphere. It was one of the worst environmental catastrophes in Lithuania's history. A huge toxic cloud hung over the city for days. Seven people died and twenty-nine were badly injured. Many others developed lung issues and heart problems, suffering for years to come.

'Of course, I remember this.' But whether her breathing problems have anything to do with that accident or not remains speculative. Most likely her longstanding lung complications are related to the many years she worked in the fiberglass factory.

What is left for her in life? Pneumoconiosis, or 'black lung disease', asthma and a small pension. Christel does as most of the Wolf Children in Lithuania do. When the money runs out at the end of the month, she fasts. However, her pension is now being subsidised by the German government, which was made possible by Wolfgang Baron von Stetten's appeals to Parliament—100 litas per month for each Wolf Child is what he has been able to get for them, so far. 'I live frugally, I don't need much. Money only becomes a problem when something unforeseen comes along, like a high energy or doctor's bill.' But, oh, Wolfgang von Stetten! Christel exclaims. He's like a father to her. 'There are no words to describe all that he's done for us over the years. Even his wife and his children—they're all so kind.'

In 1994, Wolfgang von Stetten invites her to visit Germany. There, Christel is introduced to a world that she had only ever seen on television.

> It was an experience that stayed with me for a long time. Even to think about why Mr von Stetten does this! He gave me back the belief that there really are people in this world that do good things simply because they can. And not because they expect something in return. I only wish I could do something for him as well.

Christel's eyes tear up over and over again, then she squeezes my hand, swallows, takes a deep breath and tells us more. It takes a lot of energy out of her, but she wants to tell us everything. 'What I have lived through, what was done to me, is too much for one human life. I would not wish it on my worst enemy. The last meal in Königsberg, for example. I remember it and have to shudder. Potato peels from the garbage pit, already fully black, I just couldn't …' Once again, she begins to weep. We ask her if she needs to take a break. She shakes her head, no.

'The Wolf Children are family to me, because, over the years, I had no one else. I'm all alone now, but the Wolf Children give me hope. Without them I could easily feel lost, forlorn. But we're old now and soon everything will come to an end.'

What does she mean by this, I want to know. 'What more do I have to look forward to?' she responds.

Upon our question whether she still has a lifelong dream that has not been fulfilled, she doesn't answer right away. Then, when we're about to leave, with a quivering voice, she does have something more to say. 'I do have just one more wish. To return to Königsberg just one more time. That would be so wonderful!'

We discuss the possibility of travelling to Königsberg together. But Christel's concern is that the travel visa would be expensive. And anyway, we're not sure just one day would be enough. So, there would be the overnight expense. Suddenly she second-guesses herself. Had she asked for too much? Claudia and I assure her, no, and one glance between the two of us confirms it. We know that this journey is one we'll take with her, all too gladly.

Winter in the Lithuanian countryside.

Chapter 14

Then and Now

The living and the dead—for most of us there is a clear and definitive divide that separates one from the other. Not so for the Wolf Children. For them, the distinctions are often much more ambiguous.

For some, decades can go by in which those who were absolutely believed to be dead suddenly reappear. For others, quite the opposite is true. Those who had clung to the hope of finding a long-lost relative suddenly discover that that hope was nothing more than a tragic dream. Even as we meet with the Wolf Children today, those who perhaps still wait for the return of their disappeared mother, come to sadly learn that she died in the war, and then often under unspeakable circumstances. Then there are siblings who had long been thought lost forever, who do find one another again but can hardly recognise each other, and don't even have a language in common.

Add to the list of strange paradoxes, this classified advert, searching for a person who has long been believed to be dead, Renate Kösling.

She was born near Gerdauen in 1938. Her mother, while on a begging tour in Lithuania, had lost her two daughters, Renate and Ursula. Not long thereafter, the sisters lose each other as well. Ursula makes it to Germany in 1958, but Renate remains missing and is believed to be somewhere in Lithuania. Meanwhile, she's taken a Lithuanian name, Jadvyga, which makes it nearly impossible for her family to find her.

Their father, a pilot in the German Luftwaffe, was shot down over Tauroggen and lies buried there in a German military cemetery. 'With bitter tears' and 'deep sorrow', her mother posts a classified ad in the newspaper, looking for her daughter on the date of what would have been her birthday. It seems all hope is lost, yet she trusts her intuition and does not give up.

Today, Renate is eternally grateful to her family that they never gave up believing that she survived. Renate, however, has no desire to return to Germany, even though she never had a Lithuanian family who would have wanted her to stay.

Renate was once married but has been a widow since she was 35. She has light blue eyes and a bright smile. She lives with her daughter, Juratė, in the Lithuanian countryside, where the two women have made a comfortable life for themselves. Jurate, too, was once married but is divorced.

'I don't need a man in my life to be happy,' says Renate. 'My daughter and I have a good life here.'

Renate Kösling.

The life they lead is rare for a Wolf Child. Most of the women have bound themselves to their husbands, forsaking their own happiness and unable to break away, even when they ought to, a choice Renate and her daughter have long put behind them.

> Am 15. Februar 1959, ihrem 22. Geburtstage, gedenke ich mit heißen Tränen meiner seit 1946 vermißten, lieben unvergessenen Tochter
>
> **Renate**
>
> In tiefem Schmerz
> **Ihre Mutter Frida Kösling**
> Essen-Borbeck
> Borbecker Straße 83
> **Bruder Herbert**
> Essen-Altstadt
> **Bruder Erwin,** Borbeck
> **Schwester Ursula**
>
> Letztere kam am 14. September 1958, nach 13 Jahren, aus Litauen wieder.
> Wer kennt R e n a t e und kann über ihren Verbleib Angaben machen?

On this 15. February 1959, on her 22nd birthday, we remember her with bitter tears, my beloved missing, but not forgotten, daughter,

Renate

With deepest sorrow,
    Her mother Frida Kösling, Borbecker Street 83, Essen-Borbeck
    Her brother Herbert, Essen-Altstadt
    Her brother Erwin, Borbeck
    Her sister Ursula

On September 14. 1958, after missing for thirteen years, her sister Ursula returned safely from Lithuania.
    Does anyone know Renate? Can anyone tell us of her whereabouts?

There are also men amongst the Wolf Children who have become disillusioned with their spouses. When we arrive at the Simon-Dach-House in Klaipėda, the seat of the German minority in Lithuania, Arnold Piklaps greets us at the door. He's the director of the cultural centre, which has roughly 400 members from around this city on the Baltic Sea, and he is primarily tasked with the aging group of Memel Germans in the country. 'Please, do come in. The two gentlemen are already waiting for you upstairs in one of our classrooms.'
    The two men are Siegfried Kösling (no relation to Renate Kösling) and Alfred Plink, two of the few Wolf Children who never left this area. When we enter the

Alfred Plink.

classroom, normally reserved for adult German courses, the two literally jump out of their chairs for joy.

Alfred Plink, a good-looking older gentleman with a blue double-breasted suit coat and dark turtleneck sweater, takes my right hand in both his and kisses it. At first, I'm surprised. Then it becomes clear to me that this is no exaggerated gesture on his part, rather it is an expression of his sincerity and honed manners that are—as he tells us later—'as they should be, in perfect form. It's what one does when one greets a lady. It's what was taught in my parents' home in East Prussia, how I was raised.'

Siegfried Kösling, too, welcomes us warmly, even though today is actually a sad day for him. Siegfried, who has lived in Klaipėda for many years and has become a dear friend to Alfred, is moving back to live with his adult children in Šiauliai tomorrow. He explains that when he divorced his wife and left the children with her in Šiauliai, he moved in with his new partner here in Klaipėda. Alfred, who can speak much better German than Siegfried, decides he should be the one to tell us the details of Siegfried's situation. 'He was married to a Russian, and she was not a good woman,' he says. 'Now he must move back in with his children in Šiauliai, because his second wife, also a Russian, kicked him out. Not, mind you, before she also took all his money.'

We soon learn that Siegfried is in no way the innocent one. His children don't really want anything to do with him after he left their mother for another woman. But now, because of his dire predicament, they have agreed to take him in, a most humiliating experience for Siegfried.

There are tears in Siegfried's eyes. *'Alles kaputt,'* he says, 'and my head hurts.' Alfred's hand reaches for Siegfried's. It's hard to see his friend so sad, this possibly being the last time he'll ever see him, and he wants to console him. But Siegfried just shakes his head, as if even Alfred cannot help him anymore.

We always try to visit the Wolf Children in their own homes where there are familiar surroundings. The subjects we touch on are hard enough, and being in the home can lend a sense of security. Sometimes they want to show us photos or documents, often things they had not thought about before. But today is an exception. Alfred lives with his disabled wife in a one-room home that, even without visitors, is cramped. And Siegfried doesn't even have a home to visit.

Siegfried was born in Königsberg in March 1933. A year later, his sister, Irmgard, was born. Siegfried no longer remembers when the youngest child, his brother, Günther, was born. His father, Fritz, is at the front when the Red Army arrives in Königsberg in 1945. Siegfried, his siblings and his mother, Gertrud, stay in the city where they are witness to all the gruesome atrocities that the Russians commit against the people. In 1946, his mother dies. 'Health-wise, she was already weak, but then she simply starved to death,' he tells us.

These are painful memories that still, sixty-five years later, make his voice quiver. For one brief moment, we can see in his face the 13-year-old standing there, alone with his younger brother and sister.

The three are taken to a Russian orphanage that is overseen by the military. Siegfried doesn't last long here. 'It was so terrible. We had nothing to eat, and I just couldn't wait any longer. I was simply afraid I would die of starvation.'

As many children do during this time, he embarks on the trail to Lithuania, where he offers his services to farmers as a farmhand, here one day, the next day there.

After many years, his odyssey of wandering ends when he finds work in Šiauliai on a collective farm in the early 1950s, and this is where he meets his wife in 1957. Warwara is a beautiful Russian woman, and he is smitten. In 1958, they marry and over time, they have six children. Life is not easy under Soviet rule. One of his sons, torn between his duty to the army, the political expectations of his country, and an unrequited love, falls off the deep end, and dies by suicide.

Siegfried no longer has connections to Germany, even though his father eventually does make it to the West after the war. There he marries once more, and, with his much younger wife, he has seven more children. But Siegfried never sees him again. And his father never reaches out to find him. Siegfried must have seemed like a stranger in this new life of his father's. Siegfried has no contact to his half-siblings, either.

Siegfried is tired; his headache is bothering him. When he stands up, I notice that on his right hand two half fingers are missing. I ask what happened, whether it was work related. 'And here …' he points to his eye, which looks as if it could be glass. Animatedly, he explains in Lithuanian to Alfred what happened to him back then.

Did the two men never talk about this? Apparently not. Alfred, for a good moment, is so shaken, that he can hardly speak. 'Can you imagine?' he finally says with a sigh. 'While at work, he discovered a grenade, picked it up, and … it was live! It exploded and badly injured him. He can call himself lucky. He nearly died, but all it cost him was his eyesight and two fingers.'

The room is silent for a good many minutes. It is one of those moments when we can do nothing other than just be there. I reach my hand out to Siegfried; he takes it in his and squeezes it. Finally, he puts on his longshoreman's cap and says goodbye. Alfred takes him in his arms; he wants him to stay. But Siegfried must go. Tomorrow he'll be taking the bus to Šiauliai. Everything he owns fits into a single bag.

Once he's gone, Alfred repeats what sounds like it's become his mantra: 'Can you even imagine? This poor man now has nothing, no one. He always gave all his money to his wife, and now she's thrown him out. I always told him, you must take care of yourself, put money into savings, lay something aside … Oh, this is so terrible.' It occurs to me how extraordinarily empathetic Alfred is towards his friend.

Alfred's life hasn't been easy either. 'You can't change your past, I always say. You have to be thankful for that which the Good Lord has given you.'

I have my doubts. 'Do you really?' I ask.

'Most certainly. Everything comes from The Father.'

What to our ears sounds like naivety, is, in truth, Alfred's deep, God-fearing belief. He looks at me intensely. His gaze does not soften one bit. For him there's no doubt that everything has a reason; it *must* have a reason. Otherwise, all the struggles of life would be in vain.

And he well appreciates them, the great moments that have made it all worthwhile. For example, in 1993, after forty-seven long years, he was able to hold his two sisters, Ursula and Helga, in his arms again. At the time, he had almost forgotten all his German and could hardly even express how much that moment meant to him.

The first time he visits them in Germany, he stays for four weeks. During this short time, large pieces of his vocabulary quickly return. Even the East Prussian accent comes back to him, sometimes sounding as though he's from a different era, which in a certain sense is true.

Alfred was born in a small village in the Samland in 1930. His father is an honoured veteran of the First World War. On one of the few photos that Alfred shows him, he is in his uniform, his chest decorated with numerous medals, one of which is the Iron Cross. Most impressive is the Kaiser-Wilhelm beard, with its handlebar moustache and bare chin, which his father proudly wears in this photo, professionally taken at a studio in Königsberg.

Both his father and his grandfather are masons by trade. But soon after Alfred is born, the extended family purchases a farm with 50 acres of land about 50 kilometers east of Königsberg, near Wehlau. A family photo shows his parents and grandparents with the farm in the background. Both men are standing stately erect, with his grandmother sitting in the foreground wearing a high-buttoned black dress. Alfred's mother, Anna, a slight woman, stands to the back.

Alfred remembers his life growing up as romantic. 'There was a lot of work to do on the farm, but for us children, it was a great life. There was always plenty to eat. We had animals, twenty cows and five horses, and we spent all our time outdoors, summers as well as winters.'

In 1939, his father is drafted once again. It will be his second world war. 'That was difficult for us all. We children didn't fully understand the gravity of what this meant, but for our mother it was hard. She missed the labour needed on the farm and my grandparents were terribly afraid for the life of their only son.'

In 1944, they receive the death notice. Alfred's father was killed. His mother is 42 years old, Alfred, the oldest, is 14, Helga, his youngest sister, has just turned 4.

Alfred with his older sister, Ursula, c.1937.

Next is the flight to Rauschen on the Baltic coast, where they end up living under Russian occupation. Less than a year later, his mother dies—from starvation.

His 6-year-old brother, Helmut, and his sister Helga, who just turned 5, are taken to an orphanage by the authorities, where they are given very little food. The three children are on the brink of starvation. So much so, that Helmut does not survive and dies within a year.

Ursula, the older of the two sisters, does not live in the orphanage, but she manages to always stay near her siblings. One day in 1947, she and her sister Helga are taken on a children's transport to the GDR and will later be adopted in East Germany. Alfred, the oldest, does not know any of this with certainty until 1993. When he takes off on his desperate search for food, always needing to expand his radius, he eventually loses track of the others.

> It was such a difficult time, made worse because we couldn't stay together. I was always on the search for food, but that wasn't so easy. Sometimes I worked for Russians out in the fields. Later I applied for work at the fire station in Tilsit. But there was not enough work to go around and anyway, as a German, they didn't really want me.

For the newly settled Russians, it is dangerous to hire someone like Alfred, because in this land that was once East Prussia, any ties to Germans are precarious and, anyway, illegal.

Alfred decides to move on and for the first few years, works as a farmhand on a number of farms in villages around Tauroggen, where he meets his wife. Her name is Ona, Lithuanian for Anna, like his deceased mother. She is the love of his life, and they marry in 1956. Two children, Edvardas and Dangoulė, are born.

Today, Dangoulė lives not far from her parents and helps them with their daily needs. Alfred is especially grateful as his wife has had Parkinson's disease for almost thirty years. He takes care of her as best he can, and with those things he can no longer do, his daughter gladly takes over. 'Family is the most important thing,' Alfred says. 'I'm in contact with my sisters in Germany every month. We write to one another, and we call each other. They send me a bit of money as well.'

Alfred has only a meagre pension and is happy that his relatives in Germany have not turned away from him. 'I was astonished when that first letter came through the Red Cross in 1993. I never expected to hear from them again.'

His sisters had not forgotten him all these years and remained steadfast in their search for him. Alfred understands all too well that this is far more the exception than the rule. 'There are Wolf Children whose relatives in Germany don't want to know anything about them anymore,' he muses. This is a horrible thought to Alfred, who would have been all too glad to resettle in Germany, but out of concern for his sick wife, he has never really considered it. 'I was afraid that such a move would be too difficult for her, and she would die from it.'

When, at the end of our visit, Claudia photographs him and tells him that we intend to return in the summer to give him the photos and the finished book, he beams. 'That would make me so happy. Do you know, sometimes we believed that people in Germany no longer know that we exist?'

Alfred Plink doesn't wish for much. He just does not want to be forgotten. He wants that his life will not have been lived in vain.

At the end of our visit, Arnold Piklaps shows us around the building before we say our goodbyes. The Wolf Children's association, Edelweiss, had its office here for many years, he tells us. 'Formally, they are still members, but we rarely see them anymore, maybe only twice a year. There simply aren't that many left,' he adds, something with which Luise Quitsch, the long-time chairwoman of the organisation, concurs when we visit her later in Vilnius.

Luise Quitsch has just returned from a holiday in Turkey with her daughter. Such trips are only possible for her because she, as opposed to most of the Wolf Children, had a good education and a lucrative profession and receives a decent pension. As a child, she often cursed her adoptive parents, because they always forced her to study, even when she complained. But by the time she became a teenager she was able to recognise the value in all her hard work and is eternally thankful to them. Her final grades when she graduated were good enough for her to be able to attend university and earn a degree.

As Alfreda Pipiraitė, her Lithuanian name, she became a civil engineer, working first at a construction firm in Kaunas, then, from 1986 onwards, she was head of her department at the Lithuanian Ministry of Engineering in Vilnius.

Not just in her career, but in her private life as well, her strict upbringing and her higher education seem to have paid off. 'I met my husband through a girlfriend just after I completed my degree,' says Luise. 'It was my one big love, but, for a long time, I didn't want to marry. My life always had a certain hesitation to it. I always had the feeling that something better was going to come along.'

Luise's life is not as driven, with few options, the way it is for most of the other Wolf Children. For most, even in their adult lives, they need to work hard every day to eke out even a meagre existence.

Luise's adoptive parents never expect a thank you or want anything in return, although her career certainly could provide for them. They're only too happy about how well their adopted daughter acclimatised to her foreign surroundings. Right to their death, they have a good relationship with one another. Her father dies from a heart attack, her mother passes away ten years later. By that time, Luise has had a child. She is a self-determined woman and when her big love proves to be the love of her life, she finally marries him. Neither her husband nor her daughter knows that their wife and mother, Alfreda Pipiraitė, was born Luise Quitsch.

Luise Quitsch.

Travelling is not all that important to Luise. Even visiting Turkey is something that, at first, she doesn't even want to do. But she does it because, more important than sun, sand and beaches, is the time spent with her daughter.

Luise walks with a limp when we visit her in the apartment in Vilnius where she lives with her husband. While at the ocean, a wave had knocked her over, and she sprained her ankle. 'So, I had more time to read,' she says, making light of her handicap. Her home is full of German books and magazines that today are easily available in Lithuania. Luise considers this the greatest freedom: she is finally able to admit to her German roots without the fear of reprisal.

It has been a long road, however. For many decades, Luise repressed everything that had to do with her German heritage, right to the core of her inner being—not only to others, but also to herself. She had not dreamed, even once, of her East Prussian homeland. Even her subconscious mind seemed to have erased it all.

Luise doesn't remember she is German until sometime in the early 1990s when she sees a wooden toy in a store window in Vilnius, and the word *Hampelmann*, 'jumping jack', comes to mind. She begins to have images popping intermittently in her head. Rather than full childhood memories, they are random and out of sequence and don't really relate to one another. This is no surprise. Luise wasn't even 5 when her world fell apart.

She sees herself in a room standing at a window with white curtains. She's standing on the second floor, looking down at the street, waiting for her older siblings to come home from school. Hans is the oldest, already a teenager, she remembers. Then there are others: Hilde, Wilhelm and Edith. There's one who is younger than Luise. It is little Günther. She remembers her mother's blonde hair, her father's cap and her grandfather's hat. 'I must have been curious about people's heads,' she says.

Her grandfather does not live far away, in a village whose name she eventually remembers, 'Seelheim'. There he owned a forge. 'I have an image in my head. I'm sitting somewhere at home with my Opa, and I remember yellow lilies. This I can remember. But then, what else? Dark blue tiles. These were upstairs in our children's bedroom …'

Much more vivid than the memories of her home are those Luise has of the bombings and the flight.

> Once we were in a bunker that was bombed. And in this bunker the door was locked from the outside, and we could not get out. The air was completely used up. There was an old man with a scissor. Maybe he wasn't even that old, but for me, as a small child, he was a very old man. He made a split in the door with his big scissors so that we finally got air, and after a while we were set free—or let out, somehow. I remember this bunker, and it was so good to get out and be able to breathe again! And when I was able to breathe again, I remember how good the fresh air tasted. That was sublime.

When the flight begins, the family splits up. Luise is to stay with her aunt and her cousin Trudi. From this moment on, Luise knows nothing more about what happened to the others.

More flashes of memories: bomb attacks … many, many corpses … dead horses. 'And I crawled around in it, all alone.' The most dramatic impressions are the burning forests. And the screaming women. And the stinking foreign men.

I so badly wanted a doll that was lying there at the roadside. I really wanted to take it with me. But it was strongly *verboten*. What happened to this aunt, I don't know. She was no longer alive, nor was Trudi. Why they died and I didn't, I don't know either. How we became separated, I also don't know. I only saw many corpses. That is my last memory of them.

Luise's next picture: locked inside a Russian orphanage with other children. Then there's a gap in her memory. The place is somewhere near Königsberg. There's nothing to eat. Worst of all, Luise is thirsty, but there's nothing to drink. All she has is the hope that her mother will come for her soon. But her mother never comes.

Luise doesn't learn the truth about why her mother never came until sometime in the 1990s, when she hears about a recently founded association of former Wolf Children. Through this association she meets other people who have stories similar to hers, which finally gives her the courage to start looking for possible relatives of her own in Germany.

To start this process, she decides to take a German course in order to relearn her mother tongue. Besides giving her encouragement, the Wolf Children also advise her in practical matters. Where to turn? What do you need to pay attention to when filling out the questionnaires? Luise knows that her adoptive mother had once gone to the Red Cross looking for answers but was unsuccessful. Probably the misspelling of her name had something to do with it, Luise believes today, because back then she could speak her name but certainly did not know how to spell it.

Now, when she contacts the tracing services in Lübeck, a number of different lists with names with various spellings are systematically researched. As a result, the assistants come across a query from her brother Hans, who's been looking for her. That very day she excitedly gives him a call.

Yet their communication is difficult. She cannot read the first letter she receives from Hans. It is written in *Sütterlin*, the German style of handwriting taught to schoolchildren up to 1941. Then she receives a letter from her sister Edith. Gradually, Luise discovers that Hilde and Günther are also still alive. Wilhelm, however, is still missing, and presumed to be dead. It is 1993, forty-eight years since their separation.

Luise wants to see her siblings as soon as she can. They send her an invitation for which Luise must go to the embassy to apply for a visa. It takes a very long time before the permission to travel is granted. For Luise, it seems to be an eternity. Then, out of the blue, the unexpected happens. Suddenly, Hans no longer wants to see his long-lost sister.

At first, she is deeply hurt. Today she believes it was Hans's wife who was behind it. 'She probably thought, "Now what does this poor woman from Lithuania want from us, this Russian woman?" She always called me "the Russian woman" or "the Russian sister". "She only wants to beg from us," is probably what she thought.'

The same happens with her brother Günther. He too is married, and his wife stands in the way of all contact between the two of them. Luise is not able to see him until after his wife dies. Or did the two brothers hide behind their wives, because they themselves were afraid of an encounter?

The first relative she comes in contact with is her sister Edith, who brings a former neighbour with her to their first meeting. Her maiden name was Gertrud Kabeck, and she still clearly remembers Luise as a small child. The following year, Gertrud takes Luise to visit her childhood village in Kaliningrad Oblast. Here Gertrud shows her all the places she would have known as a child. To Luise, it's as if a gate to the past has been thrown wide open. Indeed, she experiences a curious side effect. Since her past is something she no longer needs to keep secret, and all these new images come back to her mind, her memories blossom. But they also feel somewhat surreal. 'Before, these memories were sealed shut inside of me, they couldn't go anywhere, and in time, they disappeared. Now the floodgates are opening and so many memories are coming back to me, but they are fleeting memories.'

When Luise tells her husband about her inquiry at the Red Cross, he is dumbfounded. 'I had told my husband about my German roots when we first met, but he, to this day, claims that he never knew. I believe, though, that he suppressed it, or simply did not want to know it back then. It was illegal, you know. At any rate, he never believed me.' Only when Luise can 'prove' her background in the 1990s, is he willing to accept this part of her family history.

When Luise's daughter first learns about what happened to her mother in 1945, she's outraged. Unable to understand, she angrily says, 'How can your own parents do something like that to you? How could they have been in such a hurry during their escape that they lost you or would even think to give you away to someone else?' Luise cannot explain this herself in the moment. There are too many blank spots in her memory. And for someone who did not live through those times, it's hard to make sense of the chaos of war. Mother and daughter need years to process the feelings and emotions and work through them together.

Meanwhile, Luise's status in the Wolf Children association has evolved. From one seeking advice, she has become the one giving it. When a new chairperson for the organisation is needed, Luise's name comes up. She balks at the idea, citing that her German is much too poor, and there's not enough information to work with anyway. But her resistance is of no avail. She is voted in.

As the new chairwoman, Luise's background in government comes in handy. There is much work to do. Many want to immigrate to Germany and re-establish their German citizenship. As she is familiar with bureaucracy and administrations, she decides, first and foremost, to gather all data from the Wolf Children: birthdates, hometowns, former names, etc.

A strong bond develops in the group. A choir is formed, as is an ensemble. Over the years, though, the organisation becomes more and more quiet. Many Wolf Children have left Lithuania and others are sick or are having a difficult time in their old age. 'I'm probably one of the healthiest and one of the youngest,' Luise says. 'I never had such a difficult life. I never had to physically work that hard. I sat on my butt and worked with my brain, and I was always athletic. I skied and exercised regularly.'

In June 2000, Luise goes to the German reunion of East Prussians in Leipzig. Her brother Hans, who's eleven years older than her, lives in the area. This time, she decides nothing will stand in the way of their meeting. It will be the first time they see each other since the war ended. Hans can hardly believe that this adult, well-dressed woman is his sister. 'Luise, you were always such a little doll,' he says with admiration, 'hardly bigger than a pea …'

A woman whom Luise knows joins them at their table and asks her to translate two letters she has that are written in Russian but came from a former East Prussian village. This is not a problem for Luise. She knows all three languages. Others join in and want to hear what's in these letters. Soon Luise is surrounded by a group of people, and she is at the centre of attention. Hans is surprised, and also a little proud. To see his sister again, like this, is something he had not expected. On this day, he finally invites Luise to his house.

However, she's quite busy caring for matters of other Wolf Children and can only take three hours off. When Hans's stepdaughter brings them coffee and cake, Luise notices something peculiar. She is not Hans's child at all, but the child of a Russian soldier … How does this fit in with the derogatory comments her mother always made about Luise being a 'Russian sister'?

At any rate, she is now in regular contact with Hans and through the many stories her siblings tell, Luise is able to complete the puzzle of her past, piece by piece. Her father dies in 1943 from lung cancer, leaving her mother alone with the children. The Nazi regime has forbidden the evacuation, threatening them with the death penalty, until it is way too late. When their escape is finally authorised, the Red Army had already advanced to the nearest city. It is simply too late. All residents are forced out of their homes and taken to a village several kilometers away. Here, at night, the soldiers come looking for the women and rape them. Her mother is one of them. One afternoon, Günther is sitting on her lap when a soldier gestures to her that she must come once again. Because she refuses to go with him, she is shot right in front of her children. This explains another mystery. While Luise is longingly waiting in the orphanage for her mother to arrive, she is already long dead.

The other siblings are not able to stay together. Edith is stuck in the Polish sector of East Prussia. The German schools here have been closed, and she's not allowed to go to a Polish school. It is forbidden for German children, so she begins to work at a very early age. To this day, she cannot read or write. In 1958, she's allowed to immigrate to East Germany, where she is immediately hired to work in a state-owned business. She marries at age 18 or 19 and has a number of children. She divorces, and, in all, marries three times. She inherits a pile of debt from her second marriage because she cosigned a loan for her son-in-law. It's only through Günther's help that she has managed at all.

'He invited her to live with him,' Luise explains, 'but she doesn't want to. Günther is strict and she wants her freedom. She doesn't know how to manage her money, though. Günther and I are the Prussians in the family.' This is why Edith's youngest daughter, Silvia, now takes care of her, because she cannot do it on her own.

Luise takes Edith to visit their oldest sister, Hilde. She was badly traumatised and often appears as though she is not really there, like she is sick. After being raped over and over after the war, she ends up working in a Soviet barracks. Who knows what happened to her there. In 1948, she is finally able to leave the Königsberger region and is relocated to East Germany. By the time she arrives in Germany, though, she has already sunk deeply into alcoholism. And that's where her life remains. Luise describes it like this: 'She has erased herself.'

Sometimes Luise telephones Hilde.

> I say, 'This is Luise, your sister.' She responds with a deep voice, completely unrecognisable. 'What do you want from me?' she says. That's always the first question. I always answer that I don't want anything, that I'm just calling to ask how things are going for her. *'Na ja.* Well, well,' is always the next thing she says. 'How is it supposed to be going?' she once said. 'If I were to write my memoir, it would be a heartless and cruel story.' That is my sister, Hilde.

Hans dies from an asthma attack in 2005. Luise continues to stay in regular contact with Edith and Günther, however. The last time they're together is in Berlin, in 2011. They're on a walk, looking for a café, and pass a supermarket. Luise wants to buy a packet of coffee. Günther goes in and buys her five, even though she doesn't even need that many. It's his way of showing how happy he is to have finally found his sister again.

Over the years, it becomes more and more clear to Luise how different their lives turned out.

> For example, it occurred to me that in Germany there's always the question, 'What are we going to eat today?' That's a significant question! But sometimes it really makes me mad. If I receive something to eat, well and good, and if not, that's fine too. Or the question, 'What kind of ice cream should we have today?' I love them dearly, but our interests are very different. They don't read books. They're only interested in soap operas …

The experiences Luise has with her siblings teach her that her real family was the one she had in Lithuania.

Edith and Günther never return to their East Prussian homeland. 'They didn't want to; they were afraid. And they're also living in their own world. Once when I wanted to watch a documentary on television, Günther was completely aghast. "You watch those Hitler films?" he asked. They never want to be reminded of that time, whatsoever.'

Luise understands him; looking back on that time is difficult, especially when he is someone whose mother was shot while she was holding him in her lap.

> I also don't like to be reminded. But looking back has also helped me to become more peaceful within myself. The relationships with the other Wolf Children, hearing their many stories, have helped me become aware that I'm not the only one. There were many of us, and many have much worse stories. And they too lost everything. Our pasts are really all very much alike.

We meet Liesbeth Dejok at her Lithuanian sister-in-law's farmhouse just outside Jonava. Here, we sit under an old apple tree in the garden on a sunny afternoon in July.

Liesbeth and her sister-in-law have set the table: coffee, fruit, cake, baked goods, bread, homemade butter, and quark. In front of the front door lie hundreds of freshly harvested garlic bulbs that will be sold at the market in Jonava. We estimate the proceeds to be maybe fifty euros. It's hard-earned money when one considers the planting, the harvesting and finally the effort of selling them.

'All these years I've regretted that I didn't stay in East Prussia,' Liesbeth tells us. 'I would have got out, too. But I could not have known that then. If I would have had a little more patience, my life would surely have taken a different course. But when you have no food, that is the worst.'

Liesbeth is innately an optimist. She loves to laugh, and only in unobserved moments does an earnest look cross her pretty face with its fresh red cheeks. The 80-year-old appears alert, and she speaks flawless German with a hint of an East Prussian accent. It sometimes sounds a bit old-fashioned. Mostly, though, it sounds charming. 'I have a strong German accent, or at least, the Lithuanians always notice right away that I'm not from here. Even then, I've never had problems here.'

Liesbeth loves her German name and is glad that her Lithuanian family modified it only slightly to the Lithuanian pronunciation. In their home she was called Elžbieta, she tells us as soon as we arrive.

> You know, I was a daddy's girl. It was always said at home, 'Liesbeth is just like her papa.' I even had pitch-black hair just like him. Home, my

Liesbeth Dejok.

> homeland, is the Elchniederung. That's where my family has lived for over 100 years. That's where I grew up, and it's where all the beautiful memories of my childhood are from. My father always taught us to believe in the goodness of humankind. When the Red Army arrived, everyone always said, 'The Russians are coming! The Russians are coming!' He believed that the Russians, too, are only human. That's what I always told myself back then as well, that I shouldn't be afraid.

Liesbeth's father's conviction was a widespread belief throughout East Prussia ever since the First World War. Then, there was a similar flight and expulsion out of the region when the war was over, but because the people were returned rather quickly, those who lived through it believed that this second time, too, their exodus would be short-lived. Furthermore, they believed the conquerors would come to their senses and let the industrious German farmers return to their homes as soon as possible. They believed this so strongly that the wide-reaching destruction of all the agricultural lands and the infrastructure with the invasion of the Red Army was simply unimaginable.

> I was 14 years old at the end of the war. Everyone talked about Lithuania and all the food there was to eat. All the teenagers I knew were on their way there. I figured I needed to go too. My siblings at this point were not as important to me. What drove me was my hunger. We simply had too little to live on and too much to die from. In Lithuania I received as much to eat as I wanted. It was a little like the land of milk and honey. Work didn't bother me, I always did it gladly. I lived with a very kind farmer's family. I was able to help on the farm, milk the cows, herd the livestock, and I was even able to do needlework, spinning and weaving. All these were things I had already learned back home.

When the farmer wants to get proper papers for her, he discusses the matter with Liesbeth beforehand. She remembers she had relatives who used to live in the Memel Territory, and he is able to register her as a Memel German. Now, unlike most other Wolf Children, she no longer has any troubles with the authorities.

'I quickly learned to speak Lithuanian. The farmer had a daughter who was a few years older than me, and she went to school. She always told me what something was called in Lithuanian, and when you are so young, you don't forget things so easily.'

At age 20, Liesbeth marries a Lithuanian, and over the next few years they have three sons. 'Our children, unfortunately, don't speak German. They only learned English in school and, of course, Russian.' Liesbeth regrets this, but on the other hand, she feels well supported by her children, as she's no longer able to live on her own. For many years, she and her husband lived in the village where they had a small working farm, and later the two of them worked on a collective farm. She now lives in two rooms in the house of one of her sons and his wife in Kaunas. This is where we visit Liesbeth. We find a modern family home that sits on the outskirts of the city in the middle of a grove of scattered birch trees. The only thing she misses, to this day, is her siblings.

> After I left for Lithuania, my sister, her daughter and my little brother were taken to the GDR. From there they fled to West Germany, to Westphalia. For many years I didn't know where they were. Later I found them as well as our older sister through the Red Cross. In 1989, I was able to visit them in Germany for the first time. The older sister had cancer; it really scared me. She looked so bad, she was hardly recognisable.

Bruno Klein never does find connections in Germany. Today he lives with his wife, Aldona, in one of the many Communist apartment blocks in Kaunas. When the two of them meet us at the door, Bruno quickly apologises that he can no longer speak German because he has barely spoken it in sixty-seven years. When the Russian soldier hit him over the head with a rifle butt, he became deaf in one ear, and after a stroke he has lost all feeling on one side of his body. His speech is slow.

Aldona helps him wherever she can, even when he speaks. When words fail him or he cannot remember certain things, she's there to interpret. This elderly woman has pinned her long white hair up, wears a fashionable dress and appears much younger than she really is. She brings us some family papers, documents and certificates. For her family it was never an issue that Bruno is German. 'Except for our children,' she explains. 'We baptised them under my name. It was at the suggestion of a woman at the registry office. She thought it would be better that way. It would help us mitigate any problems at school.'

In 1993, the children surprise their father. Now that there are no longer legal repercussions, all three—Elvira, Danutė and Vida—change their Lithuanian surname to the paternal family name of Klein. It is a symbolic act, but it means a lot to their father. It is but one more step on his life's path to leave the Second World War behind.

Bruno is from a large family with seven siblings. His oldest brother, Heinz, was killed at age 18 in the last days of war in 1945. Heinz was a typical older brother, Bruno's role model. Aldona rummages through the black and white photographs lying in front of her. The passport photo of a very young-looking soldier is of Heinz. A cousin sent it to Bruno as a keepsake. On the reverse, it says in awkward handwriting, 'Please take good care. This is the only picture. I have no others of Heinz.'

We even find a photo of his father, Willy. It's the only one Bruno has of him. It shows a Wehrmacht soldier whose face is nearly completely hidden beneath a steel helmet. On the reverse, this time very ornately written, it says, 'Your papa in distant lands. Düsseldorf-Gerresheim, 16.3.1942, prisoner of war, army field hospital Wachzug 2/217.'

We take our time looking through all the old photos, when Bruno abruptly shows us his Lithuanian passport. 'Right here, in my passport, it says that I was born in 1933. That is, of course, not true. But because of it, I had to work an extra year and a half before I could receive my pension.'

Before the Independence of Lithuania, before he received his birth certificate from Germany, he didn't know his birth date. A medical commission at the time wrote his birth date permanently into his passport as 00.00.1933; Birthplace: Kaliningradas, Rusija. Bruno is not alone in this. That the non-existent day, 00.00, is still being used infuriates him, as it does many other Wolf Children. 'Kaliningrad' as a term for Königsberg did not exist before 1946, nor did the Russian name. It was not even part of the Soviet Union yet. How, then, could he have been born there in the early 1930s? And how could Russia have been his birthplace? Before 1945, East Prussia no more belonged to the Soviet Union than it did to Russia.

The whole thing is all the more extraordinary when one thinks about how meticulous officials, even in the Soviet Union, are about correct documentation. It is certainly not an oversight, nor is Bruno's situation unique. Even in Lithuania, after regaining its independence in 1990, a number of those people holding the same incorrect passports that had been clearly issued out of a distorted ideology needed to go through a long legal process in order to have them changed. Bruno doesn't have the energy for that. With his birth certificate from Germany, he now has all the proof he needs. Paper is patient, as he tells us, and he has experienced that more than once in his life.

How is he doing now, I ask him. 'I receive 200 litas [about 57 euros] per month as "orphan's pension". I receive no pension for the time I worked as a farmhand nor for the first years that I worked on the collective farm where I hadn't been registered properly. So, in total, I average somewhat under 700 litas a month.'

These meagre 700 litas convert to just over 200 euros, effectively the amount that constitutes the poverty line. It is only through the private donations made possible by Wolfgang von Stetten that he manages to get by. Financially it is, nevertheless, tight, especially since the co-payments for his medications are often beyond his means.

To this day, the harmonious relationship he has with Aldona is what gives him the strength to go on. How did they meet, I ask. 'At a village dance,' Aldona answers with a smile. 'He was a great dancer! We often danced the polka for hours and to do that one really needs to move! In the villages,' she explains, 'it was almost obligatory for the young people to come to the dances. Someone would begin to play, sometimes a band played, sometimes it was an accordion player—and the young people all came to dance to this.'

Aldona and Bruno Klein have been happily married for more than fifty years.

But how was it when she finally decided to marry this German man? 'Life in the village was simple. And Bruno was not the only German there. Everyone knew, but he had a good reputation as a hard-working man. That's what mattered most.'

By the time they meet, Bruno has already been working on the collective farm. Even Aldona's father is unperturbed when she tells him they want to marry. 'Love is a funny thing,' is his answer, Aldona tells us. The greater debacle comes when they move from her parents' small farm into collective farm housing.

'It was a very socialistic system,' Bruno recalls. 'Everything was communal, and one had very little privacy.' This engaged couple lives here for five years before they're finally allowed to marry in 1958. One year later, their first daughter is born. In 1960, the next one; the surprise baby arrives in 1971.

In the mid-1970s, the family moves to Kaunas. For the most part, they make this decision because of better jobs. 'There was simply more money to be made in the factories,' says Aldona, who's been a welder for most of her life. Welding for the steel industry, constructing the parts for prefabricated apartment buildings, is hard work. In the beginning, Bruno works in the brickyards, but later he changes jobs and becomes a master welder. What's not easy for the couple is that, even though they worked for decades at hard physical labour, they receive such little pension. 'That's the disadvantage of freedom,' Aldona philosophises. 'Since Independence, we have mostly had to rely on ourselves.'

Bruno travelled to Germany once, and that was only after the border reopened in 1991. He went there to visit the estate of Wolfgang von Stetten with the other Wolf Children. 'My cousins, who lived several hundred kilometers away, came to see me when I was there. That was so lovely.'

Unfortunately, because of the inability to understand each other's language, the communication fizzled. Regardless, Bruno is glad he made the trip. It was a high point in his life, he tells us. 'Everything was so different from here, but also different from how it was back then in East Prussia. It was a little like—in a fairytale.'

Even though they shared a similar fate, 72-year-old Uwe Fritz is like the 'fairy godfather' to many Wolf Children. Tauroggen is the border town in southern Lithuania where many of the destitute East Prussians first arrived when they crossed over. This is where many a child was saved from sure starvation. Here, many received their first warm meal. And yet the area in the Memel region, even today, is not especially affluent. This is, in fact, where the weakest of the Wolf Children, the sick ones, the poor and those with no connections to Germany, live. It's a good thing that Uwe is here. He cares for his 'colleagues', as he lovingly calls the other Wolf Children, and looks in on them regularly. What he brings with him when he visits are bandages for open foot wounds, items for incontinence, salves, whatever is needed, whatever those with the direst needs can use. When it comes to financial concerns, he cares for them, too. And then there are those who have difficulty reading and writing or are unable to walk anymore and cannot get to the bank on their own. He cares for these things.

When Uwe Fritz is 6, his older siblings leave him behind in Lithuania. For months they had lived in ditches, freezing, their bodies emaciated. Towards the end, his sister needs to carry him, because Uwe cannot walk any longer. They finally find shelter with a family in a small farmhouse, where they stay for a short time. There's heat and for the first time in a long time, Uwe is given something to drink. It even warms him from the inside—and he learns it is vodka.

'We'll come back to get you,' his brother and sister promise when they take off the next morning. They have to leave, as the farmer cannot care for all three of them. But they never do return. Uwe stays and is eventually adopted by the farmer. The family had lost a son who was Uwe's age and give him his name and his official papers. Uwe Fritz becomes Bronius Dapkus.

Besides working hard in the fields, Uwe is also allowed to go to school, unlike many of the other Wolf Children. He does his homework late at night, and often, by the light of an oil lamp, he falls into a deep sleep. His adopted father loves to drink, and when he comes home at night and finds Uwe asleep at the table, as difficult as everything else is, he now does not hesitate to also give Uwe Fritz a sound beating.

All the difficulties aside, Uwe is one of the few Wolf Children who receives an elementary school education and can read and write in Lithuanian. He has a small house in which he lives with one of his sons and his family. Everything is built by hand, made themselves. Uwe is proud of this.

Uwe Fritz with his adoptive family, *c*.1947.

Together we make our rounds to visit those he feels most responsible for. 'Who else do they have?' he asks me, more rhetorically than anything else.

Yet, he has plenty of his own sorrows. Not long ago his wife died, whom he had looked after for five years during her illness. The other women in the association adore him, as for the most part, they've lived with men who are much different. Uwe now has painful rheumatism and has had several heart surgeries.

'My illnesses have everything to do with my childhood,' he explains. For months on end, he lived with hypothermia, frostbite and malnutrition, which have all left their marks.

Uwe's two older siblings arrive in Germany successfully, and through the Child Tracing Service they are able to find their parents again. His sister had told them that Uwe had died in Lithuania. What her reasons were, Uwe can only speculate. 'I think it was just easier to live with the certainty of a dead brother than it was to live with the uncertainty of a missing one,' Uwe says quietly, somewhat introspectively.

He came to terms with his past long ago. It wasn't until the 1980s that he first had contact with his family in Germany. He saw his mother just once before she died in 1985. But, right to the end, she could not believe that Uwe was really her son … because he was, of course, long dead.

'When I take care of the others, I forget about my own little woes.' Uwe pushes his bad memories to the side and adds, with an impish smile, 'Besides, I believe that good deeds are good for my heart.' The glass for Uwe, it seems, is always half full.

Anna Ranglack, who lives on the sixth floor of a Communist apartment block, tries to wrest something positive from her life. For ten years she wanders through southern Lithuania until, at the age of 16, she is finally adopted. 'Salvation in the eleventh hour,' she explains in all seriousness. Anna has worked hard her entire life, and she has never attended a school. To not be able to read has caused many limitations for this 74-year-old woman. Whether it's needing to read nameplates, timetables, recipes, expiration dates or songs in the songbook at her church, Anna understands none of it. 'It's as if I were blind. Without Uwe I would be quite lost.'

Annemarie Haupt is another one of those who Uwe visits regularly. Not only does Annemarie have terrible back problems, but she's going blind. Annemarie lives in a run-down apartment building. Her one-and-a-half-room apartment even has a balcony with a view of Tauroggen, but it doesn't do her much good. Her balcony merely serves as a storage area these days. Household items, like her toilet chair that she puts next to her bed at night, are stored here during the day. Hanging on the wall over her sleeping couch is a tapestry with a blissful scene in a forest. Deer watch over Annemarie as she sleeps. It is a picture that she has tried to keep vivid in her mind over the years. With every day, a little more of Annemarie's eyesight disappears, but her memories remain. Even those of her childhood.

Annemarie Haupt.

Kurt Grävert has been bedridden for many years. When we visit him in 2011, he not only has severe back problems, but also diabetes and a number of other diagnoses that will no longer let him get out of bed. He lives with his wife in an old farmhouse. The house is neither up to date nor appropriate for their age. There is no running water, even the laundry is boiled and washed by hand, and the home is heated with firewood. With all this, Kurt mostly lies in his hospital bed. It is the only modern piece of furniture in his home. His wife helps him with his personal hygiene as best she can. The caregiver that Kurt really needs is someone the two of them cannot afford. When a representative for the Wolf Children tries to visit them in 2014 the house is empty, and a neighbour informs him that the couple had passed away recently.

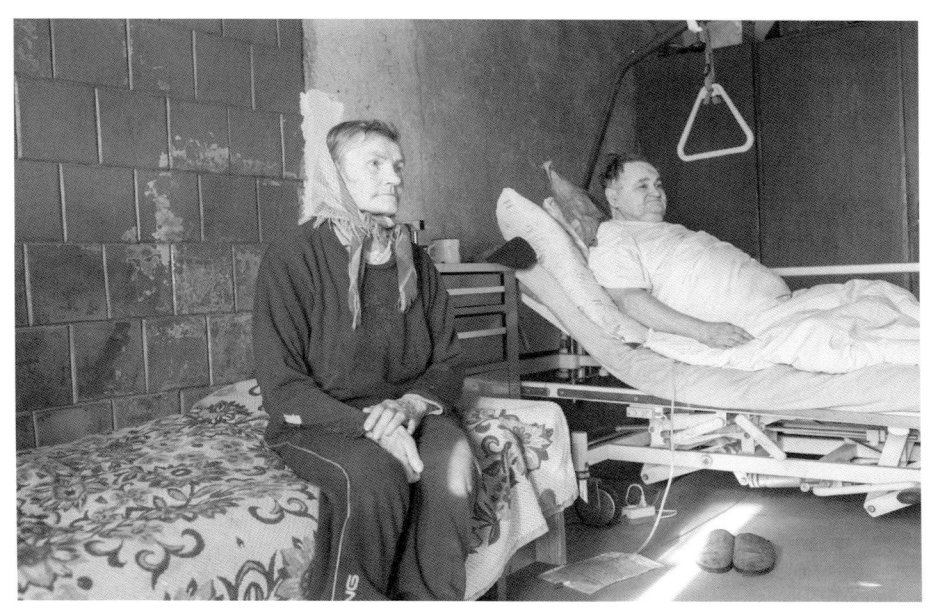

Kurt Grävert and his wife.

Karl-Heinz Methee lives not far from Kurt with his wife and two grandchildren. The youngest, a redhead in her teens who loves to play soccer, speaks German so well that her grandfather can hardly keep up with her. We are taken by her open, loving nature. Karl-Heinz, himself, has been paralysed on one side of his body after a stroke. To even go outdoors is something he hasn't been able to do for a long time. 'Everything is a struggle now,' this 76-year-old man tells us.

Käthe Rehberg lives with her daughter. 'Not how you would imagine it,' Uwe warns us. 'Rather simple …' When we visit her, we find that she lives in the basement laundry room of her son-in-law's house. Her voice quivers when she speaks. 'I have only this much and nothing else,' she tells us. 'Without the supplemental income from Germany, I would surely be dead. But even with this, I'm still not able to rent a room of my own, let alone have a place in the city.' In her 'living room', the 'salon', as she calls it, half underground, it's damp, cold, and uncomfortable. For us it's unimaginable that an old woman like this could even live here.

Our last visit on this day is somewhat further out in the country and is with Herbert Klein, who, like Uwe, comes from the Gerdauen district and is a widower. In 1948 he's picked up from his home by Russian soldiers, thrown onto a transport and taken to Siberia. In a dramatic turn of events, he manages to tear himself free while en route. With soldiers shooting at his back, Herbert swims across the Memel to safety.

Herbert Klein.

All that remains of Herbert's farmhouse.

Once settled in Lithuania, he attends tractor training school and becomes a 'tractorist', a job he works for fourteen years. After that, he moves on to become a farm smallholder. Herbert marries and he and his wife have three daughters and three sons.

He lights up when he sees us coming with Uwe. He lives all alone here at the edge of the forest in a tiny farm hut without any modern comforts. His garden house recently burned to the ground. The cause undetermined. But one thing quickly becomes clear. Among other things, Herbert has dementia. From time to time, we hear very clear German sentences coming from him, and then he disappears into a world of his own. Uwe is very worried about him, because Herbert doesn't seem to comprehend that he can't really cope by himself. 'One of his sons visits once a day and looks in on him. But he doesn't want to leave this place.'

When we are in Tauroggen again a few months later, Uwe gives us the bad news. 'Herbert's house has now also burned down! Luckily, he survived, but since then he's been living with his daughter in Klaipėda.' And sure enough, when we drive past Herbert's house in the village, it looks as if the earth had swallowed it whole. It burned right to the very foundations. Snow covers single beams that lie here and there where once a house stood. All that remains is the grey picket fence that once surrounded the house. Will the roses bloom here again when summer comes?

Seventy-five-year-old Waltraut Minnt lives near Tauroggen as well. Ever since Claudia and I met her in Germany, we knew that we absolutely wanted to see her when we came to Lithuania.

Besides friendships, there are also resentments and animosities amongst the Wolf Children. Waltraut is one of those who is perceived as odd and is even shunned by some. It takes much pleading and several attempts of asking before Uwe Fritz finally decides to take us to see her. He knows so many nice Wolf Children, hard-working, who have made something of their lives, despite their histories, he laments. And they, too, are quite poor. But he can't understand what we want with Waltraut. We remain patient, ask again and again, and finally, he agrees.

Waltraut's address is in a village near Tauroggen that stretches over a large, wooded area. We would never have found it alone, and even with Uwe's help, it's not easy. For an hour and a half, we drive in circles until, at some point, we run into one of Waltraut's daughters-in-law. She calls her daughter who lives with her grandmother in a hut at the edge of the forest. Yes, Waltraut is home, and of course we should drop by.

Completely out of breath, Waltraut runs towards us through a field. She's beside herself with joy. She has been waiting for our visit since May. It is now autumn. There are big hugs all around, and then she takes Claudia and me by the hand and shows us around.

She takes us into the little hut where she lives with her granddaughter. Two rooms and a kitchen. She shares the living and sleeping area with her teenager, which means that in this small, dark room there's a corner with a bed for the grandmother. The rest of the house belongs to her granddaughter, Aystė. On Waltraut's bed is a doll. Even this she shows us, like a proud doll-mother. In that moment, Claudia and I have the same thought: Waltraut is reliving the childhood she never had. She also shows us the handbag that she had with her in Germany. Everything that is near and dear to her fits in it. She has neither a wardrobe nor a dresser.

For our visit we sit in her kitchen. Waltraut tells us that the other day she got dizzy, fell over, and hit her head. She points to the bump on her head and the bruise. *'Ach, ach.'*

Where and when was she born, we want to know. She doesn't know this off hand; she must look it up. She finds a piece of paper. Naturally it's in her handbag. It states that she was born on 7 March 1936 in a small village in East Prussia. That's where she lived with her parents before the war—then, when everything was still in order.

Waltraut allows me to peer inside her bag. Aside from the hairpins that hold up her long dark, if much thinner, hair, I also find a small naked plastic doll, a cotton handkerchief, and a smoked sausage—the things that one just might need in life.

Waltraut Minnt.

Waltraut cannot remember the war itself. Only that her father and her oldest brother died in it. She and her four siblings stay with their mother on the farm after the war until the Red Army arrives. Two of her siblings die almost immediately—whether it is from starvation or an illness, Waltraut doesn't remember. Instead, she remembers songs that her mother taught her, and how to count. Clear as a bell and fully without an accent, she demonstrates to us, 'Eins, zwei, drei …'

Every few sentences, Waltraut begins to whisper softly as if someone might be listening in, like we're being eavesdropped upon. Often this apprehensive, reticent woman looks around. It appears as though she feels someone is watching, although far and wide, no one is here, other than us.

I ask how she met her husband. 'There were these people in the village, matchmakers. They would come and say, "I have a young man. He's older than you, but perhaps you'd be interested in him?"'

The one that is chosen for Waltraut interests her immediately and they're soon married. 'We married in the village. But then our wedding coach tipped over! Can you imagine?!' Luckily, no one was hurt. 'And anyway, I didn't have an expensive dress on or a long veil that could have been torn to shreds.'

After the wedding, the couple moves in with his parents on their farmstead. Soon they have children, six sons, all born in the 1960s. She remembers their names, but with the birth dates, things get a bit more complicated. She rummages awkwardly for papers inside her bag. Because she can hardly read, she seems to not find what she's looking for. Finally, she says Vaclavas was born in 1967. He was the youngest son and his mother's darling.

In the mid-1980s he was drafted into the Red Army, fulfilling his military obligations. Waltraut is heartbroken and has a bad premonition. Will she ever see this boy again, who was drafted into a regiment stationed deep inside Russia? Her other sons also went to the military and Waltraut never feared for any of them. But with her youngest, it's just different. And sure enough, Vaclavas, at the age of 20, is killed in a car accident while serving in the army.

All these years, Waltraut tries to lead a well-adjusted life, to be there for her children, keep up appearances and to tend to the small farmstead they have. But with Vaclavas's death, Waltraut's life falls apart. Everything that matters to her up to that point is no longer important. She now often goes into the forest, as she once did as a Wolf Child. This is where she finds her peace and serenity that were ripped away once again with the death of her son.

In all those years, she never received any support from her husband. Today she believes she would have been better off had she raised her children alone rather than stayed with this man. 'The man' was a drunk. He beat her, broke her ribs, and for years humiliated her in front of her children. There were many times when the police advised her to leave her husband, but it took years before Waltraut could find the courage to do so.

'Where would I have gone?' she asks. 'I just always prayed that peace would come to our house. Peace, peace, peace.' She wrings her hands. Two years after the death of her son and a year after the divorce, her husband dies from a stroke. That yearned-for peace finally does come to Waltraut's life.

Claudia takes pictures of her. Under no circumstance does she want to smile in any of them. Just don't open your mouth so that no one can see the bad teeth. This is not the first time we see this. Many of the Wolf Children have only a few brown stumps in their mouths, if any at all. Others have false teeth, sometimes a mouth full of silver or gold, sometimes both. But Waltraut is afraid to have the last of her teeth pulled. She would need to get a whole new set of false teeth. 'If my teeth are gone, my mouth will fall inward and how would I look then? And false teeth? I don't think I can afford that …' But she admits that her teeth are often infected and hurt rather badly.

What does she do with her time, I ask. 'I love to take walks, at all seasons of the year, especially in the summer.'

Yet, more and more, she's afraid to be alone in the woods. Heart problems bother her, and her blood pressure is not good. In the summer she often swims in a nearby river. When she does this, she brings her granddaughter along. 'No, I was never able to swim. I only go into the water up to my knees and then dunk under a little. This is how we always washed ourselves in the old days.'

There's no bathtub in her little house in the woods and no running water. In the winter they heat water to wash with on the stove in the kitchen—in the old tradition, with firewood.

What does she do during the day? *'Ach*, mostly I'm just tired. On some days I have no energy at all and I just shuffle along.'

No, she has no more desires for her life. To be alone, some tranquility, maybe. To occasionally have a piece of paper on which she can draw, and to sing, to herself. 'That's when I go back in my thoughts to my childhood.'

Waltraut shows us her pencil drawings. Ornaments, animals, mermaids. She would love to experiment with colours, but she can't afford them. 'That's something that must remain for the imagination …'

She has still not received her German passport. There's no question that she's German. Over and over, lawyers have contacted the federal offices trying to speed up the process for the exiled Wolf Children—but with little success. And Waltraut has no energy anymore to be concerned with it herself.

In the minutes from the reception for the Wolf Children with the then German President Christian Wulff at the Bellevue Palace in May 2011, there is an official notation: 'An elderly woman has lost consciousness in the salon. In order to stabilise her, she was laid upon a sofa, where, after a short time, she recovered.'

Of course, the notation is about Waltraut. To this day, the other Wolf Children are outraged at her 'circulatory issues'. 'She couldn't even keep it together at the president's residence,' Uwe Fritz groans. 'She just lay there like a princess on her settee in her castle. And right beneath a valuable oil painting! And she even looked completely happy. I don't know how she does it, always putting herself right in the centre of attention, so shamelessly.'

When I ask her about it, she giggles, 'For that one moment I was the Princess and the Pea.'

Typical scene in the countryside of Lithuania.

Chapter 15

Policies and Politics

When people in Lithuania talk about the Wolf Children these days, it's usually something like this: 'There was once a band of children from East Prussia who roamed the countryside as little beggars just after the war. Some of them ended up staying.' The stories are vague and come off as if most of these young people simply disappeared one day.

The exact numbers of how many of these wandering children there were have been puzzled over since it first became known in the early 1990s. In the Lithuanian national archives, there are numerous files with names of registered Wolf Children from the Soviet era but there are no definitive numbers. German sources allude to roughly 500 of those who stayed in Lithuania, whereas the historian Ruth Leiserowitz goes far beyond that number, believing it may well be upwards of 800—not including those who stayed behind in the Kaliningrad Oblast. One thing is certain, though: thousands of lost and abandoned children wandered through East Prussia and the Baltic States just after the war in 1945. Many of them died. Most of those who did survive were taken to the GDR or other territories in the Soviet Bloc up until 1951. But, for a few, Lithuania became their new home.

On 14 September 1991, the Wolf Children in Lithuania formed an organisation, calling themselves 'Edelweiss', named after the mountain flower so beloved in Germany that there are songs written about it.

'To make people aware of us, we published notices in all the newspapers giving information about who we were,' the Wolf Child Ruth Deske recalls, and soon their first meeting took place. Wolf Children came from all corners of the country. 'There were sixty-five Wolf Children at that first meeting. Some of them had never even disclosed to their husbands, wives or children that they had German roots.'

The group could not have been more diverse. Whereas some knew very little of their mother tongue, there were others who could still speak and write fluent German, like Rudi Herzmann. Rudi was born in the Gerdauen district in 1933, and, unlike most of the others, he never took on a Lithuania name. Others were so young when they came to Lithuania that they knew only their first names and that they once lived in East Prussia.

The founding of Edelweiss and its first years of existence were turbulent. The interests of the individuals varied tremendously and were often hugely in opposition to one another. While some hoped for financial support from the

188 The Wolf Children of the Eastern Front

Ruth Deske.

German government, others believed strongly that such expectations were wholly unrealistic and that they weren't in any position to ask for compensation. These were the people who were made to feel most guilty for the reason they needed to flee in the first place and the reason the rest of the East Prussians were expelled—even though they were only children when the war took place. This collective guilt is not surprising when one considers how long they were told the war was all their fault, especially given the anti-German propaganda that was prevalent during the Soviet era.

Claudia and I are sitting in a café in Kaunas with Margot Dudas one day in February 2012, when she suddenly has tears in her eyes. 'I don't know if I'm personally responsible for all that Hitler did to the world. But I have certainly paid bitterly for it. The most hurtful word I heard growing up was "Fascist".'

To the Communists, there was no worse form of expression against the undesirables, the pariahs of society, than this curse word. The 'Fascists' were the declared enemies of the people, embodying all that was evil in the world, and they, alone, were responsible for all the crimes that had been committed during the Second World War. They were watched day and night, discriminated against by the 'intelligence' agencies, and were not privy to certain opportunities in society, either for themselves or their children. They should be thankful, they were told, that, despite this shame, they were not also sent to the Gulag.

Rudi Herzmann barely escapes this harassment by the officials on more than one occasion.

> I was on the NKVD blacklist. I don't know how many times I was arbitrarily arrested by the secret police and then taken in for a hearing. To this day, I don't know what I did. I never did anything, but each time I was arrested, I was beaten, once over the period of three days, and always inside my prison cell, away from where others could see. I was actually almost dead after one of these beatings.

It is stories like this that the Wolf Children are finally able to share at their meetings, and, often, it is for the first time in their lives. While some Wolf Children hope Edelweiss will help them find relatives in Germany, others hope for representation on a political level. In February 1992, the board of directors sends this letter to the Lithuanian Speaker of the Parliament and highest government official at the time, Vytautas Landsbergis.

> Dear Sir,
> We turn to you, the head of our government and an individual known for his broadmindedness.
> We are children of Germans who fled East Prussia when there was no place left to go during the post-war years. Our mothers and next of kin starved to death or died in Soviet prison camps. We were young, left behind, dying of hunger, freezing, with nothing but the clothes on our backs, and, when all was said and done, treated like strangers in our own country.

Margot Dudas.

Lithuania became a good mother to us, who gave us shelter and cared for us, even though this very act of helping German children in those early post-war years was a guaranteed shuttle to a Siberian prison camp.

We are eternally grateful to the Lithuanians who were so good to us. We lost everything: our next of kin, our childhood, our names, and lastly, our own homeland. Nevertheless, East Prussia is still the place we came from. It is where the destroyed graves of our parents and ancestors lie. The churches at the graveyards that were used for shooting practice and the grounds that were so lovingly planted and cared for by our grandparents were destroyed by armoured tanks. We cannot forget these facts.

We are Lithuanian citizens and are hoping for your support. We kindly ask you to help us negotiate with Russia the following issues. ...

Three succinct requests follow:

1. For all former East Prussians now living in Lithuania, there should be some monetary compensation. 2. The Russian government is to open its secret State archives, especially as they relate to the East Prussian experience during the years 1945 to 1955. 3. All former East Prussians born before 1953 and who are now living in Lithuania should be allowed to move about freely in the Kaliningrad region. In other words, they should be given an unfettered visa.

But the Kremlin had other priorities. Since the independence of Lithuania in 1991, the Kaliningrad region lost its only shared border with the Russian heartland. Furthermore, the oblast had very little industry during the Cold War, and Russia now wanted to establish a special free trade zone in order to help create an energised economy in this otherwise underdeveloped area. By decree, Boris Yeltsin established the zone, only to abolish it again shortly afterwards. The danger of a growing separatist movement in an economically thriving exclave seemed too great a risk for Moscow.

Who within the Edelweiss committee pushed to contact the leader of the Free Trade Zone is no longer clear, but shortly after the letter to Landsbergis in August, the group petitioned the Kaliningrad governor, Yuri Matochkin. In their letter, the Wolf Children repeated what perhaps sounds somewhat naïve: they want restitution from the Soviet Union. On the whole, however, it is, if nothing more, a most remarkable attempt at civilian diplomacy:

We, Germans and children of Germans, who were forced out of East Prussia after the war and who then found shelter in Lithuania, are now turning to you. We hope for your candour and understanding of the problems that are as real to us as they currently are for you and for those people who now live in our former homeland.

The first problem regards the black cloud that hangs over our cultural heritage. The policies instituted by the governing bodies that are still in place today are worthy of criticism. Cemeteries, churches and estates have been destroyed. Yet to those people to whom these properties once belonged, who still live in their very neighbourhood, just across the border in Lithuania, they still hold meaning.

We believe with all our hearts that all of us now should work together peacefully. But this cooperation should be based on truth and humanitarianism. We believe the whole truth should be told candidly about the fate of the Germans in the post-war years in East Prussia.

What happened to the Germans in East Prussia in the early years following the war should be openly disclosed to the public. And not only us, the German children who were chased into a foreign country, but the current residents of the Kaliningrad Oblast, should honour the past.

Land, homes and property should be returned to their rightful owners. If they were destroyed, the owners should be financially compensated. We are aggrieved and astonished to learn that there are cases of illegal real estate transactions in which dishonest people have sold property that never belonged to them. It would be more ethical to ask the rightful owners if they would like to sell. This applies to the newly established Free Trade Zone in particular.

There are other problems we would like to make you aware of. For instance, what happened to the civilians from East Prussia who ended up in prison camps during the post-war years? There are several amongst us, who, as children, were victims of this very prison system.

We, and you, the past and current inhabitants of this country, need to know the truth, even if it is a bitter one. Thus, we request information on the aforementioned camps (1945–1955), the lists of prisoners taken to these camps, and the number of deaths that occurred there.

Also, we would like to ask you for the list of German children who were taken to the inner lands of the Soviet Union after the war in the years between 1945 and 1955 and where they ended up.

We ask for your humanity and understanding.

A well-composed response from the administration of the Kaliningrad Oblast, signed by the director of Nationality Issues, showed the other side was also interested in having an international understanding after the Cold War:

We would like to express our sincere gratitude for your letter that addresses our shared history. We can empathise with you, your feelings, and we understand that you, the people who suffered so terribly during the Second World War because of the disastrous circumstances that befell your parents, lost family members, lost property, and lost your homeland. However, the same is true for the former Soviet Union where over 27 million of its own citizens lost their lives.

We are making tremendous efforts to restore historic monuments in the city of Königsberg, including some of the German cemeteries in the districts of Prussian-Eylau, Gumbinnen and Insterburg. We have erected a memorial plaque at the battlefield in Großengersdorf commemorating both the Russian and the German soldiers who died there during the Seven Years' War [1756–63]. We have even re-established the Stablack cemetery near Klein Dexen in the province of Prussian-Eylau on the site where there once was a concentration camp. (A list of those people who died there is, unfortunately, impossible to obtain.)

Steps have been taken to restore cultural memorials as well. A Cultural Fund was, in fact, initiated for this effort. For example, we have invited experts from Germany to help restore the Königsberg Cathedral, and the Russian Society for the Upkeep of Memorials are closely involved in those efforts. To that regard, several notices have been published in newspapers about the reconstructions, in particular the restoration of the cathedral. …

We would like to let you know, too, that we are willing to discuss possible ways in which we can solve some of the issues regarding the children from this region who were affected by the war. …

We would, however, like to remind you that those German citizens who were forced to leave the former East Prussia were compensated for their material loss by Germany. But not all Germans applied. The process of restoring German citizenships is an ongoing process. The Russian government, along with the Interstate Council of the Germans in Russia, is reviewing all these issues, including questions of restitution.

We would also like to remind you that Russia did not start this bloody war and that the new borders were redrawn according to international treaties. Our shared goal now must be to prevent further conflicts.

We would like to express our sincere condolences and hope to continue to stay in touch with you. We would also like to let you know that we have established contact with the Republic of Lithuania. We took part in the opening of the memorial in Pagėgiai [the so-called 'Wolf Children Memorial']. We plan a similar memorial for the Kaliningrad Oblast. We agree with you that all peoples and states are called upon to work in cooperation according to the principles of humanitarianism, truth and peace.

This, one of the great moments of the Edelweiss Association, is a direct result of Lithuania's Singing Revolution and finally allows the Wolf Children to break their silence and speak out with a collective voice.

But one thing soon becomes clear: to receive any real help, it would need to come from Germany. The reinstatement of German citizenship, the ability to immigrate to the reunited Germany, or simply the improvement of their current living conditions in Lithuania—all these become the primary efforts of the Edelweiss organisation, and it is Germany that they now turn to.

In the autumn of 1993, 58-year-old Hildegard Sievers from Hanerau-Hademarschen writes a personal letter to the German president, Richard von Weizsäcker, who once served alongside Chancellor Helmut Kohl during Germany's reunification process. She is originally from Gerdauen and wants to make him aware of the lives of the Wolf Children who were left behind in the Baltic States. She writes:

> I was a 10-year-old child when I was part of the flight out of East Prussia in 1945, but I was one of the lucky ones who escaped the inferno. I am writing to you out of gratitude, and at the same time out of an obligation to the people who were hardest hit by the fate of that war.
>
> I am speaking of the Wolf Children who escaped to Lithuania in 1945 and ended up staying there. For the most part, they are now living in the direst of conditions. They were orphans whose families had died or they lost them in the chaos and confusion of the escape and never found them again. These were children who witnessed their mothers being raped and murdered. They were children who had to bury their families on their own. …
>
> One has to ask, how, after all that these children went through, did they find the courage to make the difficult journey to Lithuania where they then moved from farm to farm, begging for something to eat, sometimes for years? Who gave them the strength, when they were even separated from one another, having to figure out how to survive on their own during those first years of famine, and then needing to work hard labour as well? How do they manage today?
>
> They have life stories that one can only read and weep. How do they eke out a living, when they cannot afford clothing or shoes, and not even the most basic medications? While this plea is from my personal point of view, it is an urgent cry for help on their part. The plight of our 'Wolf Children' should be taken up by the German people out of compassion for their fellow countrymen. We cannot forget them!

On 7 December of that year, Germany's president answers her, saying he is 'deeply moved'. However, he does not directly promise anything. Instead, he advises her to contact the chairman of the German-Baltic Parliament Circle, Professor Wolfgang Baron von Stetten. He's a lawyer by profession, and a CDU (the Christian Democratic Union Party of Germany) representative in Parliament. He is the one German politician who has advocated on behalf of the Wolf Children, coordinating private donations, and persisted relentlessly to acquire federal funding for their help. Above all, he has called out the Kohl administration and other bureaucrats who have stood in the way, admonishing them for their lack of understanding, and apparent apathy.

The most pressing questions continue to be: will the East Prussians living in Lithuania regain their German citizenship? Will they be able to register as Lithuanian citizens without losing a potential German citizenship in the future? Can those who took on a Lithuanian name get their original German name back? Can their official documents be corrected to state the original German names of their birthplaces?

This last question seems to weigh on many of the Wolf Children most heavily, because, in fact, Kaliningrad did not exist when many of them were born—how can it then state in their Lithuanian passports that Kaliningrad, rather than Königsberg, was their birthplace?

In Lithuania, at this time, many are unemployed. Of those of German descent, it is about 60 per cent. Baron von Stetten, a compassionate man, personally answers all the letters he receives from Lithuania, and it soon becomes clear to him that humanitarian aid is desperately needed. He knows, too, that it will take a long time before any official support from the government will be made available, so he solicits private donations and information from places like the Red Cross and the registry for Germans living abroad, the *Standesamt 1* in Berlin. Von Stetten is a man of his word, and in his very practical way, tries to rally support.

His office manager, Monika Mandt, soon becomes quite the expert in all bureaucratic issues such as questions regarding Lithuanian name changes, the reinstatement of German citizenship, or locating lost relatives. She begins by creating lists of all the registered Wolf Children using both their Lithuanian and German names. Then she tallies the status of each individual, keeping a general overview of each of them. She eventually manages all correspondence, such as this letter written by an anonymous donor, someone who finally does disclose his identity. Because, as he puts it, he wants to make sure his (very generous) gift actually reaches the Wolf Children:

> The reason for my donation is simple: In the last months of war in 1945, I was in East Prussia in the heat of the battle, and there I met some of these so-called 'Wolf Children' personally (back then one did not call them that yet). Unfortunately, at the time I could not take any of the children with me and also could not help anyone. But their fates have haunted me to this day.

'The Wolf Children were in such a precarious situation,' von Stetten says, continuing:

> Quasi automatically, when they came of age, they were given Soviet citizenship. Then, with the independence of Lithuania, they automatically

became Lithuanian citizens. As it later became clear, this turned out to be a disastrous decision. Although they did not know, nor could they know, what the German law stated, they effectively lost their birthright to German citizenship. And, in nearly all cases, the Wolf Children actually wanted to remain German. From their understanding, this issue of German citizenship and their inability to have it reinstated had never been disclosed to them.

The failure of the German bureaucracy to do anything regarding the Wolf Children still outrages von Stetten:

Even though the Federal government sent officials to Vilnius, for weeks at a time, the ability to get anything done was a behemoth. Often the very same genealogical papers, such as marriage certificates and birth certificates, were requested again and again, documents the Wolf Children simply did not have, nor could have obtained. The fact that they did not exist was communicated to the officials, over and over, but to no avail. So not without reason, the ongoing wrongs that were done to them caused some of the Wolf Children to denounce their German fatherland for good.

Ingrid Knispel knows very little about her own past. She believes she may have been born in Königsberg in 1940, and her family might have lived in the borough of Ponarth. In 1994, she becomes the chairwoman of the Edelweiss Association. That year, the annual general meeting is held on a Sunday in May, Mother's Day. She starts the meeting with this prelude:

Let us remember our mothers today, who were driven out of their homes and, in so many cases, were disgraced, and who suffered tremendously for our sake. And let us also remember our second mothers, the Lithuanians who hid us, who cared for us and risked being taken to Siberia, for our sake.

For two long minutes there is silence in the room in honour of the German and Lithuanian mothers for whom the Wolf Children have their lives to thank.

Yet Ingrid Knispel does not mince words and she leaves no stone unturned. Especially to some of the older gentlemen, she sometimes comes off as rather rude. When she is interviewed by the daily newspaper *Lietuvos Aidas* (*The Lithuanian Echo*), she talks about the Mother's Day meeting wherein she called the German government to task and even suggests that if nothing comes from it, the Wolf Children would make their existence unequivocally clear to the German Embassy.

The indirect threat leads to a serious rift within the group.

Jonas Eidukaitis only knows his German first name, Hartmut, and believes he was born in 1944. Indignantly, he writes to Wolfgang von Stetten on behalf of those Wolf Children who are from Tauroggen to apologise for her manner:

We are most grateful for your noble and undying efforts to help us. We also want to apologise for those fellow members who continue to pester you with their endless requests. ... We do not, as a whole, support these appeals, and we are not prepared to bring the attention of an international scandal upon ourselves.

Ingrid Knispel, on the other hand, sees things much differently. She believes the German government clearly has the duty to work with the Wolf Children and that she has the constitutional right and, indeed, the duty to express her opinion publicly.

In the early years, most of the organisation's responsibilities have to do with the distribution of aid packages and Christmas presents coming from all the various sources. The historian Ruth Leiserowitz talks about the deliveries in those days. 'There was mayhem. People pushing in all directions wanting to get at the packages. I can only describe it as absolute chaos.' In her business journal she notes in 1993:

There is a noticeable social divide within the group. There are those who are quite poor and can no longer afford to travel to the meetings. Because of this, the relief packages end up going to only a few. ... I get the impression that the association was more or less founded only so that a few can enrich themselves materially at the expense of all the others.

Ruth Leiserowitz is only one of many critics of Edelweiss during these years. Wolfgang von Stetten doesn't want to get involved in internal quarrels and decides to give support to individual Wolf Children directly without going through Edelweiss.

The money comes from charities such as the 'Confrérie de la Chaîne des Rôtisseurs', a restaurateur guild of which Baron von Stetten is a member, and the Rotary Club of Germany. A notable pledge comes from an individual, Hedwig Stauder, who grew up a half-orphan. She was born in Stuttgart in 1902, and, after a successful career as an executive in the automotive industry, turned her estate over to an endowment for the Wolf Children. From the start, she champions Wolfgang von Stetten and his initiatives to support the Wolf Children. Even after her death in 1996, her endowment continues to grow. Over the twenty years since 1992, roughly €800,000 have been donated through von Stetten's efforts, all of it passed directly on to the Wolf Children without paying anything for overhead expenses.

And yet there are critics of the private donation system that Wolfgang von Stetten has created. They argue that rather than giving the Wolf Children money, they should send relief supplies instead. There's always the fear that the money could be spent on alcohol.

These are accusations that von Stetten has no interest in engaging with. And, as he says, there has yet to be someone who's done it any better:

> Because of the poor schooling they had when they were young, if at all, the Wolf Children who stayed in Lithuania were never able to pursue a career or gainful employment and thus they receive the lowest level of social security benefits. For nearly all of them, these meagre funds have them living below the poverty line. The extra money they now receive is also no greater than the lowest standard for welfare.

And he does not waver in repeating this one sentence: 'They must be able to count on our support, so that the lives of the Wolf Children will not end in the same way they began—begging in the streets.'

When Claudia and I drive through the rural areas of Lithuania to visit the Wolf Children, who for the most part live in the poorest of conditions, we think that these donations have been well invested. There are those in need of nursing care who live in farm shacks where there's not even running water. And there are those who are bedridden and yet cannot afford to pay for their medications or other medical supplies on their own. For them, this money is a matter of life and death.

It is not true that the Wolf Children only wait for handouts from the outside world. Much more accurate, and at the same time touching, is what we witness—how much they do to help one another. Whether it's Uwe Fritz in Tauroggen, Ruth Deske in Schaulen or Luise Quitsch from Vilnius, they all make themselves fully available to the poorest of the poor amongst their fellow countrymen.

Herbert Klein's farmhouse kitchen.

But even von Stetten never stops in his continuous efforts to help in whatever way he can. Above all, he wants the Wolf Children to live the waning years of their lives with a sense of security. He eventually manages to create a much-simplified application process for the Wolf Children to regain their German citizenship. Only someone who has seen the tremendous amount of paperwork the Wolf Children once needed to fill out to prove their German roots can appreciate how much this message means to them. After years of wrangling with bureaucrats on all levels, they will finally be recognised as Germans.

Now, for many, there's no longer a reason to stay in Lithuania. They fill out their applications and leave the country as soon as they are able. Those who stay behind because of family or because they are too old to make such a big move begin to receive a small supplement to their pensions, as of 2008, from the Lithuanian government. It is the so-called 'orphan's supplement' that is paid to pensioners who lost their parents during their childhood. Even with this, most of the Wolf Children receive less than the 700 litas considered to be subsistence living in Lithuania. Only through the donations that Wolfgang von Stetten sends are they able to eke out a living beyond this bare minimum.

In October 1998, Luise Quitsch is voted in as the chairwoman of the Edelweiss Association. Of the roughly 200 members who once made up the organisation, thirty-eight immigrated to Germany and twenty have died. With all the changes, those who remain will now be helped through the revised German legislation—but for many it is too late.

In July 2000, Wolfgang von Stetten receives yet one more, rather sad, letter. It is penned by Juratė Siurkienė, the daughter of Manfred Swars:

> I know how much you've done for your countrymen. So many of us were forsaken and forgotten, yet you always came through. But today, I write regarding my own situation.
>
> About five years ago, I applied at the German Embassy in Vilnius for permanent residency in Germany. The Embassy told me it would take some time. After four years, I was finally notified that I could now immigrate with my father. There were still a few papers that were needed, and I sent them to the Embassy right away. But suddenly my father became ill and died on 11 July 1999. Everything was already packed, and we would have been able to immigrate immediately. But now I've been informed by the Embassy that my reason for permanent residency in Germany is no longer valid.

Juratė is beside herself. It appears she must now start from scratch to prove that she really is German, something that has already been stated so succinctly in all the official documents she's already handed over to the officials.

> My father is no longer alive, and I cannot unbury him so that I can prove that I am actually his daughter and therefore am German, and I thus have

every right to live in Germany. I am 32 years old and I am a teacher by profession. I have two children whose mother tongue is German. My mother was exiled and spent ten years in Siberia. Other than that, I have no other relations in Lithuania.

She isn't the only one who, through the early death of a parent, loses her opportunity to immigrate to Germany. Only once Lithuania becomes a member of the European Union in 2004, does Lithuanian citizenship allow one to move freely within the EU.

In May 2011, on the twentieth anniversary of the Singing Revolution, Wolfgang von Stetten invites the Wolf Children to Germany. One of the highlights of the trip is a reception with the German president at the Bellevue Castle in Berlin, the official residence of the German president. For the thirty-five attendees, it is a moving moment when they are received by the head of state of the country that, after twenty years of negotiating, could not manage to appropriate at least a modest pension for them. But for this one short time these thoughts are forgotten. Anna Ranglack speaks for many of the women there when she says that in this moment, she 'felt like a princess'.

As a finale to the trip, there's a ceremony at the von Stetten Estate in Künzelsau. In attendance are Vytautas Landsbergis, the former Speaker of the House, the Lithuanian ambassador, as well as Antanas Račas, one of the signatories of the Lithuanian Declaration of Independence. Among the invitees is also Ursula Dorn, for whom this event is of historical significance. She too once travelled through Lithuania, begging with her mother, and considers herself to be one of the Wolf Children—even though she was technically not all by herself. Now, in the presence of one of the most senior politicians of the Republic of Lithuania, Vytautas Landsbergis, she reads from the letter she had written to him in February 1992:

Your Excellency!
You will be surprised to receive a letter from a simple woman like myself from the land of Germany. But I just had to reveal my heart to you. I want to thank, with all my heart, all the many kind and loving Lithuanian people who saved the thousands of German—now adult—people from certain death. And please make this a public announcement on the television, so that all of your fellow countrymen will know how grateful we are for the good deeds they did for our children after 1945.

Thank you, thank you, thank you. This letter is finally saying what has been weighing on my conscience for a very long time. I would love to visit your country once again. For me, that would be the greatest joy, as to me, Lithuania has become much more than just the place of my birth, Königsberg. I consider it my home.

That her feeling of gratitude and her sense of homeland relate more to Lithuania than to Germany is not out of the ordinary. Rudi Herzmann's family once owned a 120-acre piece of land near Gerdauen and belonged to the well-to-do class of East Prussian farmers. After the war, his mother loses both Rudi and his sister, Christel, while on the flight. She reaches Germany alone and assumes her children are dead. However, at the end of the 1950s, the family is able to find each other again through the Red Cross.

Christel is allowed to leave Tauroggen and go to Germany. However, for Rudi, one of only three Wolf Children who live in the tiny village of Tursučiai, to travel for a reunion with his German family is invariably denied. He goes to Moscow three times wanting to get a visa from the German Embassy so that he can visit his family. Twice, the Russian guards do not even allow him to enter.

On the third try, Rudi hides in the bushes outside the embassy and waves down a diplomat's car as it drives up. The driver, knowing well what is at hand, snaps at the Soviets in their uniforms and sees to it that Rudi is allowed to get inside. At the reception desk, the clerks help him, but later, Soviet officials once again refuse to issue Rudi the proper travel papers. The reason given is that he is still blacklisted, having once been of interest to the NKVD. Finally, he is given permission to visit his mother, but only for a short while, and Rudi's Lithuanian wife must stay behind as a 'pawn' to make sure he'll return.

In 1991, Rudi Herzmann is one of the first to fill out an application to immigrate to West Germany. It takes years before all the approvals and documents are in order, and even after that, there's still a waiting period of several years. Sadly, it's too long to be able to see his mother again. She dies in 1996, and Rudi and his wife, Romalda, are not allowed to go to Germany until a year later.

When they arrive, they are held in a resettlement camp for a week where they are treated like asylum seekers from other countries, not the German citizens they really are. Eventually they are given an apartment in a housing project in Cologne. The meagre government assistance they receive is barely enough to live on—they had, of course, never been able to contribute to the German social security fund.

Living in a big city is difficult for Rudi, who spent his entire life in the country. Furthermore, it hurts him deeply that he is perceived, not as a German, but as a foreigner, by the officials. East Prussia is by now a concept difficult for most people to grasp as anything tangible. It no longer exists, and to Germans, it has become part of a buried past. For thirteen years Rudi and Romalda stay in Cologne, trying to make life work, but finally they decide to move back to Lithuania. For Rudi, the decades-long unfulfilled dream of living in Germany is never fulfilled in the end.

'In Germany I felt more like a foreigner than I ever did in Lithuania,' Rudi tells us when we meet with him in his house back in the village near Marijampolė, where he has lived most of his life.

Chapter 16
Longing for Königsberg

As we begin to plan our next research trip for the autumn of 2011, Claudia and I discuss the organisational challenges of visiting the Russian land that was once East Prussia. We wonder if it would be better to fly directly to Kaliningrad and rent a car there or if we should drive from Lithuania and take the Wolf Children with us. While the geographical distance isn't great, entering Russia by land is quite time-consuming, as are the roads that are in terrible shape. On the other hand, we know that travelling across the border is quite stressful for the Wolf Children. If they were to meet us in Kaliningrad, we cannot be sure that they will not back out at the last minute. Claudia lives in the Netherlands, I am in Germany, and Luise Quitsch, who has been so helpful with everything concerning Lithuania, lives in Vilnius. Planning a trip to a country like Russia is never simple.

We know we absolutely want to take Christel Scheffler with us to Königsberg. She is the Wolf Child who had so openly shared her deepest desire to return to East Prussia, and she had such detailed memories of her home at the Fichteplatz in Ponarth. We would also like to have Luise Quitsch come, especially since her home had been out in the country in the district of Labiau. But at first Luise is evasive. She's used to being the one who is there for others, escorting tour groups and accompanying Wolf Children on their visits abroad. That she should now be focused upon is uncomfortable for her. Or so we think. But maybe it's the images and memories that she doesn't want to dredge up.

Christel, on the other hand, will only feel comfortable going on this venture if Luise comes along too. 'I asked Luise quite frankly if she even wants to come to Königsberg,' Claudia tells me over the phone. '"To be honest," she answered, "not really … But I'll do it anyway."' Luise doesn't want to leave us hanging, and she knows how much it would mean to Christel. I am thankful to Claudia, in the end, that in her mild-mannered way, she was able to convince her to come.

We want to also make a second trip, which would be to Gerdauen. Uwe Fritz is from the area, as is Anna Ranglack. Uwe wants to come with us, no question. He's adventuresome and, anyway, he's always so happy to see us. With Anna it's a bit more difficult. Because of family obligations, in the end, she cannot go.

Luise suddenly realises that her passport will soon expire, which means she may not be able to get a Russian visa in time. So, she applies for a new passport right away. Then there's one more problem, we realise. We also need to have an official 'invitation' to travel in Russia. As it turns out, in this now capitalistic country, we can buy even that.

Claudia and I decide we will drive from Lithuania to Königsberg, back again, and then make a second trip to Gerdauen. But a double entry on the tourist visa is something the Russian immigration office has not anticipated. For me, it takes only a few words of explanation, but for Claudia, the Russian Embassy in Amsterdam is a bit more sceptical. She's required to write a detailed travel plan and up until two days before we're to leave, we still don't know if she'll even be able to go.

The rental car gives us equally as many headaches. One cannot rent a car over the internet to cross the border into Russia, or into Kaliningrad Oblast. '*Nyet*,' is the answer, no matter where we turn. We decide to wait until we get to Lithuania to resolve the problem.

On our departure day, I arrive in Vilnius before Claudia, and I have time to visit a few of the rental car agencies at the airport. Even here they are not enthusiastic when I tell them about our plans. One rental car agent has a few cars that, in principle, will be allowed into Russia, but as a rule they need to be reserved half a year in advance. I would need to have a special kind of insurance, for which they need time to prepare. Then, ten minutes before Claudia is to land, a rental agent approaches me with a friendly smile. 'Of course, I have cars for you!' We barter a bit over size and price and come to an agreement. It's a huge load off my mind, because taking the tour in a taxi would have been our only other option.

Claudia's visa arrived shortly before she was to take off, and she has it in her hand. Now nothing more should stand in the way of our journey to retrace the Wolf Children's past. We leave early the next morning for Tauroggen, where we pick up Uwe. From there it's not far to the Königin-Luise-Brücke, the 'Queen-Louise-Bridge', which crosses the Memel River over to Tilsit. The bridge is one of the most important border crossings for automobile traffic between Lithuania and the Oblast, and yet our crossing takes hours.

To begin with, we stand in a long line of traffic in a parking area off to the side. After two hours we're at least able to see the Lithuanian border patrol house and what we assume is the famous bridge. When, and more importantly why, this line moves or does not move is not clear. Every half an hour, a few cars drive forward, and then everything stops again. It is a sunny day, and every now and then we step out to stretch our legs. Uwe chats with other drivers and sometimes returns with some tea. Finally, it is our turn. The toll gate lifts and we drive onto the bridge.

Our car once again comes to a halt. We are in the middle of the bridge and peer down at the river. The Memel looks daunting! It is unimaginable that there was a time when children tried to cross the river here, clinging onto nothing but a piece of wood. Claudia and I both have children between the ages of 9 and 11. The thought that these children were the same age when they were here alone makes us both feel sick to our stomach.

Then we start to creep forward. It is now noon. We had wanted to make the round-trip journey in one day. In kilometers, it's only a stone's throw, but that plan is looking doubtful at this point. Will the border patrol keep us so long that we really won't be able to return in one day? At times, Uwe cheers us up with jokes, at other times we have a good laugh at the Russian border policewomen, whose uniforms with their short skirts and leather boots, cap tipped to the side and long fingernails, look like they could be auditioning for a part in a James Bond film.

We finally get to the head of the line. At a small kiosk, we hand in our passports, and in exchange we are given a handful of Russian forms to fill out. No, they don't come in any other language. Yes, fill them out in Cyrillic lettering. They turn out to be customs papers for the rental car.

Two years of Russian in school finally pays off. Sister Albertina, my one Russian language teacher who still gave grades for 'good Cyrillic penmanship', would have been proud of me. Eight pages later, and with frozen fingers, I finally pass the forms back to the woman on the other side of the window. Claudia and Uwe have been waiting patiently. We all think things will get going now. We're so near our goal! But one look from the border patrol woman is enough to know that things are going to still take time. 'Not nicely enough,' she says in broken German, with a grin, and hands me new forms to fill out.

She can speak German! I am bewildered and try to negotiate with her. But there's no changing her mind. For the next half an hour, I again stand in the windy passageway and draw the cleanest and prettiest-looking Cyrillic letters I know how to make and put them into their proper tiny fields.

When I knock once again at her kiosk window, frozen and looking like a poor beggar woman, I put my friendliest smile and try to be optimistic. Surely it will work this time. '*Nyet, nyet, nyet*! Not like theese!' she shouts at me.

I can't believe it! Claudia steps out and asks what's going on. She's the more patient of the two of us, but even for her, this is the last straw. And Uwe looks distressed. He doesn't think this entry will happen at all anymore.

The third time is a charm. Together, Claudia and I fill out a new set of forms, and this time they are accepted. To us, the third try looks exactly like the first one did. It seems to be just part of the regular harassment meted out to their Lithuanian neighbours. Uwe is convinced that none of this would have happened if we had arrived with a German, or, even better, a Russian, licence plate.

At around 3.00 pm, we are finally in Wehlau. Claudia steps out to take some photographs, while we consider how to move forward. The small wooden bridge that leads into the village does not exactly instil confidence. The pedestrian bridge next to it is missing several planks, and a misstep would not be good. Is the vehicle bridge any better?

There's another problem. Ever since we exited the main highway to turn onto the road to Kaliningrad, we have not seen a single filling station. To be safe, we want to fill up before we end up stranded somewhere in the dark without petrol. In a small village, some passersby point to where we should go. We drive on, passing dilapidated Communist apartment buildings, yet we never do see a filling station. However, off in the distance there are two big oil tanks that have LUKOIL in giant red letters written on their sides. We decide to drive over to see what it is, but we find it surrounded by a barbed wire fence with an iron gate, and it is locked. A helpful watchman comes over to us and explains that we must go back in the opposite direction.

What he points to is not exactly a petrol station in the conventional sense. Without his advice we would never have found the single hand pump sitting in the middle of a dusty car park. We drive to the back of the car park, where a young man wearing sunglasses steps out of a silver Airstream mobile home and hands us a permit, allowing us to use the spigot. The readout on the pump shows only the litres, not the price. But what choice do we have?

Our journey continues. We make good time as the long tree-lined cobblestone roads are not well-travelled. We see old people sitting in front of their houses soaking in the warm afternoon sun. Sometimes schoolchildren run alongside our car. Suddenly, Uwe lights up. We've come to his home town! We are just on the outskirts of Gerdauen. To our left, through the woods, we can see a Russian Orthodox church with two shimmering blue and white onion domes. Uwe points and explains, 'Back then, this was, of course, not here.'

We drive on, straight towards a lake. The city sits on a hill just behind it. As we drive further, we pass a gristmill, the local brewery, and finally we park our car in the market square. Things look downtrodden, a bit shabby, and Uwe just shakes his head and, as if apologising, he says that it once looked much prettier. On the opposite side of the square, we notice a young policeman walking about, but we don't pay him much attention.

From a Western perspective, Gerdauen, with its population of less than 3,000, is more a village than a town. In the middle of the market square, we see a building that looks like it could be a city hall. It has a sign in the window advertising that it is actually the district information centre. Unfortunately, it is closed. A woman approaches us and asks us if we are tourists. Uwe proudly explains that he lived in Gerdauen as a child and that he has many lovely childhood memories that have beckoned him back. She and Uwe continue to exchange words for some time. The woman has a long pointy face and is wearing a nearly fashionable hat under which she has fire-red hair. I can understand only about half of what they're saying, but the two are having a rather engaged conversation. In the meantime, Claudia has wandered off. This is not unusual. She often takes off in search of subject matter to photograph, finding still moments, even here.

The circle of houses behind the market square is falling in. Some were burned out and never rebuilt. Walls framed in old German half-timbers, that even sixty-

Claudia and Uwe Fritz talking with a Russian woman in Gerdauen.

five years after the war, still hold up half the building. I can't believe that people live inside these ruins. Clothes lines run from house to house, dogs wander around, and children play in the rubble.

In the summer of 1914, Gerdauen was more destroyed than it was in all the years of the Second World War. After the First World War, with the financial support of its sister cities, Budapest and Berlin-Wilmersdorf, it had been restored to its old German style. To this day, one can still see architectural remnants of historic city planning—thatched roofs, red-brick churches, cobbled streets and timber-framed houses, the old city square.

Gerdauen was once at the crossroads between East Prussia—the breadbasket of the German Reich—and the mainland of Germany and became an important shipping centre at the turn of the twentieth century. In 1945 and the years that followed, it also became a gathering point for many Wolf Children as it lay on the main train line between Königsberg and Lithuania.

When the war ended, the borders between Poland and the Soviet Union were moved and Gerdauen was annexed into the Kaliningrad Oblast. In 1946, the city was renamed Shelesnodoroshny, which translates as 'train city'. In the first few years, the city remained well preserved, but with the new borders, the economy came to a standstill and ever since the 1960s, a marked decay has set in.

Uwe wants to show us the parish church. It is an impressive monument built in the first half of the fifteenth century and was once attached to the city wall. Over the centuries, though, it was damaged—by lightning strikes, fires and shelling. Up until the Second World War, efforts had always been made to keep it in good condition. Showing it to us is important to Uwe, because it had always been the pride of this city.

From 1948 to 1957, the building was converted to a city hall and cultural centre. Then, as so many houses of faith in East Prussia, decay set in. The Russian military had used it for target practice in the early post-war years. Later, farmers used the nave as a barn for their cows. Children, ever since, have played hide-and-seek in its dark corners. The roof finally fell in in the 1970s. Today, all that's left of the church are its foundations. The roof is missing and the interior is overgrown with weeds. In the early 1990s, a German architectural preservation group began restoring the steeple and the remaining walls, but whether the church itself will ever be used again for worship is doubtful.

The three of us wander around the ruins, and Uwe takes us to a spot he knows with a beautiful view over the Banktinsee. Suddenly we hear the laughter of children. We turn and see little fingers pointing at us. Strutting just behind them is a uniformed man. It turns out he's the police officer from the market square, and he wants to see our authorisation papers. Which authorisation papers? We aren't just acting surprised, we are.

He explains that we're inside a military restricted area and, without permission, we're not allowed to be here. I am incensed. First all the fuss at the border, and now this. Claudia shows him her passport and tells him that her visa specifically states Gerdauen as part of her travel route. That could very well be, the uniformed man says, but a travel visa will not suffice. In fact, we must now go to the *Kommandantura* in Kaliningrad to turn ourselves in.

Uwe tries a new approach: being nice. He's an old man who grew up here in Gerdauen, he explains. We really didn't want to cause any problems. Claudia and I are his granddaughters, and he only wanted to show us the place where he lived as a child. He knew nothing about a military restricted area. The police officer's face relaxes a bit. He needs to make a phone call, he says, and pulls a mobile phone from his jacket pocket to call his supervisor.

Over and over, he nods his head. '*Da. Nyet. Da. Da, ponyal.*' He hangs up and smiles at us. We should take to the road, he says, and 'don't waste any time doing it.' If he finds us here again, there will be no pardon. Uwe thanks him graciously. Claudia and I are dumbfounded, but nod and go off with Uwe on the fastest route back to the car. None of us are interested in any more of this sort of Russian red tape.

Once back at the car, we sigh with relief. Throughout the entire interrogation, Claudia and I worried that her camera equipment could be confiscated. Although she had hidden the camera and its telephoto lens under her jacket, we had no idea how long he'd been watching us, or if he knew she had it. What about the photos she took of the 'military restricted area'?

It was a short visit to Uwe's home town, but we're happy to have been there at all, and Uwe is beside himself with joy. Most of all, he's happy to have pulled one over on the Russian police officer. We are now, and forever will be, officially his granddaughters.

Uwe wants us to drive on to Allenburg. Today, it's called Druzhba, or 'Friendship', the village where he was born and where he spent part of his childhood. It lies on the way to our next destination, and he believes that the house where he lived could still be standing. He wants us to pull over at a lot that looks like an industrial wasteland. Standing in the middle of the lot is a huge brick building that has gone to ruin. 'That was once the creamery,' he tells us. 'It was where my father worked, and I could see it right from my bedroom window.'

We look over to the houses on the other side of the street. Would he like to drive over there, we ask. Uwe nods. We go down the main road until we come to a crossroads. To the left and at the end of the street is a house with a pretty garden and a picket fence. Uwe is sure this was once his family home. A little dog runs around the yard, yapping at us, and finally a kind-looking man comes out of the door. Can he help us, he asks. Uwe wipes a small tear from his eye and explains that he was born in this house. The man's wife comes out of the house to join us. She listens with intent. Uwe describes the interior of the house, and at some point, the two can no longer help but invite us in. They have renovated a little, but in general the house is just as Uwe remembers it.

We go upstairs into his former bedroom and indeed, from there, we can see directly onto the old creamery. For a moment, Uwe looks like that little boy from the past. In his mind, he tells us later, it was just like he was there. Even the old, brown tiled stove is still here. 'This is where we, as children, used to dry our wet socks and mittens in the winter,' Uwe tells us and asks Claudia to take a photo of him standing in front of it. Uwe thanks the Russian couple for having allowed us into their home, and we take our leave.

Evening is approaching and we want to start our journey home. Uwe seems to be in another world. We arrive in Tilsit and realise it is Friday evening. Evidently, we're not the only ones who still want to get to Lithuania before the weekend starts. How long are we going to have to wait this time, Uwe asks some of the other drivers. From their experience, we should count on at least six or seven hours. Claudia and I are prepared to deal with it, but we worry about Uwe. We feel it may be too much for him. We discuss it with him and come up with an idea. He should take the pedestrian walkway over the bridge, where on the other side he can catch a taxi back to Tauroggen. It's the best solution, we think, even though Claudia and I don't really want him wandering around this particular border on his own. Claudia walks him to the toll gate, says goodbye, and watches as he starts a conversation with a Lithuanian driver. The driver gives a friendly nod and lets Uwe into his car. At least we know he won't have to cross the border all alone.

Uwe Fritz standing at the cockelstove in his childhood bedroom.

Back in Vilnius the next morning, we pick up Luise and drive with her to Jonava, where Christel Scheffler lives. She's been eagerly awaiting us. Does she have the travel bug, I ask her. 'But of course! I'm so excited, I've not been able to sleep for days!'

This time we drive to the Russian border at Kybartai (Kibarten). Once again the line is at a standstill, and we pull over to wait at the side of the road. I tell the others that my Finnish grandmother thinks I'm crazy for wanting to drive to Kaliningrad. Wild horses couldn't drag her to Russia, regardless of where, she told me. Luise thinks this is funny. 'I like your grandmother!' she says. When I go on to tell about my sister who painted her house blue, and my grandmother, who passes by this house every day, nearly fainted when she saw it, Luise laughs out loud, even before I can finish making my point. 'Russian-blue!' she snorts. Grandma Helfrid seems to have made a lifelong friend.

Just past the toll gate are two lanes. The lane we are motioned to stand in is the slowest one—of course. When a car with French plates rushes by in the other lane, I ask the border guard why he's allowed to do this. He shrugs his shoulders and answers, 'Russians.'

Luise explains, 'When you have a Russian passport, you don't need to show any other documents. It's everyone else who needs to wait.'

Somehow, we have arrived during the Russian lunchtime. Nothing moves for hours. Anticipating this, Christel has packed some butter sandwiches and Luise baked her famous hazelnut cookies. At least we won't starve. But Christel is tense. We can clearly see that all this waiting is very stressful to her. The Lithuanian border patrol comes by to chat with us from time to time, but he too doesn't know what's going on. When the light on our side turns green, the next toll gate goes up, and one more car is allowed to drive into the Russian zone. Finally, by late afternoon, it is our turn. There are two more inspections and eventually we are on the A229, direction Kaliningrad.

It's only 160 kilometers, but it takes us three hours. The sky turns crimson, and we can't help but think about Königsberg as it was burning, stories the Wolf Children had told us, how the sky had turned a deep, deep red from the glow of the fire.

We finally arrive at our hotel in the Steletskaya Street near the Königstor, the 'King's Gate'. It's a newer building with modern rooms, and the four of us are happy to have arrived.

Not far from the hotel is a restaurant where we want to invite Christel and Luise for dinner. But Christel is especially overwhelmed. A mixture of culture shock, memories and insecurities has done her in. Luise asks her several times if she would like to share a hotel room with her so she won't feel so alone during the night. But Christel shakes her head, no. In the restaurant she keeps looking around, moving her head back and forth, looking first to Claudia, then to me. Eventually she says she just can't believe that we actually drove with her to Königsberg. How did she deserve this?

We try to explain that we're thankful that she was willing to share this, her personal journey, with us and she should have no more thoughts about it. When it comes to ordering our food, she meekly asks for one slice of cheesecake and a cup of herbal tea. Luise teases her a bit and Christel smiles shyly. 'You should know this is only the second time I've ever eaten in a real restaurant.'

Luise nearly falls from her chair and asks, disbelievingly, 'But why?'

'Where I live in Jonava, there's only one restaurant, and my clothes were never good enough,' is Christel's simple answer.

We don't stay long and are happy to get back to our hotel. It was a long day, and even though much of it was spent waiting, it has been very emotional. When we want to say goodnight back at the hotel, Christel waves us all into her room. She has something she wants to share with us. She unpacks two small schnapps glasses that she had carefully wrapped in tissue paper, and a small stoneware bottle of Riga Black Balsam, a traditional Latvian herbal liqueur. Christel explains it is made from linden flowers, and then adds: birch leaf buds, honey, arnica, valerian root, mint, vermouth, blueberries, raspberries, oak bark, orange peel, ginger, nutmeg, pepper and many, many other ingredients. It's time to toast and drink to our friendship, she says. Christel describes the many healing properties that this drink, with its high percentage of alcohol, has, and by which she swears. In the winter she drinks it hot, mixed with blackcurrant juice.

We all sleep well on this night.

Christel Scheffler as a young woman.

Angling from the banks of the Pregolya River, Königsberg, 2012.

Longing for Königsberg 213

Christel Scheffler holds a photo taken seventy years ago in front of the house where she once lived.

The next morning, right after breakfast, we make our way to Ponarth. We find the Fichteplatz without a problem and park our car. Moved by memories, Christel walks around the 'Platz'. Right away, she finds the entrance to the bunker where she had injured her mouth. She has tears in her eyes; she cannot believe that it still exists.

Luise wants to know if she can remember in which of the surrounding houses she used to live. Christel pauses. On the photo from her childhood that her brother Gerhard had sent her in the 1990s, she's standing in front of a door with the number 13 on it.

Hardly a thing has changed. In the middle of the horseshoe-shaped court, there's a small, forested park with some raised mounds in it. We can still see the entrances to the bunkers underneath them. Leaning against their windowsills are several elderly Russian babushkas, with their headscarves and colourful aprons, who are watching us with curiosity. When we approach the house with the number 13, one of them asks who we are and if she can help us. We explain that Christel lived here once as a child and show her the only photo that Christel still has. The door with the carvings that adorn it even today is the very same door that is in the background of the photo. Christel points to the ground floor and explains this must be where she once lived.

The woman who approached us lives next door and asks us in. She goes on to tell us she had been exiled from Kazakhstan in 1946 and was relocated here. With nothing more than the clothes on her back, she too was ripped from her

Kitty with her mother in front of 13 Fichteplatz.

homeland. Christel and our hostess are quite taken with how similar, in some respects, their stories are.

Her home consists of one room, a kitchen, and a bathroom that has only a toilet and a sink. The walls in the narrow hallway are still covered in the original wallpaper from the 1930s. With the soot from the small wood-burning stove, it now quite shows its age. Christel tells us that she lived in the exact same layout next door with three other people—her parents and her brother. For today's standards, it would be rather cramped, but back then, to have running water and a toilet was considered quite modern. The development is one of several that were built during the heyday of Königsberg. For Christel, it is the connection to the happiest time of her life. Full of emotion, she says goodbye to the woman who so kindly took us in and showed us around.

When we step back into the street, there's no way we can drive on just yet. Christel needs time. We all stand in the park and let her walk up and down the winding paths in the old playground. We watch as she runs her hands along the bars of the merry-go-round. We can see that, in her thoughts, she is once again the little girl who was once so lovingly called Kitty by her family.

Claudia discreetly takes photos. We ask Christel later what she thought in those moments on the Fichteplatz, what did she remember? She answers it was mostly feelings that came and went. 'My heart became really soft. My soul opened up.' And she had thoughts about the ways of the world. Why did life give her what was nearly impossible to endure? Why was she the one chosen to live on the shadow side of life?

These are questions for which there are no answers. We stand with her and hold these questions in our hearts with reverence. Over and over, she grabs our hands, shakes her head, walks a few steps away, and then looks back again. This is the place full of fond memories, a place where she once had a happy childhood, where she was loved, and where she had people to whom she meant so much.

We drive out of the city. The leaves on the trees are in full splendour. As we make our way through a small settlement at the edge of Kaliningrad, a speeding Maserati passes us on the right-hand side of the road and hits a chicken. Everything happens so fast. I'm happy when the car is gone, and the scare of it all is behind us. Russia, and even Kaliningrad, can be a homely place as long as the newly rich aren't around, needing to show off all they can do and all they now own.

The further we get from Kaliningrad, the quieter the roads are. We are on our way to the church where Luise was baptised. I park our car under some linden trees next to the cemetery wall. The ground is covered in leaves and with every step we take, we hear rustling under our feet. The German headstones were dismantled after the war. In their place are family plots of Russian graves surrounded by blue wrought-iron fences. Here and there is a bench and sometimes even a table. They look like miniature beer gardens, and, in fact, the graves are used as picnic spots.

On the first weekend after Easter, there is a day in the orthodox tradition in which the deceased are honoured. Throughout the year, but especially on Easter Sunday, relatives of the dead bring food and drinks, including the deceased's favourite foods, and lay them on the grave. The visitors sit, eat, and drink one or more glasses of vodka and raise a toast to those who have passed on. It's a tradition that arose during the Soviet era when churchgoing for Easter was prohibited, explains Luise.

In the lower part of the cemetery are the remains of a red-brick church, and next to it is a monument commemorating the soldiers who fell during the First World War. Lying around it are some of the remains of German headstones. In the thirteenth century, it is very likely that a holy grove had been planted here in order to win over the heathens to Christendom. Today, only the badly damaged steeple, missing its clock, and the west wall with its two buttresses are still standing. The last time the church was renovated was in 1852. The nave's star-vaulted ceiling was once one of the most beautiful in all of the Samland.

We find that the baptismal font is still undamaged. However, it is now lying under the open sky, ironically quite near the war memorial. A bit of rainwater has collected in its basin, and a single golden leaf is gently floating in circles. It is a large stone, and it is from the Middle Ages, Luise explains. For many years it lay next to the manure pile of the former rectory, and it also served as a trough for animals to drink from. A few years ago, after the fall of the Soviet Union, concerned volunteers had put it back in the cemetery grounds.

It is a solemn moment in which the four of us women stand here at this ancient stone with the church ruins as a backdrop. This is where Luise was baptised. She is back in her village for the second time in her adult life. She notices how some things have changed. What hasn't is the ancient baptismal font, lying here as a silent witness to the ages.

A typical East Prussian tree-lined road.

We are not far from the home where Luise grew up, which will be our next stop. She doesn't trust her memory and is doubtful we will find her street. She was here only once, fifteen years ago. Suddenly she thinks she recognises the small settlement where she had lived, although it is rather spread out. We drive carefully over a deeply rutted gravel road until we come to an end. It looks as though time has stood still: wide green meadows, golden birches that sway with the breeze, and a few scattered farmhouses, all painted in bright colours. But Luise shakes her head, this is not it.

We drive back to the previous crossroads. To our right is a hidden dirt track through a field. Luise is not sure … it looks too overgrown, she thinks. Nevertheless, we drive through it. It must be wide enough for a car, I think. And, indeed, after we pass four or five houses, we hear a shriek. 'Stop! This is it!' Luise becomes very excited. 'See! It was just overgrown!'

The little whitewashed semi-detached house is barely recognisable. The grass in front of it has grown tall. On the trees hang fat red-cheeked apples. But she's sure we've found her home. She points up to a dormer window on the second floor. 'Up there, that was our children's bedroom. That's where I used to wait and look out of the window to watch as the older children came home from school.'

We clear a path through the grass and look in the windows on the ground floor to see what's inside. It looks empty. Luise tells us that the last time she was here, she met the woman who had lived here then, and she had invited her into the house. Luise picks an apple and bites into it. It tastes—'like an apple, but also a little like my childhood'.

Luise standing next to the baptismal font.

We're standing in the garden where she used to play when she was young—when the world was still in order. We find the well from which they hauled their water. Red rosehips grow wild in large bushes all around. It looks rather enchanted.

Luise tells us the story of Baba Stasia who lived in the neighbouring house just after the war. 'The house used to belong to my friend Klara's family.' When the Russians took over, they gave the house to a new settler, Baba Stasia, from Central Asia. 'Klara used to come here and stand in front of the house, crying. Baba Stasia simply could not understand why she was crying. "Madame, I don't know what you want. You can always leave for Germany. Me, on the other hand, I have to stay here, forever."'

In the other half of the house, it looks as though someone is home and is working in the garden. Luise suddenly remembers Aleksei, the neighbour who so kindly had invited her in the last time she was here. She walks over to him, and indeed, an elderly gentleman in rubber boots greets her graciously. Claudia, Christel and I stand to the back, but we are immediately waved over. Luise wants to show us the house, and Aleksei tells us to go on in.

His is a simple home, three rooms and a little kitchen. And yet we can imagine how cosy it was in the winters, how lovely and uncomplicated childhood must have been in the summers. When we come back out, Aleksei is waiting for us with a bouquet of flowers he has just picked from his garden. Besides this, he gives Luise a bag with apples to take home. She is touched.

Luise's family home in Schwesternhof now stands empty.

Christel, too, is affected. These two women, the same age, with completely different histories—one an academic, the other a simple factory worker—share some of their deepest pains with each other: the loss of the safe world of their parents' home, their homeland, and their identity. Both are Germans from East Prussia—a land that does not exist anymore.

We now must make our tedious way back to Lithuania. The next day—we are back in Vilnius—we ask Luise, who at first didn't even want to come, how she feels after taking this trip. She needs to think for a moment.

Then she says quietly, 'Yesterday, I was completely petrified. Today I am happy.'

Christel and Luise tend to the Great War Memorial in the Schwesternhof cemetery. The inscription reads: '*Treue um Treue*' – always faithful.

Epilogue

by Kerstin Lieff

Nineteen forty-five—a year in which so many who had lived through the most horrendous years in modern history would rejoice. Hitler was dead; war was over. It was a time to rebuild. Yet to the few, the Wolf Children—*children* no less—the worst was yet to come. The stories in this book tell what happened to them, how they managed, how they needed to live under a new identity in order to survive. Most astonishing is that very few in the West were even aware of them. Not until the early 1990s, right after the Berlin Wall came down and the Iron Curtain began to disintegrate, did the fact of their existence begin to be known. They were adults by then; some were even grandparents. It is a most humbling honour to now be able to bring their stories to the English-speaking world.

I grew up in Minnesota, in a German home. My parents were immigrants; both lived through the war in Germany (my mother ended up in a Russian prison camp in Siberia after the war; my father, as a German officer in the Luftwaffe, landed in a British POW camp in Montreal). But in my entire childhood growing up, I never heard a word about the Wolf Children. My parents often told stories of what they had experienced and even told tales that were not widely known and certainly not taught in my school in the small town we lived in, Farmington— the horrors of living with war, the nightly bombings of Berlin, and the post-war famine in Germany. My mother often wept when she told me about *die Flucht aus Ostpreußen*—the escape out of East Prussia—or *die Flüchtlinge*—the refugees— and told me there was a time when she saw trainloads of them flooding into Berlin, frightened, disoriented, telling stories of having lost everything. A girl missing her ring finger for having run so fast when the Russians came, her ring caught on a nail, so frightened, she tore her finger right off. But my mother did not know, and certainly, my father, who had been in Canada since 1940, never knew that children had been left behind in East Prussia. Children, alone in the woods, alone in the foreign country, Lithuania, children fighting off the Russian army, alone. Never did either of them mention *die Wolfskinder*.

It was a random thing that I learned about them. I was searching the internet wanting to find stories of German children who had been orphaned by the bombings of the Second World War. I thought such a subject would be interesting to write about. After all, I am German and I had already written a book about life in Germany during the war, and this subject interested me—the little-known stories of people who came from the wrong side of history. It seemed to fit. And indeed, many such accounts exist. But I was surprised when Google sent me to numerous German sites that mentioned the lost children of East Prussia, *die Wolfskinder*. And I was astonished when I realised that almost nothing about them had been written in English. How can this be? I thought. Twenty thousand children, suddenly left to fend for themselves, the roughly 5,000 of whom survived, never given an audience for their stories?

I knew I wanted these stories to be known. I had no idea where to begin, but in hindsight, the answer was staring right at me. Of all the German books I found, there was only one that spoke simply, a book written in understandable language, in the voice of those very children. It was the book written by Sonya Winterberg with its haunting photographs by Claudia Heinermann, *Wir sind die Wolfskinder—Verlassen in Ostpreußen*, 'We are the Wolf Children—Forsaken in East Prussia'.

I was so moved by the stories, and so convinced that they needed a broader audience, that I reached out to Sonya and offered to help adapt that book for an English-speaking audience. From her voice as the narrator, I had the sense that this was no ordinary woman. A compassionate and passionate person, who would stop at nothing to get her story, Sonya spent years tracking down the few surviving Wolf Children with the intent of interviewing every one of them. At the time only about eighty were still alive. Sonya didn't stop at merely researching or relying on phone interviews. What you will see in this book is that she visited every Wolf Child she could and nearly every one of them in their own homes, where the comfort of familiar surroundings often produced unpredicted moments in which memories long buried sprang to mind.

To be able to elicit these tales from their storytellers takes tremendous patience on the part of the interviewer. It also takes humility, and trust in one's intuition to ask the right question at the right time. Indeed, many of the stories Sonya Winterberg was able to draw from her subjects were ones that had long been buried and forgotten, some out of a sheer need to survive. These people were children when the events occurred, children whose very existence was illegal until 1992. To even say you were, or anyone whom you knew were German, could land you in the Gulag. Or worse.

The publishing of this edition marks the tenth anniversary of Sonya Winterberg's book about the Wolf Children, which moved the German Parliament to revise their social security system's bylaws to finally help care for those few who were still alive. Her book became a national bestseller. Some of her characters even inspired the award-winning film *Wolfskinder* (2013) by Rick Ostermann.

In this English version, *The Wolf Children of the Eastern Front: Alone and Forgotten*, we have tried to make these stories as tangible and understandable to a non-German audience as we could. The names of cities, provinces and rivers have changed since 1945, names that will fade into obscurity because these lands no longer belong to Germany. But to a great extent, we kept their German names to help those who read this understand what this land was like, once. We sometimes used German words and phrases that have the feel of that time, and, to help visualise the geography, we've done our best to describe just that. Imagine an agricultural, pastoral, wooded land. Imagine a wild landscape, endless skies and large estates. The area is mostly Russian now, with some of it belonging to Poland.

When I wrote my first book, *Letters from Berlin*, the story of a young woman—my mother—who experienced the Second World War in Berlin, I said in its introduction: 'It was, to be sure, an era of extreme evil and extreme heroism. Yet our many bookshelves dedicated to that time have left little space for the stories of the millions of others who also suffered but whose voices were stifled because they came from the wrong side of the war.' I say this is still true. How extraordinary it is to now also know some of those stories came from children.

Editorial Note

by Sonya Winterberg

The term 'Wolf Children' has been subject to debate for many years. While some see this term as animalistic and lurid, the majority of those I spoke with still identify with it today. Admittedly, it remains a conundrum to describe these children who were in an exceptional historical situation. Another term, East Prussian war orphans, does not describe the two distinct features that were true for the Wolf Children: first, the fact that they were on their own without a parent in a hostile environment, without food or shelter under the open sky; and secondly, that they were left behind, to live behind the Iron Curtain—long after the Second World War was over.

This work depicts actual events in the lives of the protagonists. The Wolf Children have all described to me the world of their childhood, adolescence and later years as vividly and precisely as they could recall. Oral history is always shaped by the present, too. While recollections after more than sixty years may in some cases contain historical inaccuracies, it in no way diminishes the substance of their accounts. Wherever possible, statements were checked with the help of other sources and cautiously adjusted if necessary. Occasionally, dialogue consistent with the nature of the person speaking has been supplemented. All persons within are actual individuals; there are no composite characters.

For the sake of readability, the German, Lithuanian, Russian and Polish names of people and places have been used sparingly throughout this translation and might differ from the original German edition.

I am deeply grateful to Kerstin Lieff, who believed in this book long before we even met for the first time. From across the miles, her vision, encouragement and generous support turned an idea into a reality. Kerstin's wonderful translation is so much more: she truly helps bring the story of the Wolf Children to a larger audience by adapting my prose in a way that honours the loss, grief and sorrow of those who entrusted me with their stories.

The journey of this book would not have been the same without my long-time collaborator Claudia Heinermann, whose photos are also included in this edition. I will always cherish our travels together as well as the many opportunities we were given to present our work.

Lastly, I would like to acknowledge John Kay, who so graciously agreed to write the preface. While his story was a very different one, his roots in East Prussia connect him with the few remaining Wolf Children still alive today. We still marvel at the serendipity of his band's name Steppenwolf and their hit *Born to be Wild*.

It remains my hope that the Wolf Children will no longer be seen as the children of the perpetrators, but that they are recognised in their suffering as victims of the Second World War, the Stalinist regime and the Cold War. May their lives be a reminder for us all that freedom is never free.

Halifax, Nova Scotia
October 2021

Bibliography

Becher, Ursula A.J., Borodziej, Wlodzimierz & Maier, Robert (Hrsg.): *Deutschland und Polen im 20. Jahrhundert. Analysen – Quellen – didaktische Hinweise*, Bundeszentrale für politische Bildung, 2007.

Bjelfvenstam, Dorothea: *Man nannte uns Hitlermädchen*, Amicus-Verlag, 2012.

Brandes, Detlef, Sundhausen, Holm & Troebst, Stefan (Hrsg.): *Lexikon der Vertriebenen. Deportation, Zwangsaussiedlung und ethnische Säuberung im Europa des 20. Jahrhunderts*, Böhlau Verlag, 2010.

De Zayas, Alfred-Maurice: *Anmerkungen zur Vertreibung der Deutschen aus dem Osten*, Kohlhammer, 1987.

Deichelmann, Hans: *Ich sah Königsberg sterben*, Verlag S. Bublies, 2000.

Dorn, Ursula: *Ich war ein Wolfskind aus Königsberg*, edition riedenburg, 2008.

Dörr, Margarete: *Der Krieg hat uns geprägt. Wie Kinder den Zweiten Weltkrieg erlebten*, Campus, 2007.

Egremont, Max: *Forgotten Land, Journeys among the Ghosts of East Prussia*, Farrar, Straus and Giroux, 2011.

Guez, Olivier: *Heimkehr der Unerwünschten. Eine Geschichte der Juden in Deutschland nach 1945*, Piper, 2011.

Hermanowski, Georg: *Ostpreußen. Wegweiser durch ein unvergessenes Land*, Bechtermünz Verlag, 1996.

Hicks, Donna: *Dignity: Its Essential Role in Resolving Conflict*, Yale University Press, 2011.

Jacobs, Ingeborg: *Wolfskind: Die unglaubliche Lebensgeschichte des ostpreußischen Mädchens Liesabeth Otto*, Propyläen, 2010.

Kettenacker, Lothar (Hrsg.): *Ein Volk von Opfern? Die neue Debatte um den Bombenkrieg 1940–45*, Rowohlt, 2003.

Kibelka, Ruth: *Wolfskinder. Grenzgänger an der Memel*, Basisdruck, 2003.

Kibelka, Ruth: *Ostpreußens Schicksalsjahre 1944–1948*, Aufbau, 2004.

Kleindienst, Jürgen (Hrsg.): *Nachkriegs-Kinder. Kindheit in Deutschland 1945–50*, JKL Publikationen, 1998.

Köpp, Gabi: *Warum war ich bloß ein Mädchen? Das Trauma einer Flucht 1945*, Herbig, 2010.

Kossert, Andreas: *Damals in Ostpreußen. Der Untergang einer deutschen Provinz*, DVA, 2008.

Kossert, Andreas: *Kalte Heimat. Die Geschichte der deutschen Vertriebenen nach 1945*, Siedler, 2008.

Kossert, Andreas: *Ostpreußen. Geschichte und Mythos*, Siedler, 2005.

Köster-Hetzendorf, Maren: *Ich hab dich so gesucht ... Der Krieg und seine verlorenen Kinder*, Pattloch, 1995.
Leiserowitz, Ruth: *Von Ostpreußen nach Kyritz. Wolfskinder auf dem Weg nach Brandenburg*, Brandenburgische Landeszentrale für politische Bildung, 2008.
Morgenstern, Erika: *Überleben war schwerer als Sterben. Ostpreußen 1944–48*, Herbig, 2010.
Neu, Richard L.: *Edeltraut – Ramute. Wie ein 'Wolfskind' in Litauen*, Hauschild, 2007.
Nitsch, Christel: *Mein Weg durch die Dunkelheit: Vom Schicksal eines 'Wolfskindes'*, MuNe, 2008.
Nitsch, Gunter: *Eine lange Flucht aus Ostpreußen*, Ellert & Richter Verlag, 2011.
Pölking, Hermann: *Ostpreußen. Biographie einer Provinz*, be.bra verlag, 2011.
Pose, Joachim: *Ich war ein Wolfskind! Von Pommern über Ostpreußen nach Mecklenburg*, ß Verlag & Medien, 2006.
Radebold, Hartmut, Bohleber, Werner & Zinnecker, Jürgen (Hrsg.): *Transgenerationale Weitergabe kriegsbelasteter Kindheiten: Interdisziplinäre Studien zur Nachhaltigkeit historischer Erfahrungen über vier Generationen*, Juventa, 2009.
Schmidt, Winfried: *Vergessene Wolfskinder*, Projekte-Verlag, 2006.
Sumowski, Hans-Burkhard: *Jetzt war ich ganz allein auf der Welt: Erinnerungen an eine Kindheit in Königsberg 1944–1947*, btb, 2009.
Tannehill, Evelyne: *Abandoned and Forgotten. An Orphan Girl's Tale of Surviving During World War II*, Wheatmark, 2006.
Volksbund Deutscher Kriegsgräberfürsorge e. V.: *Treibgut des Krieges – Zeugnisse von Flucht und Vertreibung der Deutschen*, Eigenverlag, 2008.
Wańkowska-Sobiesiak, Johanna: *Buty Agaty/Agathes Schuhe*, Olsztyn, 2008.
Wiechert, Ernst: *Wälder und Menschen. Eine Jugend in Ostpreussen*, LangenMüller, 2007.
Wieck, Michael: *Zeugnis vom Untergang Königsbergs. Ein 'Geltungsjude berichtet'*, Beck, 2005.

Illustration Credits

Claudia Heinermann pp. 17, 18, 50, 52, 54, 69, 77, 83, 88, 93, 96, 102, 106, 110, 124, 135, 136, 138, 149, 152, 154, 155, 156, 160, 163, 170, 174, 176, 178, 179, 180, 181, 183, 186, 188, 190, 198, 209, 211, 214, 223

Archiv Bernhard Waldmann pp. viii, xi, 10, 13, 16, 22, 30, 31, 32, 35, 37, 40, 60, 64, 107

Sonya Winterberg pp. 7, 119, 206, 212, 213, 216, 217, 218, 220

Wikimedia pp. xvi, 8, 115

Deutsches Kulturforum östliches Europa p. vi

Friedland Museum p. 128

Anatoly Morozov p. 47

Panevėžys Local Lore Museum p. 74

Evelyne Tannehill p. 121

Index

Names

Briskorn, Eva, 16-20, 23, 33, 51, 63-4, 81-2
  Gisela, sister, 20, 33, 35, 51, 63
  Manfred, brother, 33, 35
  Reinhard, brother, 33
  Rudi, brother, 33, 35
  Sabine, sister, 20, 33, 35
  Siegfried, brother, 33-4
  Otto and Gisela, parents, 16-17, 19-20

Czajka, Agathe, 107-109
  Bruno, brother, 107, 109
  Johann, father, 107

Dejok, Liesbeth, 22-3, 27, 38-41, 47-8, 169-72
  Elžbieta (Dejokienė), Lith. name, 169
  Helene, sister, 27
Deske, Ruth, 44-5, 60-3, 70, 96-7, 99-100, 187-8, 198
  Birutė ([Rūta] Tamutytė), Lith. maiden name, 97
  (Birutė Gorienė, Lith. married name)
  Helga, sister, 44, 61-2
  Karl-Heinz, brother, 44, 61-3, 96-7, 99
  Siegfried, brother, 44, 61
  Irene (Gorytė), daughter, 99
  Vacys (Gorys), husband, 99
Dorn, Ursula, 200
Dudas, Margot, 95, 189-90

Eidukaitis, Jonas, 196-7
  Hartmut, Germ. name, 196
Elm, Rita, 41-2, 45
Erlach, Johanna, 79-80
  Maria and Hannah, friends, 80

Falk, Helmut, 28-9
Fischer, Horst, 101
  Kostas Galinaitis, Lith. name, 101
  Manfred, brother, 101

Fischer, Inge, xiii
  Janina Griška, Lith. name, xiii
Fischer, Konrad, 71-2, 100
  Jonas Laimonas, Lith. name, 100
  Gerhard, brother, 71
  Helmut, brother, 71
  Hugo, brother, 71-2
  Agota, adoptive mother, 72, 100
Fritz, Uwe, 175-7, 179, 181-2, 185-6, 198, 202-209
  Bronius Dapkus, Lith. name, 175

Gladstein, Hans (also Harz or Heinz), 91
  Alfred, brother, 91
Grävert, Kurt, 178
Gröning, Dieter, 27, 58, 97, 124-5
  Brigitte, sister, 124-5
  Elfriede, sister, 124-5
  Gerhard, brother, 124-5
  Gisela, sister, 124-5
  Mutti (mummy), 124-5
  Tante Ursel, 'Auntie Ursel' (orphanage house mother), 124
Gudovius, Gerhard, 4-5, 11, 20-1, 26-7, 31, 51-2, 56, 58, 70-1, 86-8, 97-8, 118-20, 129-33
  Gerhardas, Lith. name, 4, 97
  Michael, friend, 20-1
  Nachtigall, Herr, teacher, 21
  Herta, mother, 20
  Gerlinde, wife, 4-5, 130-2

Haak, Ursula, 15, 28, 53-5, 56-7, 98-9
  Erich, brother, 28
  Franz, brother, 28
  Heinz, brother, 28
  Horst, brother, 57, 98-9
  Paul, brother, 28
  Willy, brother, 28, 53, 57, 98-9
  Anna and Albert, parents, 15, 28, 54
Haupt, Annemarie, 177, 178

Heim, Gerhard, 41-2
  Hilde, sister, 42
Herzmann, Rudi, 187, 189, 201
  Christel, sister, 201
  Romalda, wife, 201
Horn, Hilde (Hildegard), 49-51, 89, 102
  Helmut, brother, 51
Hundrieser, Ursula, 80-1

Kenzler, Heinrich, 117-18
Keusling, Bernhard, 72-4, 99
  Mikas Pelgius, foster father, 73-4
Kießling, Bernhard, 41-2, 42-4
  Ilse, sister, 42-3
Klein, Bruno, 52-3, 85-6, 172-5
  Heinz, brother, 172
  Danutė, daughter, 172
  Elvira, daughter, 172
  Vida, daughter, 172
  Willy, father, 172
  Aldona, wife, 172-4
Klein, Herbert, 179-81, 198
Knispel, Ingrid, 196-7
Kösling, Renate, 153-5
  Jadvyga, Lith. name, 153
  Erwin, brother, 155
  Herbert, brother, 155
  Ursula, sister, 155
  Frida Kösling, mother, 155
  Juratė, daughter, 153
Kösling, Siegfried, 155, 157
  Günther, brother, 157
  Irmgard, sister, 157
  Fritz and Gertrud, parents, 157
  Warwara, wife, 158

Launert, Gisela, 90-1
  Karin, sister, 90
Liedke, Rudolf, 114-18
  Irmgard, sister, 114-18
  Peterchen, brother, 115
  Sieglinde, sister, 114-18
    Heinrich Kenzler, husband, 117-18
  Ulrich, brother, 114, 116-18
  Waltraud, sister, 114, 116-18
Lindenau, Rudi, 6, 7

Methee, Karl-Heinz, 179
Minnt, Waltraut, xiv-xv, 105-107, 110, 182-6
  Fritz, brother, xv

Vaclavas, son, 184
  Aystė, granddaughter, 182
Müller, Dora, 55-6, 68-9, 78-9
  Arthur, friend, 78-9
Müller, Elfriede, 104-105, 109-10
  Gustav, brother, 104-105, 109

Neumann, Hans, xii-xiii
  Jonas (Eidukaitis), Lith. name, xiii
  Gerhard, brother, xii
  Hermann, father, xiii
Nitsch, Christel, 36-7, 64-8, 84-5
  Albert, brother, 36
  Gertrud, sister, 64-5, 67
    Klaus, son, 64-5, 67
  Sofia and Josef, foster parents, 68, 84-5
    Nadja, Sofia's sister, 68

Petereit, Hans Joachim, 104, 110
Piklaps, Arnold, 155, 162
Plink, Alfred, 155-7, 158-62
  Helga, sister, 159, 161
  Helmut, brother, 161
  Ursula, sister, 159-61
  Anna, mother, 159, 161
  Ona (Plinkienė), wife, 161
  Dangoulė, daughter, 161
  Edvardas, son, 161
Plonus, Christel, 88
Pose, Joachim, 74-5, 112-14, 126-8
  Klaus, brother, 113
  Peter, brother, 113
  Auntie Bertchen, mother's sister, 113

Quitsch, Luise, 92-5, 162-9, 198-9, 202, 209-19
  Alfreda Pipiraitė, Lith. maiden name, 162
  (Alfreda Kazukauskienė, Lith. married name)
  Edith, sister, 164, 166-9
  Günther, brother, 164-9
  Hans, brother, 164-8
  Hilde, sister, 164-8
  Wilhelm, brother, 164-5
  Trudi, cousin, 164-5
  Aleksei, neighbour, 218
  Gertrud Kabeck, former neighbour, 166
  Klara (Kabeck), friend (and daughter of Gertrud Kabeck), 218

Ranglack, Anna, 177, 200, 202
Rapp, Eva, 120-3, 133-5
  Evelyne Tannehill, Amer. name, 134-5
  Douglas, brother, 120
  Erwin, brother, 120-1
  Henry, brother, 120-3, 133
  Vera, sister, 120
  Herbert, father, 120
  Agnes, roommate, 122
  Tante Elsbeth, aunt, 123
Rehberg, Käthe, 179
Riess, Erika, 82-4
  Heinz, brother, 82-4
Roscher, Günther, 101

Sauerbaum, Erika, 11-12, 136-47
Scheffler, Christel, 4, 24, 92, 100, 137-52, 201-220
  Aldona Žigmantienė, Lith. name, 92, 137, 141
  Käthe Windt, given name, 137, 139
  Keti, possible former name, 139
  Kitty, nickname, 24, 29-30, 92, 95, 139-48, 214-15

Gerhard Windt, brother, 24, 139-48
Fritz and Gertrud Windt, foster parents, 141
Paul, son, 150
Peter, son, 150
Schneider, Erna, 5-6
Schulz, Lieselotte, 104, 109
  Hannelore, sister, 109
Swars, Manfred, 199
  Siurkienė, Juratė, daughter, 199

Unkat, Günther, xii
  Anna, mother, xii

Wegner, Lothar, 24-5, 37-8
  Horst, brother, 24, 37
  Ingrid, sister, 24, 37-8
Weintke, Hannelore, 144
Willuweit, Arnold (Arno), 59-60, 75-6, 102
  Gisela, sister, 59
  Heinz, brother, 59-60, 75-6, 102
  Hilde, wife (*see* Horn, Hildegard)

General

Adenauer, Konrad, 126
Afghanistan, 150
Albertina, Sister (Order of St Francis), 204
Alcohol, alcoholic, alcoholism, 6, 87, 132, 150, 168, 197, 210
Allenburg (Russ. Druzhba), 208
Allenstein (Pol. Olsztyn), 107
Allies/Allied Forces, 41, 42
Amalienau, quarter of Königsberg (Russ. Oktyabrskye/Zentralny), 16
America, 120, 133
American, 103, 130, 134
  citizen/s, 120, 133
  controlled West Germany, ix, 129
  military, 130
  occupied zones, 129, 130
  passport, 120
Anti-Soviet Agitation *see* Gulag
Applebaum, Anne, 103
Arctic, 108
  Sea, 103
Arendt, Hannah, 49

Arnstadt, ix
Auerbachs Keller, 10
Australia, 133
Authorities, 39, 104, 122, 127, 171
  German, 127, 137, 171
  Nazi, ix
  Russian *see* Russian: authorities

Baba Stasia, 218
Baltic Sea, 9, 12, 30, 46, 71, 110, 113, 155
  evacuation attempts to cross, 37, 43
  refugees on the coast of, 161
Baltic States, xiii, 76, 187, 194
Balkans, 24
  German-Baltic Parliament Circle, 194
Banktinsee, 42, 207
Barracks:
  Biberach, 129
  Chelyabinsk, 108-109
  for children, Russian, 122
  Friedland, 129
  Kaunas, 92
  Königsberg, 56

Saxony-Anhalt, 119, 129
Soviet, 56, 92, 106, 168
Bautzen, 123
Beg, begging, x, 4, 6, 47, 59-63, 70-3, 78-9, 81, 86-7, 89, 91, 94, 95, 98, 100, 100-102, 109, 114, 116, 122, 153, 166, 194, 198, 200
  sack, 61, 78, 84
  see also Hamster-run
Belarus, 92
Bellevue Castle/Palace, Berlin, 185, 200
Berlin, xv, 14, 41-3, 46, 118, 168, 200, 221, 223
  Battle of, 113
  East, 118, 119
  Office of the Registry, 141-2
  Standesamt 1 in, 141, 195
  Wall, 1, 221
    see also Iron Curtain
  West, 119-20
Berlin-Wilmersdorf, 206
Biberach, 129
Biedermeier era, 9
Birthdates, 43, 166
Bischofswerda, 111, 118
Bitterfeld, 111, 118, 120
Bjelfvenstam, Dorothea (née Richard), 16, 25, 28
Black market, black marketeering, 45, 47
Bledau, part of Wosegau (Russ. Vishnevoye), 48
Bloody Sunday, 1-2
Blutgericht (Blood Court), 10
Bohemian protectorate, 15
Boils, blisters, 108
Border, borders, ix, 46, 118, 129, 174, 193, 206-208
  -lands, xii
  -wanderer, 60
  China, 103
  Germany, 120
  guard, 209
  Kaliningrad, 191, 202-203, 207-208
  Lithuania, 22, 45, 57, 58-60, 62, 65, 72, 74, 175, 192, 203
  patrol, 46, 203-204, 210
  Poland, 44, 62, 65, 206
  police women, 204
  Russia, 40, 191, 203, 207-209
  Ukraine, 103
  zone, 44

Brandenburg, 112
Braunschweig, xii
Bread, xv, 22, 27, 30, 40, 44-5, 48, 52, 55, 60-1, 63, 66-7, 73, 78, 81, 91, 95, 108, 124, 141, 169
  and cake, 45, 58-69
Bremerhaven, 139
British:
  air raids, 26
  bombers, bombings, 25, 139
  internment camp, 113
  military, 129
  POW camp, 221
  sector of Germany, 124
  zone, 129
Budapest, 206

Café Schwärmer, 11
Cannibalism, 47-8
Carbide, 87
Cart, v, 53, 55, 109
  hand, 26, 44
  horse, 53, 114
Castle, Neuruppin, 113
  see also Königsberg Castle
Cathedral Bridge, 9
Cemetery, 20, 136-7, 215-16, 220
  military, 19-20, 153
  Protestant, 107
  Stablack, 193
Chelyabinsk, 108-109
Chernyakhovsk *see* Insterburg
Chicago, 133
Chief Administration of Camps *see* Gulag
Chilblains, 65
Child Tracing Service (CTS), 82, 177
Children's transport, 124, 161
China, 103
Christendom, 216
  Catholic, Catholicism, xiii, 90, 99
  Christ, 126
  Protestant, 90, 99
    cemetery, 107
Christian Democratic Union Party (CDU), 194
Christmas, 15-16, 30, 37, 116, 123, 147, 197
  Orthodox, 56
Churchill, Winston, 46
Citizen, citizenship, 6, 9, 99, 146, 193
  American, 120, 133

German, 146, 166, 191, 193-6, 186, 199, 201
  Jewish, 21
  Lithuanian, 191, 195-6, 200
  Soviet, 118, 193, 195
Cold War, 1, 3, 191-2, 225
Collectivisation/collective farms, 96, 99, 105, 158, 172-4
Cologne, 201
Communism/Communist, 15, 85-6, 189
  East German, ix, 9, 118
  housing, 148, 172, 177, 205
  Party, 97
Confrérie de la Chaîne des Rôtisseurs, 197
Corpse, corpses, x, 26, 31, 34, 44, 47, 61, 132, 164-5
Cranz (Russ. Selenogradsk), 12
Cyrillic, 105, 204
Czechoslovakia, 15
Czech Republic, 41

Danzig (Pol. Gdańsk):
  Bay of, 14
  see also Gdańsk
Dehydrated, 97, 112
Delousing, 118
  see also Lice
Deport/deportation, 4-5, 48, 62, 71, 76, 84, 94-5, 97, 99, 103-105, 110, 119
Destroyed/destruction, 12, 20, 26-8, 38-9, 43, 46-8, 51-2, 59, 60, 63, 71, 76, 78, 87, 89, 101, 108, 130, 139, 142-3, 145, 150, 171, 191-2, 206
Deyma River, 16
Disease/s, 49, 58
  asthma, 151, 168
  black lung (pneumoconiosis), 151
  cancer, 167, 172
  cholera see Epidemics
  eczema, 55
  gangrene, 20
  malaria see Epidemics
  oedema, 55
  Parkinson's, 161
  pleurisy, 51
  rheumatism, 176
  scabies, 79
  tuberculosis, 56, 100, 109, 113
  typhoid see Epidemics
  typhus see Epidemics
  whooping cough, 97

Dom Brücke see Cathedral Bridge
Donated, donations, donors, 173, 195, 197, 198, 199
Dönhoff, Countess Marion von, 9
Dortmund, xiii
Dresden, 98
  Technical University of, 127
Düsseldorf, 128
Düsseldorf-Gerresheim, 173

East Prussian, 5, 12, 14, 35, 58, 95, 111, 131, 140-1, 159, 167, 191, 216
  accent, 107, 159, 169
  Citadel, 31
  Gold, 148
  East Prussian News, 111
  Exhibition Hall, 145
  farmers, 201
  homeland, 65, 76, 109, 111, 145, 164, 169, 171, 191, 193, 219
  Ostpreußenblatt, 137, 141
  people, 5, 14-15, 22, 41, 46, 58, 111, 139, 167, 175, 188, 191, 195
  virtues, 9, 15
  war orphans, 224
Easter, 15, 140, 215-16
  Pentecost, 142
Eastern (Soviet) Bloc, 1, 129, 187
Edelweiss Association, 162, 187-99
Eggesin, 116-18
Elbing (Pol. Elbląg), 29, 120
Elchniederung (Russ. Losinaja Dolina), 22, 27, 39, 56, 60, 171
Ellernbruch (Russ. Watutino), 61
Emaciated, 44, 78, 89, 109, 116, 175
  see also Famine, Hunger
England see Britain
Epidemics:
  cholera, 40, 51
  malaria, 51, 108
  typhoid, 35-6, 40, 50
  typhus, 51, 58, 80, 116, 122
  see also Diseases
Erlenrode (Russ. Prudki), 22
Essen, 155
Essen-Borbeck, 155
European Union, 200
Evacuate, evacuated, 28-30, 38, 43, 53, 57
  evacuation, 44, 167
  evacuees, 55, 101, 122
Exiled, 185, 200, 213
Expulsion, 95, 128, 171

Fachwerkhäuser, 12
Fairytales, xv, 10-11, 81, 84, 175
Famine, 6, 35, 42-5, 80, 86, 91, 104, 111, 133, 141, 194, 221
Farmstead, homestead, 66, 70-1, 73, 109, 184
Fascism, 46
Fascist, 189
   child, 8, 81, 86, 88
FDJ (Free German Youth), 118-20, 127
Fichteplatz, Fichte School, 24, 140-1, 143, 202, 213-15
Fischdorf, 12
Flee, fleeing, ix, xii, 30, 33, 35-42, 53, 71, 81, 88, 101, 121, 127-30, 188
   flight, xii, xiii, 14, 37-8, 90, 97, 122, 161, 164, 171, 194, 201
Flensburg, xii
Food, foodstuffs, x, xv, 22, 30, 36, 61, 65, 71, 78-9, 82, 85-7, 95, 116, 130, 169, 210, 215
   and orphanages, 124, 161
   in Lithuania, 60-1, 171
   rations, 23, 28, 40, 44, 52, 55, 139
   rewarded with, 27, 48, 56, 87, 108-109
   scarcity of, 30-1, 41, 43-8, 55-6, 63, 78-9, 89, 224
   search for, xiii, 31, 48, 52, 59-63, 72, 78-9, 85, 90, 161
Forest Brothers, 70-6, 99
Foster family, parents, xii, 50, 72, 74, 76, 84, 90, 95, 97-102, 137, 150
   child, children, xiv, 24, 84, 139
   daughter, xiii-xiv, 13, 85, 141
   son, 75-6
Free state, 14
Free trade zone, 191-2
Freezing, x, 33, 51-2, 60, 65, 175, 189
   frozen, x, 34, 108, 204
      Baltic Sea, 71, 110
      branches, 45
      fingers, 52, 204
      ground, 61, 65
      lagoon, 39
      Memel, 57
      pipes, 52
      potatoes, 34, 71
      tears, 56
   to death, x, 45, 60, 62
   toes, 84
Friedland transit camp, 111, 128-9

Friendship Agreement, 15
Frisches Haff, 9
Frostbite, frostbitten, 52, 84, 177
Fürstenwalde, 111-12

Gdańsk, 14
GDR *see* Germany, East
Gediminas Avenue, 1
General Steuben, 43
Gerdauen (Russ. Zheleznodorozhny), 41-5, 50-1, 61-2, 89, 96, 153, 194, 201-207
Gerdauen District, 36, 61, 64, 179, 187
German, Germany:
   army *see* Wehrmacht
   East (GDR), ix, xiv, 3, 5, 95, 97-8, 109, 111-12, 114, 117-23, 126-7, 161, 168, 172, 187
      quarantine camp, 112
      German National Trade Fair, East, 14-15
      president, 119
   economic miracle, 130
   Embassy, 165, 196, 201
      Vilnius, 199
   government, xiv, 14, 26, 29, 46, 119, 151, 188, 195-7, 201
   mainland, 22, 30, 39, 206
   Rotary Club of, 197
   Third Reich, 15
   West, ix, xiv, 3, 9, 101, 112, 118, 120, 123, 127, 133, 145, 172, 201
Gestapo, 120
Glavnoye Upravleniye Lagerej see Gulag
Gorbachev, Mikhail, 1-3
Görlitz, 122
Göttingen, 111, 129
Great Britain, 3
Great Patriotic War, 48
Gristmill, 63, 205
Gross Schönau (Russ. Peskowo), 36
Großengersdorf, 193
GST (Sport and Technology Association), 127
Gulag, GULAG, xiii, 71, 74-5, 85, 95, 103, 109-10, 126, 189, 222
   definition of, 103
   Glavnoye Upravleniye Lagerej, 103
   Wolf Children in, 105, 108-10
Gulf War, 2
Gumbinnen (Russ. Gusev), 79, 193

Haberberg, 12
Half-timbered houses, 12, 205-206
Hamburg, 116-17
Hampelmann, 164
Hamster-run, 45, 61, 79, 92
Hanerau-Hademarschen, 194
Hanover, ix, 120, 127
  Technical University, 127
Hansestadt (Hanseatic city), 11-12
Helsinki, 14
Hindenburg Lyceum, 28
Hitler, Adolf, 15-16, 21, 120, 189, 221
  films, 169
  girl, girls, 25, 28
  Heil, 28
Hochdorf, 129
Hoffmann School for Boys, 21
Homeland, 128, 134, 145, 201, 214, 219
  see also East Prussian: homeland
Honey Bridge *see* Cathedral Bridge
Horst Wessel School, 19
Hospital, 81-4, 86, 97, 145, 178
  army field, 80, 146, 173
  military, 24, 51-2
Housemaid, maid, 82, 91, 144
Hoyerswerda, 109
Hungary, 41
Hunger, hungry, ix, 1, 33, 35, 37, 51-2, 55, 59, 62-3, 65-8, 72, 75, 79, 81, 95, 100, 123-4, 137, 171, 189
  see also Famine
Hypothermia, 177

Identification card, identification papers, 28, 99-101, 110
Incarcerations, 103
Infrastructure, 43, 47-8, 58, 171
Insterburg (Russ. Chernyakhovsk), 48, 79, 108, 116, 193
International Red Cross, xii
  see also Red Cross
International Tracing Service (ITS) *see* Tracing services
Interstate Council of the Germans in Russia, 193
Interzone pass, 120
Iron Cross, 159
Iron Curtain, 1, 134, 137, 221, 224

Jewish, Jews, 21-2, 148
Jonava, 86, 92, 136, 148, 150, 169, 209-10
  chemical plant in, 150

Kaiserslautern, 130
Kaliningrad, 48, 95, 144-5, 173, 195, 202, 204, 207, 209-10, 215
  exclave, 9, 191
  governor, 191
  Oblast, 12, 166, 187, 191-3, 203, 206
  see also Königsberg
Kalvarija, 4-5, 87, 97
Karaganda, 105, 110
Karpauen (Russ. Nekrassovo), 61-2
Kaunas, xiii, 64, 86, 92, 95, 100, 104-105, 110, 117, 148, 162, 172, 174, 189
Kay, John, ix-x, 225
  Joachim Fritz Krauledat, given name, x
  Jutta (Maue-Kay), wife, ix
  Steppenwolf, band, ix, x
Kazakhstan, 105, 213
Kelmė, 61
KGB, 1
  see also USSR
Kibarten (Lith. Kybartai), 72, 84, 101, 209
Kiel, 14, 43, 147
Kindertransport, 25
  see also Children's transport
Klaipėda, 48, 91, 96, 155, 157, 181
  see also Memel
Klein Dexen (part of today's Russ. Furmanovo), 193
Kneiphof, 9-10, 12, 26
Kohl, Chancellor Helmut, 3, 194-5
Kollwitz, Käthe, 9-10
Kommandantura, 207
Königin-Luise-Brücke (Queen Louise Bridge), 59, 203
Königsberg (Russ. Kaliningrad):
  Castle, 10-12
  Cathedral, 12, 193
  Deutsche Ostmesse Königsberg see German National Trade Fair, East
  invasion of, 23-9, 31, 33, 37, 42, 59
  liberation of, 48
  memories of, 9-13
  renaming of, 48
Königstor, 210
Korea, 133
Krämer Bridge (Grocer's Bridge, Krämerbrücke), 26
Krasnoyarsk, 104
  see also Gulag
Kremlin, 191
  see also Soviet Union, USSR

Kristallnacht (Night of Broken Glass), 130
Künzelsau, 200
Kupferteich, 19
Kuybyshev (Russ., as of 1991, Samara), 126
Kyritz, Children's Village of, 112-18, 127

Labiau (Russ. Polessky District), 88, 202
Labour camp *see* Gulag
Land of milk and honey, 58, 171
Landsbergis, Vytautas, 1-2, 189, 191, 200
Langensalza, 41
Lasch, General Otto, 31
Lastadie, 11, 13
Latvia, 62, 210
Leipzig, 10, 15, 109, 167
Leiserowitz, Ruth, 95, 114, 187, 197
Lice, 55, 66, 68, 75, 79, 89
Liep, suburb of Königsberg (Russ. Oktyabrsky), 16
Litas, 6, 151, 173, 199
Lithuania, Lithuanian:
   Embassy, 164
   independence, 2, 70, 137, 150, 173-4, 191, 195
      Declaration of, 200
   Lithuanian Echo, The 196
   Ministry of Engineering, 162
   National Archives, 187
   Press House, xvi
Lübeck, 165
Lusatian Neisse, 41

Malaria *see* Diseases
Malnutrition, 80, 123, 177
   see also Famine, Hunger, Starvation
Mann, Thomas, 15
Marijampolė, 72, 201
Market, 24, 42, 45, 47, 49, 81, 87, 89, 148, 169, 205, 207
Masurian Canal, 62
Matochkin, Yuri, 191
Medical commission, 100-101, 110, 173
Medicine, medications, 149, 173, 194, 198
Mednicken (Russ. Druzhnoye), 27
Memel (Lith. Klaipėda), 48, 155, 171
   River (Neman), xiii, 22, 39-40, 48, 57-63, 90, 101, 179, 203
   Territory, 14-15, 28, 103, 171, 175
Memelland, 73, 90, 92

Molotov, Secretary of State Vyacheslav, 48
Moonshine, 87, 132
Morgenstern, Erika, 11
Moravian protectorate, 15
Moscow, 1, 14, 47-8, 108, 117, 126, 191, 201

Nasser Garten, 'Wet Garden', 12
National Socialism, Nazi Party, Nazis, ix, 9, 14-16, 25, 27-9, 33, 46, 71, 119-20, 167
Niederung *see* Elchniederung
Netherlands, the, 202
Neukuren (Russ. Pionersky), 39
Neuruppin, 113
New Year, New Year's Eve, 29-30, 39
NKVD (People's Commissariat of Internal Affairs), 74, 76, 97, 99, 189, 201

Oberteich, 12
Oder River, 41
Oedema *see* Diseases
Ordenskirche, 42
Orphan, orphans, xiv, 54, 58-9, 92, 98, 112, 114, 118, 194, 221
   orphan's supplement, 199
   war orphans, 4, 224
Orphanage, orphanages, 97, 112, 114, 116-18, 122-4, 127
   Russian, 56-7, 116, 158, 161, 165, 167

Parkhotel, 11
Partisans, 70-1, 75-6
   see also Forest Brothers
People's Commissariat for Internal Affairs *see* NKVD
Perm, 113
Petrauskas, Valdas, 1-2
Pillau (Russ. Baltijsk), 14, 30, 32, 36, 43-4
Piłsudski, Jósef, 14
Pleurisy *see* Diseases
Pneumoconiosis *see* Diseases: black lung
Pogegen (Lith. Pagėgiai), 63, 90
Poland, Polish, 9, 14-15, 22, 41-2, 44, 62, 65, 70, 107, 109, 120, 122, 134-5, 167, 206, 223-4
Ponarth, quarter of Königsberg (Russ. Dimitrowa), 12, 24, 30, 95, 141, 143, 145, 196, 202, 213

Potsdam Conference, 41, 46
POW camp, ix, 221
Powalken (Pol. Powałki), 35
Pregolya River, 8-9, 212
    see also Pregel River
Pregel River, 9-12, 26
Prison, 85, 126, 189
    camps, 94, 103-104, 109, 113, 121, 126, 133, 189, 191-2, 221
    see also Gulag
Promenadenweg, 11
Protestant see Christendom
Prussian-Eylau (Russ. Bagrationovsk), 193

Quarantine camp, 111-12, 116
Queen Louise Bridge see Königin-Luise-Brücke

Račas, Antanas, 200
Railway, 42, 53, 62, 64, 110
    buffer on, 58, 60
    cattle car on, xiv, 83, 97, 104, 111-12
    freight train, 14, 29, 43, 58, 60-1, 68, 79, 83, 91, 95, 97, 107-108
    running board on, 60-1, 65, 67
    station, xii, 12, 28-9, 60-5, 67, 72, 79, 82, 97, 101, 107, 129
Rape, raped, 33, 44-5, 80, 88, 91, 101, 106, 108, 126, 167-8, 194
Rauschen (Russ. Svetlogorsk), 12, 161
Reconstruction, 48, 127, 130
Red Army, viii, x, xii, xiii, 29-30, 32-3, 36, 39-40, 42, 44, 47-8, 53, 56, 58-9, 70-1, 76, 80, 89, 95, 101-102, 104, 114, 121, 157, 167, 171, 184
Red Cross, xiii, 82, 98, 105, 109, 116-17, 130, 137, 139, 161, 165-6, 172, 195, 201
Refugees, ix, 29-30, 34, 37, 39, 41, 43, 56, 61, 71, 90, 111, 127, 129, 221
Resettlement, 128, 201
Restitution, 191, 193
Restoration, 193
Return migration, 41
Reunification, 3, 6, 128, 194
Reutlingen, 4-5, 129-31
Rhineland, 101
Rīga (Latv.), 14
    Black Balsam, 210
Romantic era, 9
Rosenau-Speichersdorf (East Prussia), 145

Royal Air Force, 27
Rügen, 139
Ruin, ruins, 31, 39, 49, 55, 206-207, 216
Russia, 1, 12, 36, 44, 46, 59, 68, 70, 104, 126, 131, 145, 173, 184, 191, 193, 202-203, 209, 215
    see also Soviet
Russian:
    aristocracy, 12
    authorities, 48-9, 86, 99, 111, 161
    Communists, 85
    Embassy, Amsterdam, 203
    Empire, 70
    government, 47, 70, 96, 98-9, 118, 191, 193
    guards, 201
    immigration, 203
    language, 204
    military, 33-4, 47-8, 75, 81, 92, 131, 158, 207
        aircraft, 42, 55
        duties, obligations, 99, 101-102, 184
        front, ix, 47, 101
        occupation of Baltic States, 51, 76, 88, 111, 161
        police, 65, 85
        troops, xvi, 2, 30, 46, 76, 107
    Orthodox Church, 205, 215
    passport, 209
    police, 48, 61-3, 99, 189, 207-208
    Rusija, 173
    settlers, 48, 56, 59, 76
Society for the Upkeep of Memorials, 193
soldiers, 2-4, 23, 25, 29-30, 34, 36, 38-40, 44, 46, 51-6, 62, 65, 70-4, 76, 79-80, 87-8, 91, 95-7, 105-108, 114, 116, 121, 167, 172, 179
territory, 58
USSR, 1, 3, 74, 112
    definition of, 103
visa, 202
zone, 118, 210

Sackheim, quarter of Königsberg, 9
    Gate, 19, 24
Samara, 126
    see also Kuybyshev
Samland, 39, 44, 82, 159, 216
    Sambia Peninsula, 39
Sassnitz, 139

Saxony, Saxon, 5, 28-9, 41, 109, 112, 118, 129-30, 139
Schaulen (Lith. Šiauliai), 198
Schwesternhof (East Prussia), 218, 220
Secret trial *see* Prisons
SED (Socialist Unity Party), 118, 128
Seedienst Ostpreussen, 14
Seelheim (East Prussia, Pol. Cisy), 164
Šiauliai, 6, 63, 91, 96, 157-8
  see also Schaulen
Siberia, xiii, 1, 36, 62, 71-2, 75, 85, 94-5, 97-8, 103-105, 107-10, 122, 179, 191, 196, 200, 221
  see also Gulag
Sievers, Hildegard, 194
Simon-Dach-House, 155
Singing Revolution, 2, 193, 200
  see also Lithuania: independence
Smolensk (Russ.), 99
Socialist, 103, 112, 114, 118
Soldau (Pol. Działdowo), 14
Sovetsk, 59
  see also Tilsit
Soviet:
  Air Force, 30, 37
  Bloc (Eastern), 129, 187
  citizenship, 118, 195
  era, 136, 140, 148, 187, 189, 216
  prison camps *see* Gulag
  settlements, 85, 215
  spies, 76
  Union, xiv, 1, 41, 44, 46, 70, 90, 95, 103-105, 111, 114, 150, 173, 191-3, 206, 216
    Supreme Council of, 3
  see also Russia
SS (Schutzstaffel, 'Protection Squadron'), 46, 148
Stalin, Josef, 1, 46, 70, 119
Stalingrad, Battle of, 28
Starvation, starve, x, xiii, 4, 48-9, 52, 58, 60-1, 69, 72, 80-1, 157-8, 161, 174-5, 184, 189, 209
Stauder, Hedwig, 197
Stetten, Baron Wolfgang von, xiv, 151, 173-4, 194-200
Stockholm, 14, 16
Stowaway, 59-60, 85, 104
Stresemann, Gustav, 14
Stribai, 75
  see also Partisans

Stuttgart, 139, 197
Sudetenland, 15
Sumowski, Burkhard, 12
Sütterlin script, 19, 165
Swabian, 4-5, 129, 131
Swastika, 26
Swinemünde, 14
Switzerland, 133
Synagogue, 20, 130
  Street, 20

Tauragė *see* Tauroggen
Tauroggen (Lith. Tauragė), 48, 63, 89, 98, 102, 109-10, 153, 161, 175, 177, 181-2, 196, 198, 201, 203, 208
Teutonic Order, 16, 41
Thuringia, ix, 41, 112, 150
Tilsit (Russ. Sovetsk), vii, ix, 2, 15, 27-8, 48, 53, 55-9, 61-3, 72, 74, 97-8, 126, 161, 203, 208
Tilsiter cheese, 11, 15-16
Todt Organization, 25
Toronto, Canada, ix
Tracing services, xiii, 123, 165
  Child, children, 82, 113, 177
  International (ITS), xii-xiii, xiv, 3
Transports, 5, 25, 28, 41, 95, 97, 111-12, 116, 122, 124, 129, 161, 179
Travemünde, 14
Trek, trekkers, ix, 34, 39, 43, 53, 55, 90, 123
Trenches, x, 23-4, 34
Trofimov, Russian chief of police Anatoly, 48
Truman, Harry, 46
Tuberculosis *see* Diseases
Turkey, 162-3
Two Plus Four Agreement, 3
Typhoid *see* Epidemics
Typhus *see* Epidemics

Ukraine, Ukrainian, 103, 117
  Tursučiai, 201
United States, 3, 103, 120-1, 130, 133
  army, military, 130, 133
Ural Mountains, 126
USSR *see* Russia

Versailles Treaty, 14-15
Vilnius, 1-2, 64, 67, 81, 85, 162-4, 196, 198, 202-203, 209, 219

German Embassy in, 199
Parliament building in, 1-2
Press House in, xvi
Red Cross in, 117
see also Wilna
Vogtland, 5
Vokietukai, 1, 71

Warfare:
- artillery, artillery fire, x, 26, 31, 34, 38, 53, 132
- bombs, bombings, 26, 27-9, 30, 37, 42, 53, 57, 132, 137, 139, 164, 221-2
  - phosphorus, 25
- fire storm, 28
- firing squad, 97, 107
- flamethrowers, 26
- grenades, 38, 123, 158
- guns, 2, 26, 38, 40, 53
- machine guns, 38, 71, 74
- strafing, 42
- tanks, 1-2, 38, 43, 55, 106, 133, 191, 205
- torpedoes, 29, 43

Wehlau (Russ. Snamensk), 67, 101, 114, 159, 204

Wehrmacht, 15, 22, 51, 53, 70, 113, 172
Weizäcker, Richard von, 194
West Prussia, 14, 51, 63
Westphalia, 172
Whooping cough *see* Diseases
Wieck, Michael, 10, 47
Wilhelm I, Kaiser, 10
  beard, 159
Wilna (Lith. Vilnius), 67
  see also Vilnius
Wolf Children:
  Association *see* Edelweiss
  Memorial, 193
Wolfen, 111
World War:
  First, 14, 23, 26, 126, 132, 159, 171, 206, 216
  Second, ix, xiii, 1, 41, 126, 130, 148, 159, 172, 189, 192, 206, 222-5
World Youth Festival, 118-19
Wulff, Christian, 185

Yeltsin, Boris, 191

Zhukov, General Georgy, 46
Zuckertüte ('sugar cone'), 20